T0354541

Bishop Martin J. O'Connor, Rector,
in front of the Pontifical North American College, 1953
Photo courtesy of NAC Archives

THE SECOND FOUNDER

**Bishop Martin J. O'Connor
and the Pontifical North American College**

Monsignor Stephen M. DiGiovanni

Order this book online at www.trafford.com
or email orders@trafford.com

Most Trafford titles are also available at major online book retailers.

Printed in the United States of America.

ISBN: 978-1-4669-6150-0 (sc)
ISBN: 978-1-4669-6149-4 (hc)
ISBN: 978-1-4669-6151-7 (e)

Library of Congress Control Number: 2012922620

The Second Founder: Bishop Martin J. O'Connor and the Pontifical North American College,
by Monsignor Stephen M. DiGiovanni,
is published with ecclesiastical approval.

+ Timothy Michael Cardinal Dolan
Archbishop of New York

January 23, 2013

Trafford rev. 02/14/2013

 www.trafford.com

North America & international
toll-free: 1 888 232 4444 (USA & Canada)
phone: 250 383 6864 ♦ fax: 812 355 4082

*Dedicated
to the
Alumni
of the
Pontifical
North American College,
the Spiritual Sons
of
Martin J. O'Connor*

Contents

Abbreviations

The major archives visited for this study, and the abbreviations used here for each in the footnotes, are:

APF: The Archives of the Congregation *de Propaganda Fide*, Rome, housing all original documents about the founding of the College.

CUA: The American Catholic History Research Center and University Archives, The Catholic University of America, Washington, D.C., housing the Archbishop O'Connor Papers.

KC: The Archives of the Knights of Columbus Museum, New Haven, Connecticut, housing the Count Enrico Galeazzi Papers.

NAC: The Archives of the Pontifical North American College, Vatican City State, housing the Francesco Silvestri Papers.

NYC: The Archives of the Archdiocese of New York, housing the Cardinal Spellman Papers.

N.D.: No date indicated in a document.

N.P.: No place of origin indicated in a document.

Foreword by Raymond Leo Cardinal Burke

The Pontifical North American College, the Church in the United States of America and indeed the universal Church owe a great debt of gratitude to Monsignor Stephen M. DiGiovanni for his careful and thorough research of the formidable task of not only opening anew the Pontifical North American College after the ravages of the Second World War but also of equipping the College to provide for the ever greater need of its particular service of preparing, in the Eternal City under the fatherly care of the Vicar of Christ on earth, worthy shepherds for the flock in the United States. I refer not only to the preparation of seminarians to present themselves for priestly ordination but also to the higher education of priests for the sake of their priestly life and ministry in their dioceses. The Rector to be appointed after the conclusion of World War II would have the ultimate responsibility for the accomplishment of such an important, indeed critical, work of the Church.

As you, the reader, are about to discover, in ample and well-documented historical detail, the task was indeed formidable, for it involved the restoration of the original seat of the College on the Via dell'Umiltà as a residence for United States diocesan priests sent to undertake the study of the sacred sciences at the pontifical universities and institutes, the restoration of the Villa Santa Caterina, the summer residence of the College, and the building of a new and much larger college to accommodate the requests of many Bishops from the United States to have a worthy place for their seminarians to receive priestly formation in the City of Saints Peter and Paul. The Rector's responsibilities clearly also included the weighty responsibility of caring for the seminarians and priests of the North American College who were already undertaking their studies during the time of the restoration and new construction.

The complexity of the situation was considerably augmented by the fact that the office of Rector must necessarily be entrusted to a priest or Bishop from the United States who, at one and the same time, would have the responsibility both to direct and supervise major construction works in Italy during a period when she was struggling to recover from the tremendous losses, both human and material, caused by the War, and to cultivate the best possible communication with the Bishops of the United States upon whom the College and all of its programs depended for necessary and not insignificant support. To fulfill both responsibilities the new Rector would have to draw heavily upon the human and Christian strength, the human and Christian virtues, which had been cultivated in the home and through years of seminary studies and priestly life. In what you are about to read you will discover that there were many thorny situations and difficult relationships which could understandably have been the cause of profound discouragement in the mission or even of its abandonment. One must also not forget the state of communications at the time, which not infrequently witnessed letters and responses to letters crossing each other in the mail, with resulting misunderstanding and confusion. The first priest chosen for the work of Rector, in fact, with sadness resigned the position not long after accepting it because its many demands seemed beyond what his physical strength and health could sustain.

The then Bishop Martin J. O'Connor, an alumnus of the College and, at the time, happily the Auxiliary Bishop of his home diocese of Scranton, accepted the great burden of the preparation of the reopening of the College, at the Via dell'Umiltà, on the Janiculum Hill, the site chosen for the new seminary building, and at the Villa Santa Caterina. Conscious of his own limitations, especially a severe hearing impediment which also naturally affected his manner of speaking, he took up the work out of deep love of the Church and of her Supreme Pastor, the Roman Pontiff. Having been privileged, as a young seminarian for the Diocese of Scranton, to prepare for priestly ordination in Rome, he was thoroughly convinced of the importance of providing the same possibility for the young seminarians from his homeland in the 1950s and into the future. He was, in no way, naïve about the weighty responsibilities placed upon his shoulders and about the evident severe challenges to be met. Not giving way to fear or discouragement before the mission, in all of its complexity, he, with great competence and tireless tenacity, went forward, staying the course until the work was brought to its remarkable completion.

There seems little doubt that the spirituality of Saint Thérèse of Lisieux, which had nurtured his life in Christ as a child, a seminarian, priest and Bishop, fortified in him the humility and confident abandonment to Divine Providence so much required for the task which he nobly and efficaciously undertook and brought to completion. His choice to include roses of the Little Flower in his episcopal coat-of-arms was a sign of how powerfully Saint Thérèse's Little Way had assisted him as a priest and would, he trusted, assist him as Bishop. In many ways, the deepest meaning of the story which Monsignor DiGiovanni so ably recounts is best apprehended in the context of the Little Way.

At the beginning of the great work which Bishop O'Connor undertook, Cardinal Dennis Dougherty of Philadelphia with good reason wrote to him: "You may now meritoriously be considered the second founder of the American College, Rome."[1] Hence, the title of Monsignor DiGiovanni's important study. What must not be forgotten is that the formidable work of founding anew the College enjoyed the unfailing blessing and support of the Roman Pontiff, the Venerable Pope Pius XII, and of those who worked most closely with him. In that respect, Bishop O'Connor would insist that the second founder of the College was truly Pope Pius XII, under whose benevolent and generous care, he carried out his mission.

All that it would mean to fulfill the responsibility of a second founder loomed before the dedicated and hardworking Bishop who began the work, as he continued to accomplish it throughout the years which ensued, with complete trust that he was doing the will of God. Bishop O'Connor's response to the letter of the Apostolic Delegate, Archbishop Amleto Cicognani, inquiring about his willingness to accept the appointment of Rector, expressed the mind and heart with which he carried out his exceptional service. He wrote to the Apostolic Delegate: "Since I do not seek this office, I consider the decision of the Committee as a manifestation of God's

---

[1]   Philadelphia August 21, 1948, Dougherty to O'Connor, CUA, *O'Connor Papers*, Box 42: *NAC subfiles*.

will for me. This gives me strength to assume such a responsibility."[2] Early on, the distinguished Italians who provided him with essential assistance, above all, Count Enrico Galeazzi, the architect of the College, whose earthly remains are most fittingly entombed in the crypt of the Chapel of the College, and Francesco Silvestri, the lawyer of the College, recognized Bishop O'Connor's extraordinary talent and dedication placed with humility and trust at the service of the Church. At the same time, the Second Founder was never lacking in his acknowledgment of the essential and highly qualified service of Galeazzi, Silvestri and other Italian collaborators.

During my years of study, first at the College on the Janiculum, from August of 1971 to July of 1975, and then at the College on the Via dell'Umiltà, from September of 1980 to April of 1984, I had frequent occasion to be grateful for the excellent facilities provided by the Bishops of the United States for their seminarians and priests studying in Rome. Apart from the objective reflection upon the tremendous sacrifices involved in restoring, building and maintaining the facilities, I also heard about the extraordinary priestly dedication and leadership of Bishop, later Archbishop, O'Connor from those who had worked with him.

Bishop Frederick W. Freking, Bishop of La Crosse, my home diocese, who sent me both for seminary studies and graduate studies to the Pontifical North American College, had served as Spiritual Director of the Pontifical North American College in the years soon after its reopening, from 1953 to 1957. More than once, he spoke with great admiration and affection of Archbishop O'Connor. In particular, I remember him mentioning that the Archbishop would talk to him about "the big picture" which must be kept in mind for the good of the College. The "big picture" included the love of the universal Church at her heart in the See of Peter, which the Pontifical North American had the distinct responsibility to cultivate in priests and seminarians, and the love of the Church in the United States for whom the Pontifical North American College was preparing

---

2   Wilkes-Barre, PA, n.d., Martin J. O'Connor to Cicognani, CUA, *O'Connor Papers*, Box 59, Folder: *Confidential Papers*.

worthy shepherds and assisting those already ordained to perfect their learning for the fuller pastoral care of the faithful.

Since taking up my service at the Supreme Tribunal of the Apostolic Signatura in August of 2008, I, as a member of the Roman Curia, have had frequent occasion to observe directly the life of the Pontifical North American College and to hear from others their impressions of the College. It was also my blessing to be able to send seminarians and priests to the Pontifical North American and to follow their studies, during my some fourteen years of service as Bishop of La Crosse and Archbishop of Saint Louis, from February 22, 1995 to June 28, 2008. There can be no question that the College is flourishing in all of the essential aspects of priestly formation and life. Bishop O'Connor's years of tireless and dauntless work to refound the Pontifical North American College continue to bear enduring, truly eternal, good fruit for the Church in the United States today.

Before concluding, I express the hope that Monsignor DiGiovanni's highly credible and thorough study will inspire a greater appreciation of the irreplaceable and outstanding service of Bishop Martin J. O'Connor to the Pontifical North American College at a truly critical period of her history. Sadly, the hermeneutic of rupture and discontinuity, to which Pope Paul VI made reference in his striking homily for the Solemnity of Saints Peter and Paul in 1972,[3] and which Pope Benedict XVI masterfully analyzed in his Christmas address to the College of Cardinals and the Roman Curia on December 22, 2005,[4] has led to a forgetfulness of all that the then Bishop O'Connor had accomplished for the College and

---

[3]   Paulus PP. VI, "Per il nono anniversario dell'Incoronazione di Sua Santità: «Resistite fortes in fide», 29 giugno 1972, in *Insegnamenti di Paolo VI*, Vol. 10 (1972), Città del Vaticano: Tipografia Poliglotta Vaticana, 1973, pp. 703-709.

[4]   Benedictus PP. XVI, Allocutio "Ad Romanam Curiam ob omina natalicia," 22 Decembris 2005, *Acta Apostolicae Sedis* 98 (2006), pp. 40-53. English translation: Pope Benedict XVI, "Address of His Holiness Benedict XVI to the Roman Curia Offering Them His Christmas Greetings," 22 December 2005, *L'Osservatore Romano Weekly Edition in English*, 4 January 2006, pp. 4-6.

a consequent lack of appreciation of how much the College today continues to owe to his outstanding and indeed heroic service.

Having its roots already in the 1950s and flowering in the 1960s and 1970s, the hermeneutic of rupture and discontinuity has viewed everything which has gone before in the life of the Church as suspect and even aberrant before the age of love, joy and freedom of a so-called "new Church." The time-tested disciplines of priestly formation and life, which Bishop O'Connor exemplified, were ridiculed and set aside without consideration. The spirituality of the Little Way which inspired his labors was considered out-of-date and inferior to so-called new insights into the spiritual life.

The pride of the adherents of the hermeneutic of rupture and discontinuity led them to exaggerate the human frailties and foibles of Bishop O'Connor, and to ridicule him who had literally spent his every energy to provide for seminarians and priests a fitting and worthy place to carry out the sacred work of priestly formation and of priestly studies. The manner in which Bishop O'Connor was treated at the end of his years of service to the College is one of the saddest chapters in her history. To the extent that the hermeneutic of rupture and discontinuity infected the life of the Pontifical North American College, as it infected every aspect of the Church's life, especially in the period following the Second Vatican Ecumenical Council, the memory of Bishop Martin J. O'Connor and of his extraordinary service to the Pontifical North American College was forgotten. More seriously, the solid program of priestly formation and priestly life, nurtured under the fatherly gaze of the Successor of Saint Peter, to which he was so deeply dedicated, was compromised, to a greater or lesser degree, for many years.

But, thanks be to God, the hermeneutic of reform and continuity, which is coherent with the organic nature of the life of the Church, has once again prevailed under the providential leadership of Blessed Pope John Paul II and Pope Benedict XVI. Monsignor DiGiovanni's work on the service of Bishop O'Connor to the Pontifical North American College is a wonderful example of the hermeneutic at work in telling the important story of the refounding of the College after World War II. It is my hope that, with the study of the fruits of Monsignor DiGiovanni's research, some additional tribute to the memory of one of the greatest rectors of the Pontifical North American College, indeed, as Cardinal Dennis Dougherty declared, her "second founder," will be undertaken at the College which he loved so deeply and served so well.

In conclusion, in the name of all who will be blessed to read *The Second Founder: Bishop Martin J. O'Connor and the Pontifical North American College*, I express the deepest esteem and gratitude to Monsignor Stephen M. DiGiovanni for his thoroughness and care in writing the history of a most significant period in the life of the Pontifical North American College. In our gratitude to Monsignor DiGiovanni, let us pray for God's continued blessing upon the important service of the Pontifical North American College to the Church in the United States of America and far beyond, in continuity with the great and perennial tradition of seminary education to which Bishop Martin J. O'Connor was dedicated in an extraordinary way.

Raymond Leo Cardinal BURKE
Prefect of the Supreme Tribunal of the Apostolic Signatura
10 November 2012—Saint Leo the Great, Pope and Doctor

Introduction

On August 26, 1973, my classmates and I sailed from New York Harbor on the Italian Line ship *Raffaelo* headed for four years of studies in Rome. We were the *New Men*, accepted into the ordination class of 1977 at the Pontifical North American College. Most of us were in our early '20's, just recently graduated from various colleges in the United States. For me, and for most of my classmates, this was our first Atlantic crossing, and would be our first experience in Europe. It was exciting!

After seven days on the open sea, living a life of relative luxury, making new friendships among the 60 or so of us, along with some College faculty members, we had our first taste of Italy even before landing. Scheduled to land in Naples, we were informed that a cholera epidemic was raging, and we would disembark in Genoa, instead. Cholera!!!??? It was modern times in 1973, for Heaven's sake! And WE were the New Men of the Pontifical College! How could cholera be permitted to interfere with our glorious destiny? Italian reality would knock us down a notch or two by the time we arrived on the Janiculum Hill.

Even we were naïve in those heady days, as most Americans are about the workings of Italy and, even more so, of the workings of the Vatican, or of Roman universities. So, we landed in the city of Christopher Columbus and immediately boarded our un-air conditioned second class compartments in the slow train south, in sweltering weather. By the time we arrived at the Rome's Stazione Termini, we were dead tired, drenched to the skin with perspiration, and fearful that the epidemic had moved north. We boarded a tourist bus, sent to meet us at the station, and plodded through Roman traffic towards the Tiber River.

Only when we turned left onto the Via della Conciliazione and saw the dome of Saint Peter's did our hearts rise again. As we moved up the Janiculum Hill, we could hear the three College bells ringing our welcome. The large iron gates opened wide, and we turned to the right along the northern side of the chapel, coming to a stop at the formal seminary entrance along the avenue of pines, facing Saint Peter's Basilica. Some members of the faculty and upperclassmen who had worked on the welcoming arrangements met us at the stairs, applauding us and shaking our hands as we entered the chapel to meet the Rector, and begin College life with a prayer of thanksgiving.

During the first week the Rector, Bishop James Hickey, led us on daily pilgrimages, celebrating Mass for us in the catacombs, shrines of martyrs and saints, and the seven Basilicas of the city, and introduced us to the rich history of the Church in Rome. For the subsequent six weeks we studied Italian in the City, became acquainted with one another and the College, and settled into seminary life. University classes began in mid-October. Little was mentioned about the history of the College, other than its beginnings in 1859, and the fact that the present building was opened in 1953, built by the Rector, Bishop Martin J. O'Connor. For us in our early 20's, that was ancient history.

On Thanksgiving Day, after the traditional holiday banquet, we were ushered into the auditorium to watch two movies, annually shown on that day: the 1959 epic *Ben-Hur*, during which we all howled in agreement at the words, "Rome will rule the world", and an odd 1950's period piece, featuring Bishop O'Connor. *Person-to-Person* was a weekly American television show, and, soon after the opening of the new College on the Janiculum, the man who built the place was interviewed. And there, for the first time, we were introduced to Martin J. O'Connor. He was a plump, bespectacled bishop, dressed in a pre-Vatican II ecclesiastical outfit, speaking in odd tones and halting phrases, who introduced himself and the College to an American audience of the 1950's, and to us, the recently arrived *New Men*, who had been born when this piece was first filmed.

During the next years, we were frequently reminded that the College had been built in the period before the Second Vatican Council. Those times were described by various seminary faculty members in unflattering terms, as an unfortunate period in the Church's history, dark and dreary, as compared with the openness and light of the post-Vatican II era. And Martin J. O'Connor, *Oaky* or *The Oakball*, as he was commonly called by faculty and students alike, was the bumbling embodiment of all that was wrong with the pre-conciliar Church. This was common fare in the 1970's, as I learned in my first four college seminary years in the States, and not unique to the Pontifical College in Rome. Happily, all that changed at the College, beginning with the renewing years when Monsignor Edwin O'Brien and Monsignor Timothy Dolan served as College Rectors.

Who was this man, Martin J. O'Connor, and what happened to him? After having completed the new College, O'Connor was rumored to become the archbishop of Chicago, or of Philadelphia, or of New York, or to succeed to an important Vatican post. Instead, he was pushed out of the College, occupied a few posts of little significance, and simply disappeared from history, living a lonely life in Rome, never invited to the College, dying in 1986. Likewise, as if in pharoanic Egypt, his name has been all but removed from the institutional memory of the College by the Rectors who succeeded him, and his life's greatest accomplishment is not even mentioned on his tombstone.

Yet, even as a student, annually watching *Person-to-Person*, chuckling with my classmates when *Oaky* appeared as just another comic character akin to Ralph Kramden in *The Honeymooners*, there was a doubt in my young mind that continued for years: if, as we had been led to believe, the pre-conciliar Church was so backward, and *The Oakball* such an incompetent, how did the huge building known as *The College* get built in post-war Rome, and how did that little round man with his comic voice and inarticulate gestures accomplish such a task? That is the genesis of this monograph.

As in most efforts, the influence of personalities is an important factor. The re-opening of the Pontifical North American College in Rome after World War II, and the building of the new College atop the Janiculum Hill, are no exceptions. The personalities involved were large: Pope Pius XII; Francis Cardinal Spellman, Archbishop of New York; Dennis Cardinal Dougherty, Archbishop of Philadelphia; Edward Cardinal Mooney, Archbishop of Detroit; Samuel Cardinal Stritch, Archbishop of Chicago; Count Enrico Galeazzi, papal and College architect; Francesco Silvestri, College lawyer; and Bishop Martin J. O'Connor, the College Rector. And it is simply my self-appointed goal to help set the record straight about Martin J. O'Connor and his greatest work as the second founder of the Pontifical North American College.

* * *

In researching this book, I am grateful to the archivists and their staffs at each of these archival repositories: William J. Shepherd at The American Catholic History Research Center and University Archives at the Catholic University of America in Washington, DC; Susan Brosnan at the Archives at the Knights of Columbus Museum in New Haven, CT; Laura Panarese at the Archives of the Pontifical North American College in Rome; and Sister Margarita Smith, O.P., who originally organized the Archives of the Archdiocese of New York during the past decades, and her able successor, Father Michael Morris. Thank you, all.

My thanks also go to His Eminence Edward Cardinal Egan, Archbishop Emeritus of New York, to the Most Reverend Daniel Cronin, Archbishop Emeritus of Hartford, and to Mr. Thomas McKee. All three were students under Bishop O'Connor: a young Dan Cronin arrived in Rome in 1949; Ed Egan and Tom McKee in 1954.[5] I am grateful to them, for they have been kind enough to share their memories of Bishop O'Connor with me, and generous enough to encourage me in my work. I thank His Eminence Raymond Leo Cardinal Burke for the beautiful foreword to this work concerning the College we both love. I am also thankful to Mr. Christopher Brayshears, a seminarian studying at the College, for his beautiful photographs of the College chapel and the tomb of Count Galeazzi. Likewise, I am very grateful to Dr. Joseph McAleer, *Oxon* for his editorial suggestions, proofreading and guidance. His professional expertise as a journalist and author helped make this narrative readable.

---

[5] Throughout this book, alumni of the North American College will be indicated by [NAC and the year of ordination or of departure from the College] after their names.

Chapter 1

Pope Pius IX and the founding of an American seminary in Rome

---

"You should set up, here in this venerable City of Ours, your own College for clerics from your own nation. For you, in your wisdom, are well aware what great advantages would accrue to your dioceses from such an institution."
—Blessed Pope Pius IX, 1855

Cardinal Giovanni Maria Mastai Ferretti took the name of Pius IX upon his election as Pope on June 16, 1846. Until his death in 1878, he guided the Catholic Church during one of the most turbulent periods of European history. Among his many accomplishments was the founding of the Pontifical North American College, which opened in 1859.

The idea for a national seminary to train Americans in Rome first came from Archbishop Gaetano Bedini following his visit to the United States in 1853.[1] The Catholic Church in America impressed the Vatican visitor—at least he considered the laity impressive. His report about some of the clergy was less than complimentary. He was shocked at the enormous diocesan and parochial debts, and what he

---

[1] Gaetano Bedini (1806-1864) was a priest of the Diocese of Sinigaglia. He became Titular Archbishop of Thebes in 1852 and named Apostolic Nuncio to Brazil. With thoughts to establish diplomatic relations between the Holy See and the United States, Pope Pius IX sent Bedini in 1853 to visit informally the United States, to tour the country and to submit a report on the state of the Church in America. Following his return to Rome in 1855 he was named Secretary to the Propaganda Fide. He was elevated to the see of Viterbo-Toscanella and created Cardinal Priest of Santa Maria Sopra Minerva in 1861.

1

termed "too much selfishness and too great a spirit of independence" among the priests.[2] The debts were the natural result of the poverty of American Catholics, the majority having been European immigrants who arrived in the United States impoverished. The poor quality of some priests was caused by much the same reason: most were themselves penniless immigrants, sometimes poorly educated, and a few came to America seeking to escape their stern bishops or the law.[3] A better crop of priests was required to serve the growing Church in America, and Bedini knew how to provide them. The Archbishop made two recommendations upon his return to Rome: that diplomatic relations between the Holy See and the United States be established; and that an American seminary be founded in the Eternal City.[4]

The establishment of a seminary for Americans was mentioned by the Pope himself, soon after Bedini's return. On New Year's Day, 1855, he wrote John Hughes, Archbishop of New York:

> In order that you may be able to provide more easily for the needs of your dioceses, and have diligent and industrious laborers to assist you in cultivating the vineyard of the Lord, We strongly desire ... that after mutual consultation and collaboration [among the American bishops], you should set up, here in this venerable City of Ours, your own College for clerics from your own nation. For you, in your wisdom, are

---

[2] Wister, Robert [NAC, 1969], *The Establishment of the Apostolic Delegation in the United States of America: The Satolli Mission, 1892-1896*, doctoral dissertation, Pontificia Universitas Gregoriana, Rome 1981, p. 10.

[3] DiGiovanni, Stephen [NAC 1977], *Archbishop Corrigan and the Italian Immigrants*, Huntington, IN, 1994, pp 82 ff.

[4] The North American College is not based on an American model, which usually provides both residence and courses of study. Rather, it is similar to others in Europe: primarily a residence for students, providing room and board. As a seminary, it also provides spiritual and pastoral formation as training for future priests. The academic programs in philosophy and theology are provided by the various pontifical universities throughout Rome.

well aware what great advantages would accrue to your dioceses from such an institution.[5]

On July 19, 1858, the Church's missionary authority, the Congregation *de Propaganda Fide*, while discussing the decisions of the Ninth Provincial Council of Baltimore, considered Bedini's proposal for an American seminary, writing in its report:

> One of the greatest works of Catholic wisdom of the successors of Saint Peter is the foundation in Rome of many Pontifical colleges which were built here and still prosper in goodly number with the most noble end of welcoming young men from diverse nations more or less infected with error, and here instructing them in true doctrine, forming in them all virtues, then sending them as priests to their countries to work all their lives to preserve Catholics in the faith and to lead back those in error to the ways of truth and justice.[6]

Another reason for the establishment of an American College in Rome was the concern Propaganda had about the unity of the American bishops among themselves and with the Holy See. A national college in Rome could provide one more link between the Successor of Saint Peter in Rome and the successors of the apostles in the United States.

The Pope, however, had greater concerns about the well-being of the Universal Church, and greater confidence in the Americans than did either Bedini or the Propaganda officials. He saw the United States of America as a land of great promise, in which the ancient

---

[5]   Pius IX, January 1, 1855, *Obsequentissimas Litteras,* quoted in McNamara, Robert [NAC, 1936], *The American College in Rome, 1855-1955,* Rochester, 1956, p 17.

[6]   APF, "Ristretto con sommario sugli atti del Concilio IX Provinciale di Baltimora e sull'erezione in Roma di un Seminario per le chiese degli Stati Uniti nell'America Settentrionale 19 iul. 1858", Acta 1858, vol. 222, f 327-329.

Catholic Church could flourish. And it was the Church in America that the Pope was betting on for the future of the Universal Church. The Church in Europe had been under attack for centuries, and nearly destroyed by various kings, governments and revolutions. It was to America, whose first President, George Washington, was one of Pius' heroes, in which the Church could find her sea legs once again and preach the Gospel freely, even as she was being attacked throughout Europe.[7] In America, the land of immigrants, a standardized Roman training of her priests would prove useful in forming a unified Catholic Church to meet the challenges of the future.[8]

Pius expressed his hopes for the Church in America during his inaugural visit to the North American College on January 29, 1860, housed in the former Visitation convent on the Via dell'Umiltà, located around the corner from the Trevi Fountain, and down the street from the former papal palace on the Quirinal Hill (today the palace of the President of the Republic of Italy). It was the feast of Saint Francis de Sales, founder of the Visitation Sisters. While a seminarian, the future Pope had frequently visited the Umiltà convent and served Mass for the Sisters; as a young priest, he often came to the old convent on that feast day to offer Mass for the Sisters, and did so again on July 2, 1846, soon after his election as Pope. And, it was in this chapel that he had made public the decree of heroic sanctity of Sister Margaret Mary Alacoque, the Visitation sister visionary of the Sacred Heart, a few weeks later on August 23rd. He returned to that former convent, now the new American College, as an old friend.

He told the newly assembled first class of twelve American students that the political violence, and the possible loss of the Papal States did not weigh terribly upon his mind. He continued:

---

[7] McNamara, op. cit., p. 81. During his visit to the College, Pius stopped before a bust of George Washington by Thomas Crawford, the American sculptor. Pointing to the statue, he addressed the new students, saying "This is the portrait of a great man: the father of his country."

[8] Martina, Giacomo, *Pio IX (1851-1866)*, *Miscellanea Historiae Pontificiae*, vol. 51, Roma 1986, pp 251-252.

What afflicts Us and frightens Us far more is the perversion of ideas: this horrible evil of falsifying everything. Vice, in fact, is taken for virtue; and virtue for vice. Yet while they lavish acclaim and praise upon the most wicked men and deeds, they have the effrontery to brand as 'hypocrisy,' 'fanaticism', and 'abuse of religion,' firmness in the faith and the very constancy of the bishops in the defense of its sacred rights and its good works.

Now, more than ever before, is the time to take vengeance upon them, in the name of God! And the vengeance of the priesthood and of the Vicar of Christ can only be prayer and supplication that they may all be converted and live. The worst of evils, we know only too well, is the corruption of the heart and the damaging of the mind; and it can be overcome only by the greatest miracle which God can work—and which we must beg Him to accomplish.[9]

The Pope was a realist, and this he clearly demonstrated in the opening of the College. While the days were numbered for the temporal reality of the papal states, which would cease to exist within ten years, there shone a bright future for the Universal Church in America. Pius IX saw himself not so much as the custodian of an outdated political structure, but "as the custodian of the highest principles of good" before those of evil about to burst forth in Europe.[10]

While Pius IX enthusiastically supported the project, the American bishops did not—at least not at first. Unsure of themselves or their ability to provide seminarians for the new College, and with limited finances, since many dioceses were very poor, they held back from any commitment. Some bishops also thought that Americans should be trained in America, where they would serve as priests,

---

[9]   Quoted in McNamara, op. cit., p. 80.
[10]   Martina, Giacomo, *Pio IX*, vol. 51, Roma 1986, p. 252.

and not trained abroad in Europe. Yet the officials of Propaganda along with Bedini urged the Pope forward, and forward the project went with a decision on May 9, 1859 that the new American College would open the following November, whether the American bishops were on board or not.

It was decided that the Propaganda Fide would purchase the older portion of the vacant convent of Visitation nuns on the Via dell'Umiltà, once forcibly occupied by Napoleon's troops. The Americans were not given the property title, but perpetual use of the building and land at no cost, and would be required only to cover the operating expenses and maintenance costs, and to pay for the furnishing of the new College. Circular letters were sent to the American bishops informing them that their new seminary was about to open, requesting that they send students (along with an annual tuition of $150 per student, a considerable sum at that time), and suggest the names of candidates who might be chosen as the institution's first Rector.[11]

Once the decision was made to open the seminary for the American students, the work of reconstruction of the long abandoned convent, damaged by French troops, began under the personal direction of Archbishop Bedini. He guided the architect, Andrea Busiri, as well as the workmen in the extensive renovations of every part of the old buildings, often helping with his own hands. Reuben Parsons of New York, one of the first seminarians, recalled:

> . . . an instance of the zealous prelate's muscular exertions even unto profuse perspiration, as he endeavored to render the long-dismantled College church fit for divine worship. After a cursory inspection of the refectory and the students' rooms we entered the church; and there, amid a cloud of dust, divested of his cassock, resplendent in shirt-sleeves

---

[11]   McNamara, p. 39.

and knee-breeches, was Archbishop Bedini polishing candlesticks, scrubbing marbles . . .[12]

The Archbishop replaced the original ancient chapel painting of the Madonna which had been stolen by Napoleon's troops, with an exact copy of his own favorite Madonna: Mary the Mother of Mercy, from the church of Santa Chiara in Rimini. Bedini made her the patroness of the College, located on the Via dell'Umiltà—"Humility Street," under the title of Our Lady of Humility. Bedini's painting resides within the baroque altarpiece above the high altar today. The Archbishop also provided a marble sculpture of the patroness of the United States: Our Lady of the Immaculate Conception, and placed the lovely statue atop a stone column, which can still be seen in the main courtyard of the old College on Humility Street.

The first Rector of the College was a New York priest, Reverend Doctor William McCloskey.[13] He was appointed on November 14, 1859, but could not possibly complete the Atlantic crossing in time for the planned opening on December 8th. An Irish Benedictine monk, Dom Bernard Smith, was named the temporary "Pro-Rector".

The College formally began on December 7, 1859 with the entrance into the College of the twelve new *Nordamericani*, led by their prefect, Edward McGlynn, a New York seminarian who had begun his Roman studies at the missionary Propaganda College. With the solemn inauguration of the College the next day, and the papal visit on January 29th, the College opened to welcome an ever-increasing number of young Americans studying for the priesthood. Within a few decades, it had outgrown its Umiltà home.

---

[12] Brann, Henry, H*istory of the American College of the Roman Catholic Church of the United States, Rome, Italy*, New York, 1910, pp 461-462.

[13] Father McCloskey (1823-1909) was a priest of the Archdiocese of New York, and Rector of Mount Saint Mary's Seminary, Emmitsburg, MD [1853-1857]. He was highly regarded by many American bishops, including his own Ordinary, Archbishop John Hughes, whose recommendation sealed McCloskey's appointment as the first Rector of the College. Six of the original *Nordamericani* had studied under McCloskey at the Mount. He later became fifth Bishop of Louisville.

*   *   *

During the years 1859-1910, 649 seminarians lived at the North American College on the Via dell'Umiltà. The College also grew by means of purchasing property and buildings. In 1878, the College built a mortuary chapel in Campo Verano; in 1899, the Villa Santa Caterina in Castel Gandolfo; and in 1901, the Pilotta wing [Palazzo Tomba] contiguous to the Umiltà seminary.

Pope Saint Pius X had urged the Americans to build a larger seminary in 1907. While immediate construction was impossible, fundraising for the future was begun by the Rector, Monsignor Thomas F. Kennedy [NAC 1887], whose building fund eventually amassed $50,000.00 [approximately $1,170,000 in 2012 dollars][14] for a new college.[15]

More substantial plans for a larger College began following World War I. At first, the College trustees thought to expand the Umiltà site. But the Holy See intervened, suggesting that the American Hierarchy consider joining forces with the Congregation *de Propaganda Fide* to purchase a large site on the top of the Janiculum Hill for the construction of a new Collegio Urbano and a new Collegio Americano.

The reason was to forestall any possible attempt by Protestant groups to purchase that property overlooking the Vatican, as American Methodists had done earlier atop Monte Mario. The only reason for the failure to construct a Protestant Vatican on Monte Mario "200 spiritual feet higher than Catholicism,"[16] towering over Saint Peter's, was popular Roman sentiment that led even the anti-clerical Roman government to refuse zoning and building permits. The Vatican preferred to forestall any possible future attempts at similar Protestant construction by urging the American bishops to purchase the land, the perfect location for a new American

---

[14] See www.usinflationcalculator.com. All monetary inflation calculations come from this source. Throughout this book, dollar amounts in brackets represent the equivalent value in 2012 U.S. dollars.

[15] McNamara, p. 382-385.

[16] Ibid., pp. 502-504.

seminary, where America's future priests could forge stronger bonds with the Successors of Saint Peter.

The American Hierarchy agreed, and, during their September 1924 meeting, formally approved the purchase of twelve acres [4 ½ hectares] on the Janiculum Hill.[17] The property had been the site of the former mental hospital of Santa Maria della Pieta. The College Rector, Monsignor Charles A. O'Hern [NAC 1906], was given the task of visiting American dioceses in an attempt to secure the $600,000 [$8,073,157.89] needed for the purchase of the parcel of land. Armed with a letter from the Pope supporting the new College, reprinted with photographs of the Vatican in an elegant advertising portfolio designed to inspire generous support, O'Hern secured pledges for $120,000 [$1,577,725.71] within a few weeks. An agreement was reached in July 1925 between the Propaganda Fide and the Italian Ministry of Justice, and the property agreement was concluded.

During these years, the American bishops moved quickly to raise funds and develop designs for a new College. Monsignor Eugene S. Burke [NAC 1911] was named the Rector in 1925, "And then the job of erecting a new college was given me and in old Navy spirit I started to complete the job", he wrote to a potential donor. "I want a building that is a credit to our land and our church and a plant large enough to answer the needs of the present day."[18]

Almost immediately after the agreement to purchase the Janiculum site, the Roman government announced, via newspaper accounts, their plans and designs to cut a new street and tunnel directly through the American's portion of the Janiculum property, dividing in two the site of the new American College. The rest of the area around the new street was to be transformed into parkland, in which

---

[17] NAC, *NAC Construction*, 1925-1954, #224: Folder: *Fund Drive*. Originally, sale of the Umiltà site was considered, but Cardinals Hayes of New York and O'Connell [NAC 1884] of Boston protested that little would be raised from the sale, a large portion of which would be used to repay the Propaganda Fide for use of the building. Both Cardinals suggested the Umiltà complex be retained as a future site for priest graduate students.

[18] Rome October 12, 1925, Msgr. Eugene S. Burke to Mr. William P. McPhee, NAC, *NAC Construction, 1925-1954*, #224, Envelope: *Building Fund-1926*.

development and construction would be prohibited. The Vatican/ American purchase, therefore, would be rendered useless—at least for the Americans—and the Italian government and the Propaganda knew this when the property sale had been finalized.[19] Months of protests followed, resulting in the redesign of the Roman street project, and the closing on the property sale and contract was signed with the American Hierarchy on March 5, 1926.[20]

The next Italian government threat to the College was rumored in the early 1930's, made real in 1938. Once again, the Americans were informed by means of Roman newspapers. The Propaganda Fide officials knew of the plan, but refused to give any information to the College Rector, who finally approached the United States ambassador to Rome. In correspondence between the ambassador and Roman city officials, blueprints emerged that would create a new boulevard cutting through the Umiltà property, destroying all the College buildings, preserving only the historic chapel.[21] In the meantime, the Propaganda Fide refused to negotiate a private entrance for the proposed American College on the Janiculum, making an American facility independent of the new Propaganda College impossible. The final obstacle concerning title to the Umiltà property, and a precise decision about the boundary lines of the Janiculum site was, once again, Propaganda Fide.

Burke was authorized by the American bishops to hire Ettore Rossi as architect to begin plans for the Janiculum building.[22]

---

[19] Rome December 24, 1925, Msgr. Eugene S. Burke to American Bishops, NAC, ibid, #224, H-34.

[20] CUA, *O'Connor Papers*. Box 36, Folder: *Kealy, Msgr. J. Gerald*. The agreement divided the property into three tracts: one owned by the American Hierarchy, one by the Propaganda Fide, and the third held jointly by both.

[21] This was not the first threat to the Umiltà property by the Italian government. In 1884, Roman authorities decreed that the American College property would be confiscated, as the Italian government had confiscated all Church property in Rome after 1870. Archbishop Michael Corrigan led the charge to protect the College. Responding to letters by the American Hierarchy, President Chester A. Arthur intervened, and the Italian government backed down. *Records of the U.S. 48th Congress*, 1st Session, Ex. Doc., No. 143.

[22] Rome June 5, 1940, Ettore Rossi to Bishop Ralph L. Hayes, KC, *Enrico Galeazzi Papers*, No. Amer. Coll, Corresp with and about Architect Ettore

Rossi and Burke toured England, Ireland, and the United States, visiting seminaries and ecclesiastical buildings, which inspired numerous and detailed architectural plans. The plans are grandiose, incorporating architectural elements from classical Roman buildings such as the Coliseum and the Palazzo Barberini, and mimicking the monumental size of American seminaries then being built in the United States, such as Saint Charles Borromeo in Overbrook, Pennsylvania and Our Lady of the Lake Seminary in Mundelein, Illinois. The fantastic, sometimes over-the-top architectural sketches reflected the American post-war self-confidence, and helped Burke in his fundraising efforts.

But, with the arrival of the Great Depression, and the numerous construction projects in nearly every Catholic diocese in the United States, donations dwindled. There was another reason that support began to evaporate, in that many priest and bishop alumni were opposed to supporting any project of a new seminary building, preferring that the Umiltà property remain the seminary's home, and that any new construction should be there, where the College was born.[23]

During their 1935 bishops' meeting, the College Episcopal Board reported that, to date, O'Hern and Burke had been able to collect only $469,055.00 [$7,877,556.18] for the Seminary Building Fund. Considering all expenses of the College, including the payment of the debt to Propaganda for purchasing the Janiculum property, the Building Fund was in debt to the principal College Fund for $13,061.21 [$219,356.83]. This was partially due to the lowered exchange rate of the American dollar, having decreased in value in Italy by 40%. The one department of the College paying its own way was the house for graduate priests, located in one of the old buildings on the American portion of the Janiculum property, the Casa San Giovanni. An important observation was made that would

---

Rossi, 1940-1943, 1948, Box 29, File 16.

[23] Buffalo June 27, 1939, Bishop John A. Duffy [NAC 1908] to Mons. Ralph L. Hayes, NAC, #224, H34: *NAC Construction, 1925-1954*, Folder: *Fund Drive-1926.*

affect the future decision to build the new seminary on the Janiculum and not on the Umiltà:

> Because of special advantages and privileges derived from its location, part of this Institution shows an operating surplus. The Janiculum site is extra-territorial, and as a consequence, property located there is tax-free. The Graduate School, moreover, enjoys the privilege of purchasing staple supplies in the Vatican City where food imports are not levied. A college erected on the new site would continue to enjoy these significant advantages and notably decrease its maintenance costs.[24]

The Second World War brought these fundraising efforts, architectural dreams and plans to a halt. The College closed in 1939 and the students and faculty returned home. But, not before the recently elected Pope Pius XII called upon the Americans not to forget their College in his encyclical letter, *Sertum laetitiae*, on the occasion of sesquicentennial anniversary of the establishment of the American Hierarchy:

> We greatly appreciate, too, your desire to erect in Roma a more worthy and suitable building for the Pontifical College which receives for their ecclesiastical education students from the United States.[25]

---

[24] "Report and Suggestions of the Sub-Committee of the Episcopal Committee for the North American College, Rome" [1935], NAC, #224, H34: *NAC Construction, 1925-1954*; Folder: *Fund Drive-1926*.

[25] *Sertum Laetitiae*, 32, 33: "It is indeed true that the elite of our youth profit by travel abroad to complete their education, a long and happy experience shows that candidates for the priesthood derive very great profit when they are educated here close to the See of Peter, where the source of faith is purest, where so many monuments of Christian antiquity and so many traces of the Saints incite generous hearts to magnanimous enterprises."

The Americans did not forget their Roman seminary, and a new Rector, Bishop Ralph Leo Hayes [NAC 1909], and a Vice Rector, Monsignor Allen Babcock [NAC 1925], technically held their College positions during the war, even though from the vantage point of the United States. Various proposals were made to the Rector that he rent the Umiltà and the College summer villa at Castel Gandolfo[26] in order to have some income with which to pay the Roman property taxes, and to provide some security, since the groups renting would be responsible for protecting the buildings.[27] The Rector refused them all,[28] until Cardinal Fumasoni-Biondi, Cardinal Prefect of the Propaganda, informed him in 1941 that the Propaganda had rented a portion of the old Orsini Palace wing of the Umiltà property to the Italian civil authorities, for which Propaganda received rent.[29]

Likewise, in 1942, the Vatican urged the College to rent the Villa Santa Caterina in Castel Gandolfo to the Italian government to house orphans, "in order to avoid drastic consequences that might result from refusal."[30] Despite warnings from the American government that Americans were prohibited from doing business with the enemy Italian government during wartime, the American

---

26   The Villa Santa Caterina was purchased by the Rector, Father William O'Connell [NAC 1884] in 1899 and served as the summer home for the College until the early 1970's, in the days when the seminarians did not return home until after their ordination to the priesthood. The Villa had been built in 1830 by the Orsini Family, which had also built the Palazzo Orsini on the Via dell'Umiltà, which was the original home of the College.

27   Rome September 4, 1940, Silvestri to Hayes, NAC: Coll. Amer., *Corrispond. Rettori, Card Spellman—M.C. Geough* [sic], Sub-folder: *Corrispond. Rettore S.E. Mons. Hayes.*

28   Crafton, Pennsylvania September 13, 1940, Hayes to Silvestri, NAC: Coll. Amer., *Corrispond. Rettori, Card Spellman—M.C. Geough* [sic], Sub-folder: *Corrispond. Rettore S.E. Mons. Hayes*: "La risposta e assolutamente definitivamente negativa."

29   N.p. October 10, 1941 Hayes to Spellman, NYC, Box S/C-73, Folder 1: *To Card. Spellman, N. Amer. Coll.* Hayes suggested that any rental fees from this should be deposited in the College account at the Vatican Bank. The College lawyer, Francesco Silvestri, watched over the College properties, defending its legal rights as best he could during the war.

30   Washington, D.C. January 9, 1943, Cicognani to Spellman, NYC, Box S/C-73, Folder 2: *To Card. Spellman, N. Amer. Coll.*

bishops were powerless to prevent the Italian government seizure and use of their lands, nor the Propaganda's renting portions of it to the Italian government.[31] "In this matter, ever since I left Rome, I have been hoping for the best and expecting the worst,"[32] wrote the Rector. Nothing could be done until the war's end.

Ultimately, the College buildings were taken over by Mussolini's government: the Umiltà Seminary housed war orphans, and the Villa Santa Caterina by the Commune di Castel Gandolfo to house repatriated children and families left homeless by the war.[33] The only College properties not taken over by the government were the College Mausoleum in the Campo Verano, and the Casa San Giovanni, atop the American portion of the Janiculum Hill property, watched over by two American priests, Fathers Joseph McGeough [NAC 1930], and Walter Carroll [NAC 1935].[34]

On November 11, 1944, the College Rector, Bishop Hayes was named the Bishop of Davenport, and a new College Rector

---

[31]   Washington, D.C. February 15, 1943, Mr. Adolf A. Berle, Jr. to Msgr. Michael Ready, NYC, Box S/C-73, Folder 2: *To Card. Spellman, N.Amer. Coll.* Berle was the United States Assistant Secretary of State.

[32]   Pittsburg, February 20, 1943, Hayes to Mons. John J. Casey [NAC 1927], NYC, Box S/C-73, Folder 2: *To Card. Spellman, N. Amer. Coll.*

[33]   NYC, Box S/C-73, Folder 1:*To Card. Spellman, N. Amer. College.* This file contains 1941-1943 correspondence between Spellman and American bishops and Francesco Silvestri, the College lawyer, and the Vatican concerning the question of "renting" the College property to the Italian government, rather than wait for the inevitable government confiscation. Spellman had been elected secretary of the Episcopal Board of the North American College in February 1941. The Castel Gandolfo property housed 1,500 Italians during the war years; the Umiltà housed "several thousand boys" during the war years.

[34]   Rome November 26, 1940, Bp. Ralph Hayes to Francesco Silvestri, NAC, *Corrisp. Rettori, Card. Spellman*, Folder: *Corrisp. Col Rett. S.E. Mons. Hayes.* The American priests working in the Vatican and living at the Casa San Giovanni agreed to pay their own housekeeping expenses, since the College had no operational income during the war years. Still, the College was responsible for the upkeep of its buildings, costly repairs, utility costs, and the paying of Roman property taxes on the Umiltà property, which they sent via the Propaganda Fide. The NAC Archives has a large number of letters dating 1940-1944 concerning the terrible physical and financial state of the College during the war years.

was needed. The President of the College Episcopal Board of Trustees, Dennis Cardinal Dougherty [NAC 1890], Archbishop of Philadelphia, sought the names of possible candidates from the other Board members.

During the summer of 1945, the Episcopal Board asked Francesco Silvestri, the College lawyer, to visit the College properties to assess their condition, and to draw up a report to assist a new Rector. He submitted his report, appropriately, on July 4, 1945, concluding that the Umiltà was a disaster, and still inhabited by Italian refugees. That left only the Villa Santa Caterina in Castel Gandolfo as the one viable location to re-open the College, and that was a complete mess: broken windows and doors, wrecked water and sewage systems, a non-functioning electrical system, no heating because it was a summer house, and no furniture or household equipment. Both Silvestri and Count Enrico Galeazzi,[35] the College architect, judged the Villa uninhabitable, even if emergency repairs were made costing an estimated 201,354,000 lire, which estimate included neither new hydraulic nor heating systems nor related construction.[36] The Episcopal Board of the College decided to finance the repairs using

---

[35] Enrico Galeazzi (1896-1986): A gifted Roman architect, was friend and trusted adviser of Pope Pius XII, who served the Pope during the war years as acting governor of Vatican City State, and personal representative of the Pope to President Roosevelt, bearing a letter to him in 1943 following the bombing of Rome. He also assisted in implementing Pius XII's policy to save the Jews of Rome, by helping coordinate the efforts of various religious orders to hide Jewish families. One famous incident, when Nazi soldiers forced their way into the Basilica of Saint Paul's Outside the Walls, Galeazzi personally stood in their way, protecting the scores of Jewish families hiding in the Basilica. Following the war, Galeazzi was the regular architect for the Reverenda Fabbrica San Pietro, whose work included the architectural planning for the excavations beneath Saint Peter's Basilica. For decades, Galeazzi was the official representative of the Knights of Columbus in Rome, and architect for numerous sports fields and youth organizations supported by the Knights for impoverished Italian children.

[36] Vatican July 4, 1945, Silvestri to Spellman, NYC, Box S/C-73, Folder 5: *To Card. Spellman, N. Amer. Coll.*

the few funds left in the Rector's bank account, even though it held only $18,577.81 [$237,470.86].[37]

By December 1945, both Silvestri and Galeazzi submitted a second, nineteen-page report to Francis Cardinal Spellman [NAC 1916], Archbishop of New York. The first and fundamental question was the location of the College once it re-opened: at the Via dell'Umiltà, at Castel Gandolfo, on the Janiculum property, or at another site somewhere in Rome.

They reported that temporary repairs to the Villa Santa Caterina, and the installation of a heating system "would resolve the old question whether the Villa could continue to be used only during the summer months, and would improve the property." They warned Spellman that the American bishops must keep in mind the continued possible threat of the City of Rome's master plan to cut a wide boulevard directly through the Umiltà property, as well as the need to define the legal relationship of the Propaganda Fide with the College concerning the Janiculum property. Likewise, if the College abandoned and sold the Umiltà site, the College would lose its unique relationship *ad beneplacitum Sanctae Sedis*, ["at the pleasure of the Holy See"], whatever that actually meant, and become simply a co-owner of property with the Propaganda Fide atop the Janiculum.[38]

Armed with these reports, the Board sought a priest of deep faith, immense talent, and experience for the job of Rector. Dennis Cardinal Dougherty sent a circular letter to the Board members on June 27th, asking their candidates and background information about each one.[39] Spellman sent two names in reply. His first choice was Monsignor Thomas F. Markham [NAC 1917], Pastor of St. Peter Church in Lowell, Massachusetts, one of Spellman's College friends. His second choice was Monsignor J. Gerald Kealy [NAC 1916],

---

[37] New York August 11, 1945, Spellman to Dougherty, NYC, Box S/C-73, Folder 5: *To Card. Spellman, N. Amer. Coll.*
[38] Rome, December 1945, Francesco Silvestri to Spellman, NAC, H 30.
[39] Philadelphia June 20, 1945, Dougherty to Spellman, NYC, Box S/C-73, Folder 5: *To Card. Spellman, N. Amer. Coll.* Philadelphia, June 27, 1945, same to same, NYC, in above ref.

Pastor of Saint Gertrude Parish in Chicago, Illinois, Spellman's College classmate and close friend.[40]

The Episcopal Board met at The Catholic University of America on July 18, 1945 to vote on the five final candidates, whose names were presented in alphabetical order. After a secret ballot, Markham received the highest number of votes, followed by Kealy, with Martin J. O'Connor [NAC 1924], Auxiliary Bishop of Scranton, in third place.[41] These three names made up the *terna*[42] that Dougherty sent along with the voting results to Cardinal Giuseppe Pizzardo, Prefect of the Congregation for Seminaries and University Studies, who would later be named Cardinal Protector of the College. When the Apostolic Delegate contacted Markham to announce the news, he was dumbfounded when Markham promptly refused the appointment![43] After some embarrassed scurrying about, the second choice of Spellman and the Board was named the new Rector, Monsignor J. Gerald Kealy of Chicago, who received notification of his appointment by January 1946, and left for Rome soon after.

Kealy was a close friend of both Spellman and Archbishop Amleto Cicognani, Apostolic Delegate to the United States.[44] Besides friendship, both Archbishops were aware of Kealy's strengths and talents, as well as his experience as a founding Rector of Our Lady of the Lake Seminary in the Archdiocese of Chicago.

---

[40] New York June 30, 1945, Spellman to Dougherty, NYC, Box S/C-73, Folder 5: *To Card. Spellman, N. Amer. Coll.*

[41] Philadelphia August 10, 1945 Dougherty to Pizzardo, NYC, Box S/C-73, Folder 5: *To Card. Spellman, N. Amer. College. Dougherty*: The alphabetical *terna* was, Msgr. Allen Babcock of Detroit; Msgr. J. Gerald Kealy of Chicago; Msgr. Thomas F. Markham of Boston; Bp. Martin J. O'Connor of Scranton; Bp. Thomas Boland of Newark [NAC 1922] "was added to the list during the meeting".

[42] Spellman Diary, July 18, 1945: "Meeting for American College election for Rector. Mons. Markham; Mons Kealey [sic], + Bp. O'Connor on Terna. Visited Apostolic Delegate with Abp Cushing + Bp. McIntyre returned to NY." NYC, Spellman Diary, vol. 23.

[43] Stamford, CT May 5, 2011, Interview with Archbishop Daniel Cronin [NAC 1953] by the author.

[44] Chicago January 29, 1946, Abp Samuel Stritch to Kealy, CUA, *O'Connor Papers*, Box 37, Folder: *Kealy, Msgr. J. Gerald.*

Throughout the winter and spring, Kealy visited the American College sites, met with Vatican officials, corresponded with American bishops and alumni, the College lawyer, Francesco Silvestri, and the College architect, Count Enrico Galeazzi in order to assess the situation and make recommendations to the Episcopal Board.

Spellman was also interested in the possibility that the Americans might acquire another Roman site for their seminary. Kealy was instructed to inquire about the purchase of the Hotel De La Ville, atop the Spanish Steps near the Hassler Hotel,[45] and to study the feasibility of purchasing another property further up the Janiculum Hill, the Villa Abamalek. The property had been owned by Prince Abamelek-Lazarev, cousin to Tsar Nicholas II, who had willed the property to the "Tsar and the Russian People", and was killed prior to the 1917 Revolution. After the Revolution, the Bolshevik government claimed ownership, which claims were repeated after World War II by Stalin's government against the claim to ownership by the Prince's exiled family.

Just as the Vatican had urged the American bishops to purchase the Janiculum property overlooking the Vatican in 1924 to forestall its development by an American Methodist group, so now they hoped the Americans might wrest the Villa Abamelek further up the Janiculum from the possible ownership by the Communist government of the Soviet Union.[46]

The Vatican's efforts to undermine the growing influence of Communism in Italy were very real, and the American bishops were pressed into service to assist in a variety of ways in the United States and in Europe, helping to provide vast amounts of funds, food and supplies to impoverished post-war Italy and throughout Europe, and to urge the American government to assist the rebuilding of Europe and derail Communist influence.[47]

---

[45] Stamford, CT May 5, 2011 Interview with Archbishop Daniel Cronin by the author. The Hotel De La Ville is today the Rome Intercontinental Hotel.

[46] Rome April 22, 1946, Silvestri to Kealy, CUA, *O'Connor Papers*, Box 37.

[47] New York June 21, 1948, Spellman to Galeazzi, NYC, S/C-20, Folder 14. Washington, D.C. July 8, 1948, Msgr. Edward Swanstrom to Spellman, NYC, S/C-20, Folder 14. New York July 14, 1948, Spellman to Galeazzi, NYC, S/C-20, Folder 14; New York August 7, 1948, Spellman to Galeazzi, NYC,

Following the consistory in February 1946, the American cardinals visited the Villa Abamalek site, and agreed it would be a more suitable property for the new College than their site lower down the Janiculum Hill, and would be free of any strings or hindrances by the Propaganda. Cardinals Stritch and Spellman supported the purchase. Kealy appreciated the location and beauty of the Villa, but thought the deal too risky, and the Abamelek family member urging the purchase to be untrustworthy.[48] Nevertheless, Galeazzi and Silvestri were instructed to look into the details for acquiring the property and buildings.[49] All design work for the new College was suspended until the purchase could be affected.[50] Eventually, the Italian government prohibited the sale, in favor of claims by the Soviet Union. The Villa Abamelek eventually became the residence for the Soviet ambassador to Italy, and remains so today, and the decision about the future site of the College was again focused on either the Umiltà or the Janiculum sites.[51]

In his first and only report to the College Episcopal Board, Monsignor Kealy wrote that the construction of a new College

---

S/C-20, Folder 14: This last letter involved Spellman providing $15,000 to De Gasperi, from American businessmen for the Catholic War Relief Services, to be deposited in the Vatican Bank and used in Italy.

[48]   Chicago May 21, 1946, Kealy to Spellman, NYC, Box S/C-73, Folder 6: *To Card. Spellman, N. Amer. Coll*: Kealy reported that he had visited the Villa Abamelek twice with Galeazzi. "It is a magnificent piece of property and in many respects would be preferable to the property on the Janiculum. But it seems to me its acquisition would involve political and financial difficulties and would further complicate the affairs of the College." New York May 27, 1946, Spellman to Kealy, NYC above reference: Spellman suggested that Kealy discuss the matter with Stritch. ". . . and if any action is to be taken and any authorization for action required, I shall be pleased to attend a meeting any time and place it is called."

[49]   Rome April 22, 1946, Silvestri to Kealy, CUA, *O'Connor Papers*, Box 37, File: Kealy, Msgr. J. Gerald.

[50]   Rome April 26, 1946, Galeazzi to Spellman, NYC, S/C-20, Folder 11: *To Card. Spellman from Count Galeazzi*.

[51]   Vatican June 18, 1946, Galeazzi to Kealy, CUA, *O'Connor Papers*, Box 44: NAC, File: *Reports*. Vatican June 19, 1946, Galeazzi "Report to the Committee of Bishops for the North American College in Rome", CUA, Box 44: *NAC Reports*.

would take at least three years.[52] During that time, the College should re-open as soon as possible, either at the Villa Santa Caterina or on the Via dell'Umiltà as temporary housing for the students: either choice would mean the expenditure of large sums of money. "We cannot use the buildings in their present condition. The Bishops must be in agreement to spend this money now if the College is to open in 1947." Kealy suggested that the College Building Fund not be touched for rehabilitation of these properties, preferring that an appeal be made to the American bishops and alumni to pay for the work. He estimated the Villa renovation would cost approximately $200,000 [$2,063,542.60]. Because the Villa had only been used by the seminarians during the summer months, the largest expense would be a heating system, as well as repairs and improvements to the buildings for all-year occupancy. He hoped the Villa would accommodate 175 students, "and would serve American College purposes until the erection of a new College in the City."[53]

Kealy next gave his recommendations for the Umiltà property which, "since 1940 has undergone tragic deterioration." Suggestions had been made to rehabilitate only the Palazzo Tomba, that portion of the Umiltà seminary complex that the Americans actually owned and held title to, and that they not touch the Palazzo Orsini portion of the Umiltà seminary, although that included the chapel, refectory and Rector's apartment, technically owned by the Propaganda. He recommended that the entire property be remodeled and repaired. But, Kealy observed, that would be inadequate for future use as a seminary for Americans, and a waste of money. It could be retained for future use as a house for American post-graduate student priests. He wrote,

> In the judgment of qualified technical experts in Rome, rehabilitation of the present buildings [on the Via dell'Umiltà] is out of the question. The walls

---

[52]   Rome June 8, 1946, Kealy to Episcopal Board, CUA, *O'Connor Papers*, Box 42: NAC, File: *Galeazzi Proposals and Estimates (1947-1950)*.
[53]   Rome June 8, 1946, Kealy Memorandum, CUA, *O'Connor Papers*, Box 42: NAC, Folder: *Galeazzi Proposals and Estimates (1947-50)*.

and foundations, due to age, are unsafe; utilities are completely ruined.

He continued:

> We yield to no one in loyal attachment to the hallowed traditions and revered memories of our Alma Mater, but in forming a decision affecting the future of the College, we must face actual facts and consider the future needs of the College. We must plan now, not plan for a generation but for several generations.

That new College, if built on the Janiculum site could accommodate 400 students, and would offer all American dioceses the possibility of sending students. The facility and grounds were very adequate, and a full and independent seminary might be considered, "constructing lecture-halls to obviate the necessity of students going elsewhere. A large enrollment would permit of our procuring the best professors in Rome for lecture courses in the various sciences."

The Rector concluded his memorandum that "The sooner a beginning is made, the sooner will the American College assume its rightful place among Roman institutions to the profit of the Church in the United States." He suggested an American architect be commissioned as a consultant, "in order that the College be built according to American standards and needs."

Galeazzi sent a lengthy report to the bishops, agreeing with Kealy and recommending that they not rush to re-open the College. It was his opinion that the Umiltà property was unsuitable and too small for a modern seminary, especially since its foundations were damaged. The only practical answer would be to demolish the buildings, except for the chapel, and construct a modern seminary, if the bishops preferred the Umiltà site. But the cost would be prohibitive, $1,200,000 [$14,159,076.92] and, since the site was small, the new building would have to rise eight stories to provide a suitable "modern" building. Therefore, the Villa Santa Caterina should be renovated for year-round occupancy, until a new building could be completed on the Janiculum property. He wrote:

> Neither must we be afraid that the eventual necessary expense might be excessive or badly employed, because this Villa is a most important property, which will ever be most useful to the College, located in a pleasant and healthy spot very close to Rome.[54]

Once title to the Palazzo Orsini at the Umiltà property was obtained from the Propaganda, the old buildings could be destroyed, except for the chapel, library, and refectory, and a new eight story seminary would rise, whose exterior walls would blend with the surroundings, the result would be "a prudent union of a small internal . . . skyscraper with the traditional Roman architecture of a Monastery."[55] The new building would nearly triple the size of the present Umiltà facility to roughly 90,000 cubic meters, with 330 single student rooms, besides the chapel, refectory, library, auditorium, gymnasium, faculty rooms and other facilities, with the main entrance moved to the Piazza della Pilotta. The title for the Umiltà would need to be transferred from the Propaganda to the American bishops, the deal possibly sweetened by the concession of the shared portion of the Janiculum property to sole ownership by the Propaganda. But, Galeazzi insisted, the entire Janiculum property should be retained by the Americans "in order to keep legally an extraterritorial ground in Rome. This might prove of some benefit in the future."

As progress seemed to be made, Kealy surprised everyone, submitting his resignation on August 15th, catching everyone off guard. Galeazzi gave voice to his and Spellman's consternation and sadness at Kealy's resignation when he wrote the Archbishop of New York, "He always had great sense, and entered well into the spirit

---

[54] Vatican June 19, 1946, Count Galeazzi, "Report to the Committee of Bishops for the North American College in Rome", NYC, Box S/C-73, Folder 6: *To Card. Spellman, N. Amer. Coll.*

[55] Vatican June 18, 1946, Galeazzi to Kealy, CUA, *O'Connor Papers*, Box 44: *NAC Reports*; Folder: *Report to the Board.*

of the difficulties of the College".[56] With Kealy, the College project seemed finally to be moving; now all was back to square one.

In his formal letter of resignation to Cardinal Pizzardo, Kealy mentioned surgery and daily medication for stomach ailments as the reasons for his decision. Since the treatment and recuperation would take some time, he thought it unjust to retain the office if he could not fulfill his duties in a timely fashion:

> From the depths of my heart, I am saddened by the resignation of this office, in which I had hoped to work for the greater Glory of God. But I am moved in justice and comforted knowing that God always gives us the grace to offer whatever sacrifice He calls us to make.[57]

During his few months as the Rector, Kealy had been faced with vast and numerous challenges in post-war Rome, whose economy and government were still in shambles. He was also faced with ruined College buildings, an immense building program for which he had insufficient funds, no assistant faculty, and no authority to make decisions in Rome without Board approval, and he was 3,500 miles from home. His loneliness, uncertain living conditions and isolation in post-war Rome may have exacerbated his health problems. In an age when international travel was difficult and communication limited, Kealy did what he could: he visited the College properties,

---

[56]   Rome August 13, 1946 Galeazzi to Spellman, NYC, S/C-20, Folder 11: *To Card. Spellman from Count Galeazzi.*

[57]   Chicago August 15, 1946 Kealy to Pizzardo, CUA, *O'Connor Papers*, Box 37, Folder: *Kealy, Msgr. J. Gerald.* In an email to the author, Robert Kealy wrote that his uncle's resignation was prompted by both illness and loneliness in Rome. He said his uncle suffered from ulcers, a very serious malady in the 1940's, often requiring surgery. Knowing this, Kealy made an agreement with his archbishop that he would accept the position as Rector only on the condition that one of his four assistant priests be named administrator of Saint Gertrude Parish, so that, if Kealy felt it necessary to resign from the College, he could return as pastor of Saint Gertrude's. Cicognani expressed his surprise at Kealy's decision, alluding to reasons besides poor health for Kealy's resignation, in his November 6, 1946 letter to Spellman.

met with Vatican officials, architects and lawyers, and ordered further studies, site maps and reports, which would form the basis for the American hierarchy's decisions about re-opening the College. Even after his resignation, Kealy continued for years to forward his opinions for the new seminary to Spellman, who used them as a foil to those of Kealy's successor, Bishop Martin J. O'Connor.[58]

---

[58] Rome November 5, 1946, Galeazzi to Spellman, NYC, S/C-20, Folder 11: *To Card. Spellman from Count Galeazzi.* "My dear Friend" is Galeazzi's salutation to the Cardinal Archbishop of New York.

Chapter 2

The New Rector and Post-War Dreams

"Since I do not seek this office, I consider the decision of the Committee as a manifestation of God's will for me. This gives me strength to assume such a responsibility."
—Bishop Martin J. O'Connor, 1946

Once again, names of candidates for the Rectorate were requested of the Episcopal Board members. In a letter to Count Galeazzi, Cardinal Spellman gave his rendition of the Board meeting in Philadelphia that drew up the new *terna* of candidates for Rome, even though he had been absent, attending the funeral of the wife of the Mayor of New York. Spellman listed the candidates: Bishop Martin J. O'Connor and Monsignor John J. Russell [NAC 1923], Pastor of Saint Patrick's Parish, Washington, D.C., were the choices of Edward Cardinal Mooney, Archbishop of Detroit. Monsignor John J. Wright [NAC 1935], secretary to the Archbishop of Boston, was supported by Archbishop Richard Cushing. Monsignor Allen Babcock [NAC 1925], Rector of the Cathedral in Detroit, was put forward by Bishop Ralph L. Hayes of Davenport. Monsignor John J. Hartigan [NAC 1923], was Spellman's choice. The *terna* sent to Rome was *Dignissimus* O'Connor, *Dignior* Babcock, and *Dignus* Hartigan.[59]

Following the meeting, Spellman met with the Apostolic Delegate, and informed him of the *terna*. But since Spellman had

---

[59] New York October 1946, Spellman to Galeazzi, KC, *Enrico Galeazzi Papers, No. Amer. Coll. Correspondence*, Box 30, File 16. Spellman and Galeazzi were great friends: this, and many other letters, are addressed "Dear Enrico", and signed "Frank Spellman."

already secured the appointment of his two failed earlier candidates, Markham and Kealy, Cicognani wanted to make sure another embarrassing nomination was not made. The Delegate wrote to those on the *terna* to ascertain if each would accept the appointment if offered the job by the Holy See.[60] After receiving the Delegate's letter, O'Connor phoned him to arrange a meeting. "When I saw him [O'Connor] last Monday," the Apostolic Delegate later wrote Spellman, "I immediately explained that the reason for wishing to know his mind on the question of his own appointment was to provide against the possibility that the post would again be declined by a designated candidate."[61]

Martin J. O'Connor was named Rector of the North American College on November 15, 1946, effective November 21st, as Cicognani informed Spellman in a handwritten note, just after the cable from Rome arrived in Washington, D.C., "at—5:00 pm."[62] Spellman had expressed his opinion of O'Connor a month earlier to Count Galeazzi: "He [O'Connor] would be satisfactory but no ball of fire. I shall be surprised if he accepts because he is already a bishop, happily situated and not too strong."[63]

After the new Rector's appointment, and after having met and spoken with O'Connor, the Archbishop of New York offered a more pragmatic opinion to Galeazzi, possibly because he knew they both would be working with O'Connor on the new College: "I believe that you will find him [O'Connor] a devoted, capable and earnest person. He is much interested in the college and most reasonable to deal with in matters concerning it."[64] Spellman was less than enthusiastic

---

[60] Washington, D.C. October 31, 1946, Cicognani to O'Connor, CUA, *O'Connor Papers*, Box 59, Folder: *Confidential*.

[61] Washington, D.C. November 6, 1946, Cicognani to Spellman, NYC, Box S/C-73, Folder 6: *To Card. Spellman, N. Amer. Colleg.*

[62] Washington, D.C. November 15, 1946, Cicognani to Spellman, NYC, above ref.

[63] New York October 1946, Spellman to Galeazzi, KC, *Enrico Galeazzi Papers, No. Amer. Coll. Correspondence*, Box 30, File 16. The official letter of appointment as Rector is in CUA, *O'Connor Papers*, Folder: *Confidential Abp O'Connor*.

[64] New York November 30, 1946, Spellman to Galeazzi, KC, *Enrico Galeazzi Papers*, above ref., Box 30, File 16.

about O'Connor's appointment, because, if contemporary clerical gossip be believed, O'Connor had not been Spellman's choice for the job, and had hoped his friends, namely, Markham, Kealy, and Hardigan, would have succeeded.[65] Yet, very soon after O'Connor's appointment, Spellman gave him $5,000 for the College.[66]

Martin J. O'Connor was born to Martin and Belinda [nee Caffrey] O'Connor, on May 18, 1900 in Scranton, Pennsylvania. He received a Catholic education and enlisted in the United States Army in 1918. Following World War I, he began studies for the priesthood, first at Saint Mary's Seminary in Baltimore, followed by his theological studies at the Pontifical Institute of Saint Apollinaris in Rome. He was a member of the North American College priestly ordination class of 1924. O'Connor served in various chancery posts in his home diocese, was a pastor, and was named to the titular see of Thespia on November 11, 1942, and appointed Auxiliary Bishop to the Bishop of Scranton.[67]

O'Connor had shown himself a capable priest and administrator. But he was not flashy, either personally or religiously speaking, compared to his predecessor. Monsignor Kealy cut a dashing figure and could have been the embodiment of the post-war American Catholic priest, capable of commanding the respect of the new American seminarians, many of whom were war veterans.[68] Kealy was prayerful, intellectually astute, personable, and a charming

---

[65]   Washington, D.C. December 11, 1952, Msgr. Joseph P. Christopher to Msgr. Florence D. Cohalan, NYC, Box S/B-12, Folder 2: *About Card. Spellman.* Likewise, O'Connor became a close friend with Galeazzi, and through Galeazzi, became known and trusted by Pius XII and Madre Pascalina, who had served as Pius' housekeeper and trusted head of the papal staff for years, thus adding a personal aspect to any future decision-making about the College that involved the Archbishop of New York.

[66]   New York, November 30, 1946, Spellman to O'Connor, NYC, Box S/C-73, Folder 6: *To Card. Spellman, N. Amer. Coll.*

[67]   *New York Times*, January 28, 1943, p. 14: Monsignor Fulton J. Sheen preached the sermon at O'Connor's episcopal consecration.

[68]   Rome, May 9 & May 24, 1947, Fr. Joseph Lacy to O'Connor, CUA, *O'Connor Papers*, Box 25, Folder 11: *Misc.* U.S. Government checks were sent to the College for many war vet seminarians, whose educational expenses were covered under the Servicemen's Readjustment Act of 1944: the G.I. Bill.

conversationalist, athletic, handsome, an accomplished administrator, seminary rector, and pastor.

At first glance, O'Connor was his antithesis: round, un-athletic, quiet, and apparently uncomfortable in society, a man more accustomed to deskwork and clerical circles. He was also subject to health problems, serious for the time, which he endured quietly while continuing his work. And he spoke in an awkward manner, with an accent and phrasing more Gilbert and Sullivanesque than modern mid-20th century American. This was partially the result of hearing problems he suffered throughout his life, about which few were aware. In his later years, he wore two hearing aids. His pronunciation was as much the product of what he perceived he had heard as it was due to any training he received or efforts he made. "He never heard well, and imitated in speech what he heard", even if his poor hearing distorted the actual speech of the one speaking to him. "He read peoples' lips as much as heard what they said."[69] His was not the "type" portrayed by Hollywood as having won the war or as a dashing American priest.

For all these traits, O'Connor was misjudged too often as pompous and stuffy, and dismissed as inept and old fashioned. Yet, he was a man of deep faith and piety, a thoroughly dedicated priest who loved the Church and the priesthood. He also had a superb yet dry sense of humor,[70] and a streak of generosity and understanding only recognized by the more astute observers and co-workers. And, he was smart. In his reply to Archbishop Cicognani's October 31, 1946 letter asking if he would accept the appointment as Rector, O'Connor answered he would, if named, then continued:

---

[69] Stamford, June 14, 2011, interview by the author of His Eminence Edward Cardinal Egan [NAC 1954].

[70] Stories about "OKY" or "THE OAKBALL" abound. Years ago, one of his students told me that, as he sneaked through the Rector's garden at the Villa to take a quick and prohibited early morning swim in the pool, he was stunned to see O'Connor hauling himself out of the water. O'Connor came up to the petrified seminarian and told him, "Tell no man of this vision", then returned to the Villa to dress for the day's work.

> May I assure Your Excellency that I regard the recommendation of the Bishops' Committee as a sign of great confidence for I look upon the training of young men for the priesthood in this National College as a work of the highest importance for the Church in America.

> Since I do not seek this office, I consider the decision of the Committee as a manifestation of God's will for me. This gives me strength to assume such a responsibility.[71]

O'Connor and Kealy were at opposite poles, humanly speaking, yet they balanced each other, for they were identical in their dedication to the Church, and love for the College and the priesthood. Both were superbly capable priests, in their own ways, with their own talents and strengths.

O'Connor's deep faith and humble priestly piety supplied him strength as he entered into the difficult task of re-opening the College and building a new seminary in post-war Rome. This can be seen in his numerous letters to bishops and priests, notes to Count Galeazzi, who became his very close friend, to Francesco Silvestri, the College lawyer, and to the members of the College faculty who carried out his plans during his frequent trips back home to secure support, funding and students for the College. Many of these communications included requests for prayers for strength and guidance, Mass intentions for success of the seminary project, and repeated statements of appreciation for God's grace and strength that came to him through his friends and staff.[72] All the

---

[71]   Wilkes-Barre, PA, n.d., Bp Martin J. O'Connor to Abp. Amleto Cicognani, CUA, *O'Connor Papers*, Box 59, Folder: *Confidential Papers*. Cicognani immediately passed on O'Connor's reply to Spellman in his letter of November 6, 1946, NYC, Box S/C-73, Folder 6: *To Card. Spellman, N. Amer. Coll.*

[72]   Stamford, June 14, 2011 interview by the author of Edward Cardinal Egan, who was one of O'Connor's students and served as a chapel organist soon after the new College opened. Cardinal Egan told me that one day, the Rector

archival collections containing O'Connor's correspondence about the College during his years as Rector bear witness to his deep sense of duty and piety, and a special devotion to Saint Therese of Lisieux.[73]

The new Rector spent his first days on the job visiting Cardinals Dougherty, Spellman, Stritch, and Mooney "and [I] have ascertained their minds in relation to the preparation of a report for the Episcopal committee after I have had an opportunity to make a study of the conditions in Rome concerning the American College."[74] Spellman informed him that the plans discussed in Rome the past February "whereby the Villa was to be put into condition to receive classes pending the erection of a new college on the Janiculum", and:

> that at the meeting in Philadelphia the opinion seemed to favor the conditioning of the old college on the Via dell'Umiltà as a temporary site for the college with the idea that it might be used at some future date for priest-students of the college and for post-graduate priest-students.[75]

---

was to receive the vows of some religious sisters during a Mass at a nearby convent. The sisters had phoned to ask if he could bring along an organist, and the Rector sent the young seminarian from Chicago a message asking if he would step in at the last minute. Egan went to O'Connor's apartment to give his answer early that evening. The Rector thanked him and then, as he was showing Egan to the door, they passed by his private chapel. Egan noticed the candles lit, and the Rector explained that it was his custom to spend the entire night before ordinations or solemn professions of sisters in his private chapel in prayer before the exposed Blessed Sacrament

[73] Rome July 5, 1954, O'Connor to Galeazzi, KC, *Enrico Galeazzi Papers*, N. Amer. Coll, Corresp: *Most Rev. Martin J. O'Connor, 1953-1954*, Box 30, File 13: O'Connor included roses in his Episcopal coat of arms in honor of Saint Therese of Lisieux.

[74] Scranton December 2, 1946, O'Connor to Cicognani, CUA, *O'Connor Papers*, Box 46, Folder: *O'Connor, personal.*

[75] New York January 4, 1947, Spellman to Kealy, NYC, Box S/C-73, Folder 8: *To Card. Spellman, N. Amer. Coll.*

The Rector also met with Kealy while in Chicago, to obtain his predecessor's observations and ideas.[76]

O'Connor arrived in Rome on December 13, 1946. He had informed the Apostolic Delegate of his plans to live at the Casa San Giovanni, the only habitable building of the North American College, located on the Janiculum property, which Kealy had re-opened for graduate student priests.[77] While living there, O'Connor followed the daily rule and schedule of the priests' residence, then under the supervision of house superior, Father Edward Glavin [NAC 1935], even personally making the expected student priest payment for room and board "of $50.00 a month for expenses of living in his own college!"[78]

The Episcopal Board asked O'Connor to prepare a report for an executive session [Cardinals Dougherty, Mooney, Spellman & Stritch] during their upcoming April, 1947 meeting. That meeting would set the course for the College, underscoring the major challenges for Americans building in post-war Rome, and reveal the strength of personalities working on one project, while a world apart from each other, in many ways.

As he visited the College properties, and met with Galeazzi and Silvestri, O'Connor designed his report to answer the basic questions left unanswered for decades. The first question was the location for the College: whether to restore, rebuild, and modernize, or to tear

---

[76] New York November 30, 1946 Spellman to Kealy, NYC, Box S/X-73, Folder 6: *To Card. Spellman, No. Amer. Coll.*

[77] Scranton December 2, 1946, O'Connor to Cicognani, CUA, *O'Connor Papers*, Box 46.

[78] "Memorandum concerning the Holy See approval of the opening of the Casa with Father Glavin in Charge", NAC, H18: *Casa San Giovanni*, #9. Vatican September 24, 1946, Cardinal Pizzardo to Mons. Giovanni Montini, NAC, *Casa San Giovanni*, #9, H18: The opening of the Casa San Giovanni for American graduate priest studies was approved by the Holy See on September 24, 1946, with Monsignor Joseph McGeough to continue as pro-procurator of the College until the arrival of Father Edward Glavin. Rome October 25, 1946, Msgr. Joseph McGeough to Fr. Edward Glavin, NAC, in above reference: The Casa followed a normal seminary schedule of 6-8 a.m. private meditation and Mass; community meals in silence with readings; scheduled community devotions.

down the Via dell'Umiltà site; or to build a new building atop the Janiculum; or to scrap both and purchase another site.[79] All these possibilities had been considered seriously by the bishops since the war's end. Another reality became clear to the Rector: he would be traveling to and from the United States frequently to rally the support of bishops, alumni, bankers and lay donors, and to seek the approval of the Episcopal Board for nearly every aspect of the project, since he had no authority to make decisions or to sign contracts.

He also realized the extent of his duties and responsibilities: to administer the graduate studies program at the Casa San Giovanni; to restore the various College buildings; to re-open and administer one of them as the temporary home of the College; to build the new College; to secure the financial and moral support of the American hierarchy; and to recruit new students. Likewise, he found himself crossing the Atlantic and crisscrossing the United States in an era when international and domestic commercial air travel was very expensive, tediously cumbersome, and as unpredictable as the weather.

Once he understood that his work would be both in Rome and all around the United States, O'Connor needed to build a team to help with the work on the ground in Rome while he was in the States. Francisco Silvestri continued as the College lawyer, and worked well with O'Connor, writing him, "Your capacity in assimilating and solving the many problems of the American College in Rome, remind [sic] me of the English sentence: 'The right man in the right place.'"[80] He needed a seminary faculty, and an architect had to be named, although Count Galeazzi unofficially continued to fill that post. One of O'Connor's first requests was the appointment of a Vice Rector and a Business Manager, who could run the College operations on the ground in Rome while he himself worked as a traveling salesman for the College at home. His request illustrated the red tape that had frustrated Kealy, and threatened to undermine the entire project: the Rector had no authority to make decisions in

---

[79]   Rome December 1945, Francesco Silvestri to Spellman, NAC, H 30.
[80]   Rome March 30, 1947, Silvestri to O'Connor, NAC, Coll. Amer., *Corrispondenza Rettori, Card. Spellman.*

Rome, because Spellman insisted that the Episcopal Board vote on nearly everything.

O'Connor wrote the Archbishop of New York in February 1947, requesting the appointment of Father Richard Burns [NAC 1937] as his Vice Rector. Burns, a priest of the Diocese of Rochester, was already in Rome, working in the offices of the Oriental Congregation. O'Connor had already spoken with his boss, Cardinal Tisserant, about releasing the priest from his Vatican post.[81] Galeazzi also wrote Spellman, telling him of O'Connor's intention to hire Burns as Vice-Rector. Galeazzi agreed with the Rector, telling the Archbishop of New York that he thought O'Connor should have a Business Manager as well:

> I agree fully that he should not be alone. The American rectorship should be complete and efficient all the time (while the Rector is in the States also) during the progress of these important works. The rector is active, very prudent, conservative and diligent.[82]

Spellman began by writing to the Bishop of Rochester asking if he would release Burns for the new work at the College, and then he wrote all the Board members asking their opinions. "I think that Bishop O'Connor should have anyone he desires to work with him in the capacity of Vice-Rector of the American College", Archbishop Cushing wrote in reply to Spellman, of the opinion that the Bishop-Rector should be making his own decisions.[83] One month later, after written responses had been obtained from all the Board members, and the Apostolic Delegate informed, Spellman notified O'Connor that he had his Vice Rector. By the end of April, the College also had a Business Manager, Fr. Joseph Lacy [NAC 1938]

---

[81] Rome February 1, 1947, O'Connor to Spellman, CUA, *O'Connor Papers*, Box 36, Folder: *Burns*.

[82] Rome February 3, 1947, Galeazzi to Spellman, NYC, S/C-20, Folder 12: *To Card. Spellman from Count Galeazzi*.

[83] Brighton February 15, 1947, Cushing to Spellman, NYC, Box S/C-73, Folder 9: *To Card. Spellman, N. Amer. Coll.*

of Hartford, and a Spiritual Director, Monsignor Charles Fitzgerald [NAC 1916].[84]

The final member of the Roman team was the architect. O'Connor suggested that an American architect be given the commission to design the new College, since it would be an American design for American seminarians, albeit in Rome. Spellman sought the counsel of Count Galeazzi, hoping his position as College architect would be confirmed by the Episcopal Board, even though Galeazzi had told his friend in November 1946 not to feel any obligation to secure him the post.[85] Galeazzi thought the architect should be an Italian, familiar with Rome, knowledgeable of the building materials available locally, and having an understanding of the unions, whose designs and plans might be sent to an American architect for comments.[86]

O'Connor returned to the States in the spring of 1947 for the bishops' meetings, insisting that he personally make the presentations about the College to the bishops. The executive committee of the Episcopal Board [Cardinals Dougherty, Stritch, Mooney and Spellman] decided to grant the commission to design the new College to Count Galeazzi, after Spellman's urging, during their April 23, 1947, meeting at Saint Charles Seminary outside Philadelphia.[87] The Board also approved Spellman's suggestion that Galeazzi's architectural plans be reviewed by a "special" office of the Archdiocese of New York, which would choose a consultant architect to assist Galeazzi in his work. All decisions about the new building, from design and construction to finances, were to be made through the Archdiocese of New York, through the offices of Monsignor John Maguire [NAC 1928], and the archdiocesan architect Thomas A. Kelly.

---

[84] New York April 28, 1947, Spellman to O'Connor, CUA, *O'Connor Papers*, Box 44, NAC.

[85] Rome November 5, 1946, Galeazzi to Spellman, NYC, S/C-20, Folder 11: *To Card. Spellman from Count Galeazzi.*

[86] Rome February 3, 1947, Galeazzi to Spellman, NYC, S/C-20, Folder 12: *To Card. Spellman from Count Galeazzi.*

[87] Wilkes-Barre April 25, 1947, O'Connor's "Report for His Eminence, Francis Cardinal Spellman", CUA, *O'Connor Papers*, Box 44: *NAC.*

At the same meeting, the bishops decided that the Umiltà property be studied and renovated for future use by student priests; that Galeazzi begin work on designs and studies for the new home of the College on the Janiculum to house 300 students; and that the Villa Santa Caterina in Castel Gandolfo be studied and renovated for temporary student use until the Umiltà was repaired. The seminarians would then move into the Umiltà to await the construction of the new College; graduate student priests should be accepted for the Casa San Giovanni on the Janiculum property; and, the new College faculty was approved and their salaries set.[88] The College re-opening would be deferred until October, 1948 with fifty students, 25 in first year philosophy, 25 in first year theology, and their annual tuition would be set at $720.00 [$7,428.62] per student. The Rector was instructed to study the admissions requirements of other seminaries, as well as to conduct another study about the College rules, and to report his findings to the bishops. The Board even voted on the amount and type of clothing each student should bring!—"two cassocks, shoes, hat and necessary underclothing."[89]

The next subject was the title to the College properties. The Episcopal Board empowered the Rector to secure the title to the Orsini Palace portion of the Umiltà property, still owned by the Propaganda Fide, for which the College paid an annual tax to the Roman government, since the fall of the Papal States in 1870.[90] Likewise, a portion of the Janiculum property was co-owned by both

[88] Wilkes-Barre April 25, 1947, O'Connor's "Report for His Eminence", section 12, above ref: The Vice Rector's annual salary was $1,200; the business manager's, $600; the Rector's, $2,000. The Board, however, failed to include the salaries in the budget, which caused practical problems.

[89] Wilkes-Barre April 25, 1947, O'Connor's "Report to His Eminence", sections 4 & 5, above ref.

[90] Detroit April 9, 1941, Mooney to Spellman, NYC, Box S/C-73, Folder 1: *To Card. Spellman, N. Amer. Coll.* Mooney wrote that in 1924, when negotiating the purchase of the Janiculum property, "I came to know of the agreement by which Propaganda gave the American College perpetual use of the property on the Via dell'Umiltà. This agreement had to do with that part of the building which faces on the Umiltà and the Archetto, running back to a point somewhat beyond the 'Green Door.' The newer part of the building, facing on the Piazza Pilotta, was purchased during Archbishop Kennedy's

the American bishops and the Propaganda Fide, and clarification of the property lines was needed. O'Connor was also to settle a property dispute with the town authorities of Castel Gandolfo concerning the Villa Santa Caterina, and to restore the College Mausoleum.

The final element necessary to re-open the College was funding. But the bishops decided only to discuss the College operational budget for 1947, which did not include anything about the funding for new construction on the Janiculum.[91] The Rector was instructed to stay in correspondence with Spellman "as questions would arise." Likewise, he was given authority "for an expenditure of a sum not to exceed $2,500 [$25,794.28] at any given time". In everything, O'Connor was to report to the Archbishop of New York.[92]

O'Connor's final duty while in the States was to attend the annual alumni meeting in Chicago in May 1947. This was an important event, because the support of the priest and bishop alumni was essential to the College project. Many of the alumni and bishops favored remaining at the Via dell'Umiltà. But most had no idea how seriously damaged the buildings were, or that post-war Rome was another world, remembering only their student days in a city and a College very much changed by the war.

In response to the traditional toast to the College, the Rector offered his observations, making the point that the new College

---

time and belongs absolutely to the College." He knew there was a tax on the Propaganda portion of the building.

[91] Wilkes-Barre April 25, 1947, O'Connor's "Report for His Eminence, Francis Cardinal Spellman", CUA, *O'Connor Papers*, Box 44: *NAC*. $100,000 was appropriated for the immediate renovation of the Villa Santa Caterina in Castel Gandolfo, to serve as the temporary home of the College once it re-opened in 1948. Likewise, an additional $5,000 was appropriated to settle with the town authorities, who wanted the College to build and pay for housing for displaced Italian families in the town, before beginning discussions about the College property. Fees for Galeazzi and Silvestri were also granted, and the Rector empowered to restore the mausoleum, to purchase a small bus for student transportation, a refrigerator and general repairs for the House of Studies. Wilkes-Barre May 13, 1947, O'Connor to Burns, CUA, *O'Connor Papers*, Box 36: Folder: *Burns*: The student priests had been using an old "decrepit" army ambulance to get around Rome.

[92] Ibid, section 11: "Instructions."

would still be the College remembered and loved by the alumni. To emphasize this, O'Connor had secured the active support and assistance of his three predecessors: Bishop Eugene S. Burke, Bishop Ralph L. Hayes, and Monsignor J. Gerald Kealy. He told the alumni that, soon after arriving in Rome, he offered Mass for the living and deceased alumni in the private chapel of a College alumnus, Monsignor William Hemmick [NAC 1905], in the Palazzo Doria:

> My particular reason for the Mass there was because long ago there was a young man ordained privately on this site, who had a great deal to do with the foundation of our Alma Mater. That young man later became His Holiness, Pope Pius IX. I mention this because all of us at this meeting will return as emissaries to our respective dioceses with a spirit of harmony and unity of thought in supporting the policy of the Episcopal Administrative Committee in everything that concerns this Seminary.[93]

O'Connor described the ruinous state of the College properties, and told the alumni that the Board had decided to restore the Villa Santa Caterina as the temporary home of the College, which would re-open for the fall term of 1948. Once the Umiltà property was repaired, the students would move back to the city, and there await the completion of the new College on the Janiculum. O'Connor then described the city—so very changed after the war, but still the city they all loved:

> Rome is a large and far flung metropolitan city. Where you and I walked in the country, we now find roads and apartment houses. A city that fifty years ago had a small population, now numbers 1,700,000 souls. We all love the old site on the Via dell'Umiltà.

---

[93]   Chicago May 8, 1947, "Address to NAC Alumni Association meeting," CUA, *O'Connor Papers*, Box 46.

We would like to have it as a permanent site for the College if possible. But it is practically impossible to erect a satisfactory building within the limited space provided on the site of the old College, unless the College remained with a very small student body.

The Janiculum property was purchased twenty years earlier, he told the alumni, for the very purpose of erecting a new North American College, close by the Successor of Saint Peter and the Tomb of the Prince of the Apostles. The Janiculum was no longer on the outskirts of the city, and it was extra-territorial:

In other words, we have outgrown our present location [Umiltà], but we will not abandon it if our priest students use it in the future. Unless we wish to leave Rome altogether and live eight or ten kilometers from the city, there is no desirable site left for us in the heart of things except on the Janiculum Hill. We are all confident that it is God's work. However, we must be prepared for the interference of the devil in such an important fundamental undertaking as the re-establishment of this Seminary in Rome. I am certain that those two outstanding marks of a Christian—a lively conscious faith, and readiness to do God's will are the characteristics of every alumnus of the North American College and will, on your part and mine, help to restore our Alma Mater to a bright place in the sun of the Eternal City.

Following the reunion, the Rector wrote separately to Monsignor Burns, Father Lacy, Count Galeazzi, and Francesco Silvestri, reporting the Board's decisions, and parceling out tasks to each: the priests were to continue administering the Casa San Giovanni and visit the Villa Santa Caterina weekly to make sure repair work progressed; Galeazzi was to begin drawing up exact architectural plans of the buildings and properties on the Umiltà, Castel Gandolfo, and on the Janiculum, and begin plans for renovation at all sites;

Silvestri was to begin looking into the property titles for all the College properties.[94] Trying to cut costs, he instructed all to make only the most basic repairs necessary for use of the buildings, and to make no improvements, since the costs were so high and the budget limited.[95] He sailed back to Rome on June 27, 1947.[96]

During the summer months, following the Board's instructions, O'Connor wrote each American ordinary, announcing the College re-opening in October 1948, asking each bishop to send candidates of "sound health, emotional stability and a very satisfactory preliminary general scholastic record, especially in the study of Latin," the language of the university lectures.[97] Fulfilling the instructions of the Episcopal Board from their meeting in April 24, 1947, O'Connor and his team worked to complete renovation estimates and architectural drawings of the College properties, to make preliminary architectural drawings for the new college, and to conclude questions of property titles with the Propaganda and the town of Castel Gandolfo.

Lengthy reports were prepared by all the Roman team members, as the background for O'Connor's report, scheduled to be presented

---

94   Rome June 18, 1947, O'Connor to Burns, CUA, *O'Connor Papers*, Box 36, Folder: *Burns*. The College had hired permanent help to watch over the College properties and make repairs, as well as a driver for the Rector who was Primo Spaghetti. Cardinal Egan told me the students had loosely translated his name, and called him the "Prime Noodle", during the 1950's. O'Connor also found cars for Galeazzi and Silvestri, whose automobiles had been confiscated during the war, as well as replacement car parts, tires and food for the 16 student-priests, all of which was provided by the War Relief Services.

95   Scranton May 29, 1947, O'Connor to Galeazzi, KC, *Galeazzi Papers*, Box 30, File 7: Writing about the remodeling of the Umiltà property: "Outside of plumbing, heating, electricity and the absolutely necessary repairs, I would not suggest radical changes or great improvements, in order to lower the costs if possible. May I suggest that one alternative include hot running water at convenient places on each floor, but not in the [student] rooms."

96   *New York Times*, June 28, 1947, "The American College in Rome will reopen in the fall of 1948, the Most Rev Martin J. O'Connor, new director of the educational institute, said before sailing yesterday aboard the Italian liner *Saturnia*."

97   Rome August 23, 1947, O'Connor to USA Bishops, NAC, H30.

during the October 17, 1947 Philadelphia meeting of the four cardinals on the College's Executive Committee. Since Cardinal Mooney could not attend, the meeting was re-scheduled at the last minute to November 10, 1947, for Curley Hall at The Catholic University of America in Washington, D.C.[98] The Rector sent detailed reports by Galeazzi and Silvestri, as well as preliminary sketches for the renovations of the old College and the construction of the new College, which formed the basis of his own report, at the end of which were his suggestions about the "next step in the future of the College."[99]

He also sent along his own observations about the financing of the College and the construction of the new seminary. The numbers were staggering. Because the buildings of the original College on the Via dell'Umiltà were in generally bad condition, the renovation cost was estimated to be $550,000 [$5,158,856.50], and "20% for contingencies" and new furnishings, since the furniture left behind at the beginning of the war had been destroyed or rendered unusable by the Italian war orphans. It was estimated that a full year would be necessary for the work to be completed, hopefully by October 1, 1948. The construction of the new seminary on the Janiculum Hill, designed to house 300 students, was estimated to cost $2,740,000 [$28,270,533.63]. The restoration work of the summer Villa Santa Caterina in Castel Gandolfo was under way. The installation of a heating system for year-round occupancy at the Villa was begun, since the College would re-open there until the Umiltà was completed. In April, the bishops had given O'Connor $100,000 [$1,031,771.30], as well as an additional $25,000 [$257,942.83] for the repairs at the Villa. The Casa San Giovanni on the Janiculum property, which was housing the student priests, had required $3,500 [$36,112.00] for repairs during the summer, and the repairs of the College mausoleum at Campo Verano, costing $1,500 [$15,476.57], were nearly completed.

---

[98] Scranton October 15, 1947, O'Connor to Burns, CUA, *O'Connor Papers*, Box 36, Folder: *Burns*.
[99] Rome October 15, 1947, O'Connor to Episcopal Board, CUA, *O'Connor Papers*, Box 36, Folder: *Burns*.

The negotiations concerning the boundaries of the American property on the Janiculum and the transfer of the ownership title of the old College buildings to the American bishops, both with Propaganda Fide, were completed, except for the formalities; those with the town of Castel Gandolfo had broken down.[100]

From this point, the major decisions were reached concerning the future of the North American College, and the major challenges identified, which would occupy O'Connor and his team, as well as the Executive Committee of the Board for the subsequent six years.

One should remember that while these challenges were being met, the Rector and his team would also be involved in the daily operation of the student priest graduate house on the Janiculum Hill; the daily running of a seminary, once it re-opened in October 1948; the entire construction project on the Janiculum; frequent labor strikes; post-war shortages of building materials; the solicitation of American bishops to send new seminarians; interminable meetings with Propaganda and Vatican officials about property titles to the College lands and buildings; endless meetings with the Italian government for the removal of war orphans; the return of College property; blocked lire negotiations to fund the construction; numerous meetings with the city government of Rome for permits for restoration of historic buildings and new construction on the Umiltà property; the opening and staffing of a new office to accommodate the tens of thousands of American pilgrims to the Vatican during the Holy Year of 1950 and the Marian Year of 1954; and the extending of hospitality to American cardinals, bishops, priests and laity, who came to see the construction and the College. Add to these Bishop O'Connor's numerous and deteriorating health issues, and his dealing with the personal relationships of all involved, and one has an idea of O'Connor's challenges during the next years.

Likewise, put all this in the international context of a post-war world. Both the Vatican and the United States worked together to

---

[100] "Report of the Rector", October 17, 1947, CUA, *O'Connor Papers*, Box 44: *NAC*. The exchange rate noted in the report was 600 Lire per $1. Another difficulty was the removal of the children and some families from the old College, not a high priority for the Italian government at war's end.

rebuild Europe, directing massive international relocation efforts of refugees, supplying vast quantities of money, food, medicines, and clothing, as well as working to protect Western Europe from the widening Communist influence of the Soviet Union. In Rome, and in all Italy, the influence of the Communist party was very real, especially among trade unions. In the general elections of 1948, the United States, the Vatican and the Christian Democratic Party, led by Alcide De Gasperi, joined forces to urge Italians to reject the blandishments of Communist idealism, by providing financial assistance and goods to the Italian government, and by providing jobs in projects such as the construction of the North American College. Food rationing, shortages in building materials, serious outbreaks of disease, frequent labor strikes, and the effect on the exchange rates and commodities markets by the Korean War, all made the construction of a massive modern reinforced concrete building in post-war Rome a task of Herculean proportions, set upon the shoulders of a man who certainly did not look like a citizen of Olympus. And none of these challenges was faced independently of one another, they were unrelenting and simultaneous, a fact often forgotten.[101]

And yet, the *OAKBALL*, supported and guided by Galeazzi and Silvestri, fulfilled the dual-duty for which he was sent to Rome: to re-open the North American College after the war, and to build its new home on the *Gianicolo*. Among the many challenges he faced completing his task were the securing of the property titles of the College sites from Propaganda Fide, and finding the necessary funding for the construction of the Janiculum seminary.

---

[101] Another *OAKBALL* story is told that, soon after the Umiltà repairs were completed and the students took up residence in 1949, an American priest visited. Ignorant of the extent of the repairs recently completed, he expressed surprise that it had taken so long to re-open the College, since he thought only a new paint job had been needed. The Rector reportedly snorted, "Yes young man, a $700,000 paint job!"

Bishop Martin J. O'Connor's Episcopal Coat-of-Arms.

Pontifical North American College Coat-of-Arms.

Blessed Pope Pius IX.

(courtesy Basilica of Saint John Archives)

Like the colonies there were thirteen originals. Seated in the middle is Edward McGlynn, upperclassman from the Propaganda College assigned as temporary prefect of the twelve new " Romani. "

The original "Nordamericani", 1860.

(courtesy Pontifical North American College Archives)

THE AMERICAN COLLEGE FACING ON VIA DELL' UMILTÀ

The College on Via dell'Umiltà, circa 1900.

Rome - North American College - Portico and court

The Umiltà Seminary:
Main courtyard with Bedini's Madonna, circa 1900.

N. 6 - Rome - North American College - Grand Staircase

Umiltà Grand Staircase, circa 1900.

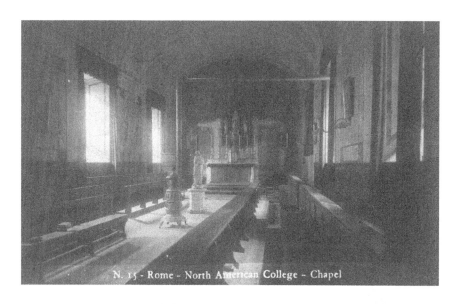

Umiltà student chapel (above); main chapel (below), circa 1900.

Umiltà seminary refectory, circa 1900.

Villa Santa Caterina in Castel Gandolfo and Chapel, circa 1900.

Two designs by Ettore Rossi for the new North American College.

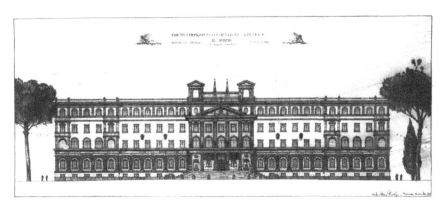

Casa San Giovanni, on the Janiculum Hill.

Martin J. O'Connor as a seminarian at the North American College.

Bishop Martin J. O'Connor departing for Rome in 1948.

(FX3) PHILADELPHIA, April 19--SIGNING MESSAGE TO POPE--Thousands of residents of Philadelphia's "Little Italy" section celebrate news of early returns from Italy's Sunday elections by signing 200-foot parchment scroll to be sent to Pope Pius XII. The message to the Pope reads: "We the undersigned humbly and sincerely rejoice with Your Holiness in this great victory over communism." (AP WIREPHOTO) (LL22025wmw) 1948

Italian immigrants and Italo-Americans in Philadelphia sign a petition against the Communist Party in the 1948 Italian General Election.

October 18, 1948: The "official" ground breaking ceremony for the new College. Bishop Martin J. O'Connor is in the center. To his right is Count Caleazzi and Francesco Slivestri, lawyer for the College.

October 18, 1948: The "official" ground breaking ceremony.
Bishop Martin J. O'Connor with shovel, and Count Galeazzi at the far right

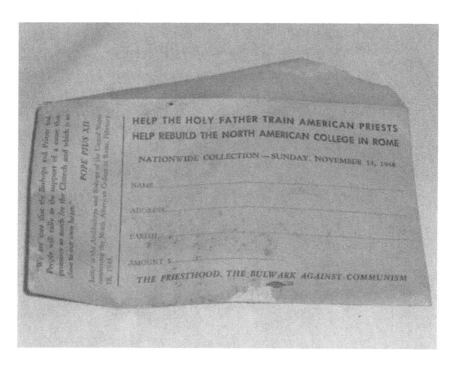

*Fundraising envelope for nationwide parish collection
to fund the construction of the new College, November 14, 1948.*

Plastic model of the revised "P" plan for the College.

Plastic model of the revised "P" plan for the College.

Chapter 3

Securing the Property Titles

> *"From a strictly juridical point of view, Propaganda has presented its evidence concerning its rights. However, this point of view is superseded by the honor so well deserved* [doveroso omaggio] *by the Episcopate of the United States."*
>
> —Pope Pius XII, 1948

When Blessed Pope Pius IX founded the North American College on the Via dell'Umiltà in 1859, he granted the American bishops the use of the land and buildings *ad beneplacitum Sanctae Sedis*, the title for which would remain in the name of the missionary Congregation *de Propaganda Fide*. The arrangement made sense, since the Catholic Church in the United States was then mission territory, subject to the jurisdiction of the Propaganda. The American bishops agreed to take responsibility for the upkeep and maintenance of the buildings, and the North American College was incorporated as an American institution in the State of Maryland. At the time, no one imagined the fall of the Papal States in 1870, and the effect the *Risorgimento* would have on Church property rights in the City of Rome.[102]

Following World War II, the Americans began thinking once again to build a new seminary and to restore the Umiltà property. They also decided that it was time that they held title to the Palazzo Orsini portion of the Umiltà property that the North American

---

[102] In 1901, Monsignor Thomas Kennedy, the College Rector, purchased the building contiguous to the seminary known as the Palazzo Tomba, which had been put up for public auction, leaving only the Palazzo Orsini in the hands of Propaganda.

College had occupied for nearly 100 years, upon which they had lavished a small fortune in capital repairs and improvements, and for which they had paid taxes to the Italian government. One of the tasks assigned the new Rector was to secure the property title of the Umiltà property for the American bishops. While this was one of the most fundamental of duties, it proved to be the most nettlesome of the challenges faced by Bishop Martin J. O'Connor, his Roman team, and the Episcopal Board of the College as they worked to reestablish the American seminary after the war.

After only a few months on the job, the Rector reported to the American bishops that negotiations with Propaganda Fide about the title transfer were completed, with only some legal formalities remaining. That was the result perceived by Bishop O'Connor, Count Galeazzi and Francisco Silvestri, of the verbal negotiations with the Propaganda officials, including the Cardinal Prefect of Propaganda Fide, Cardinal Fumasoni-Biondi, Monsignor Celso Costantini and Prince Carlo Pacelli, during their formal meeting of July 24, 1947.[103] During the meeting, O'Connor expressed to the Cardinal Prefect the hopes of the College Episcopal Board about the title for the Palazzo Orsini portion of the Umiltà property, the clarifying of the College's Janiculum property lines, and the opening of a new entrance road or driveway there for the American College. To sweeten the deal, O'Connor suggested the exchange of the College's rights of co-ownership on the Janiculum property site in exchange for Propaganda's rights to the Orsini Palace portion of the College.

The Cardinal Prefect suggested to O'Connor that the Congregation *de Propaganda Fide* might consider retaining control of the Umiltà property, and the Americans might continue simply to use the buildings, as at present. O'Connor replied that, since vast sums of money had already been spent by the American bishops on the upkeep and improvement of the Umiltà property for nearly

---

[103]   Rome July 25, 1947, O'Connor: "Memorandum for Cardinal Spellman and Board of Trustees", CUA, *O'Connor Papers*, Box 44. At the July 24th meeting, O'Connor claimed that Fumasoni-Biondi had given him verbal assurances that he approved the plan for a new entrance for the College on the Janiculum property, and that the renovation work for the Umiltà could be begun once the American bishops approved the plan.

a century, the American bishops preferred to own the property themselves. Fumasoni-Biondi ended the meeting by simply brushing the differences aside, expressing his hope that all would be worked out in the discussions between the lawyers of the College and the Propaganda, and that the Rector should pursue his construction projects even before those negotiations concluded. But it was not the legal reality, nor the intention of the Propaganda officials to settle so easily with the Americans, if at all. The Americans came to realize this only slowly.

Believing the negotiations with Propaganda Fide concerning the Umiltà and Janiculum property titles concluded, O'Connor wrote his Roman team with instructions, approved by Spellman and Dougherty, to move ahead with the various construction and renovation projects at the Umiltà and Castel Gandolfo sites, the signing of contracts and the purchase of construction materials.[104]

But, on October 13, 1947, Fumasoni-Biondi sent a letter to the College for the Rector, who was already in the States for the upcoming November bishops' meetings. The Vice-Rector forwarded the letter to Silvestri, who forwarded it to O'Connor with his own comments, which O'Connor received by November 2nd. The Cardinal Prefect wrote that he was preparing to present the College's requests about the Umiltà and Janiculum properties at the upcoming plenary session of the Propaganda. He asked the Rector to clarify three points. First, why should the Americans ask for the transfer of the Palazzo Orsini on the old College site, when they were granted control of the site in perpetuity, *ad beneplacitum Sanctae Sedis*, as approved by Pope Pius IX in his audience of March 23, 1862? Subsequently, during the decades that followed, the Propaganda itself discussed the question of transferring the property title to the College Board of Trustees, but Roman political turmoil, anti-clerical governments, and world wars prevented the transfer.

---

[104] Cable: New York, October 18, 1947, O'Connor to Galeazzi, CUA, *O'Connor Papers*, Box 36: *O'Connor*. The Rector received authorization from Cardinals Dougherty and Spellman to instruct Galeazzi to purchase 100 tons of steel in answer to the Count's cable indicating the unexpected availability of this large amount of so rare and coveted a commodity in post-war Italy. This would be used for the Umiltà restoration.

The second question asked if the American bishops would consider ceding to the Propaganda that portion of the Janiculum property owned jointly by the Propaganda Fide and the American College. Finally, there was a need to determine a new property line on the Janiculum providing a private entrance for the American College. It appears that Fumasoni-Biondi simply wanted written clarification of the verbal understanding arrived at between himself and O'Connor during their summer meeting.[105] At least, that is how O'Connor perceived it, as he wrote the College lawyer in response to his October 23rd letter,

> "As His Eminence, the Cardinal [Fumasoni-Biondi] was very gracious and the memorandum of our conversation, which I left with you, covers the essential points, I think we can look forward to an early and satisfactory solution of this problem".[106]

Silvestri wrote a formal answer to Fumasoni-Biondi on November 3, 1947, signed by the Vice Rector in O'Connor's name: all were in agreement on two of the three points, but the American bishops insisted on the property title to the Orsini Palace. He ended his letter asking that the definition of the exact relationship between the Propaganda and College be made *hinc et inde*, since these questions had already been discussed and settled, most recently during the July 24, 1947 meeting of the Rector and the Cardinal Prefect.[107]

The November 10, 1947 meeting of the College Episcopal Board was a great success for the Rector: Galeazzi's project designs for the Umiltà, Castel Gandolfo, and the Janiculum were approved, funding provided, and permission given to solicit construction bids by the

---

[105] Rome November 1, 1947, Silvestri to Galeazzi, KC, *Enrico Galeazzi Papers*, N. Amer Coll. Correspondence, Box 29, File 7.

[106] Scranton November 2, 1947, O'Connor to Silvestri, NAC, *Coll. Amer. Corrisp. Rettori; Card. Spellman—M.C. Geough* [sic].

[107] Rome November 5, 1947, Burns to O'Connor, CUA, *O'Connor Papers*, Box 36: *Msgr. Burns*.

College's Roman team.[108] O'Connor also met with 103 bishops in Chicago at the Church Extension Society meeting, and there reported the good progress of the College projects.[109] The Board members were equally elated that all was moving ahead. Spellman sent letters to his seminary classmates asking them to contribute towards the cost of the High Altar in the new College chapel,[110] and sent a circular letter to all American bishops, reporting the decisions by the Episcopal Board, and asking their support for the imminent construction of the new College.[111] By December 2nd, contracts for the restoration work on the Umiltà and the Villa in Castel Gandolfo were signed.[112]

No notifications were issued from Propaganda Fide, and the presumption was that the summer verbal understanding between the Rector and the Prefect had been approved during the plenary session. But after O'Connor returned to Rome in December, he met with Fumasoni-Biondi, and was surprised to discover that the question had not been discussed during the November plenary meeting, but had been postponed until the next plenary session of the Congregation in February 1948.

Sensing danger, O'Connor set to work immediately. Assisted by Silvestri and Galeazzi, he wrote the entire history of the College property title question in a long report to Fumason-Biondi, dated January 25, 1948. In it he expressed clearly the frustration of the American bishops, especially since construction contracts had been signed and huge sums of money already spent on the basis

---

[108] Scranton November 12, 1947 O'Connor to Burns, CUA, *O'Connor Papers*, above ref. Scranton November 14, 1947 O'Connor to Galeazzi, CUA, *O'Connor Papers*, above ref. Scranton November 14, 1947, O'Connor to Silvestri, NAC, *Coll. Amer: Coll. Amer. Corrisp Rettori; Card. Spellman—M.C.Geough* [sic].

[109] Scranton November 22, 1947 O'Connor to Burns, CUA, *O'Connor Papers*, Box 36: *Msgr. Burns.*

[110] New York November 15, 1947, Spellman to Fr. Laurence Killian [NAC 1915], NYC, Box S/C-73, Folder 11: *To Card. Spellman, N. Amer. Coll.*

[111] New York November 20, 1947 Spellman to American ordinaries, NYC, Box S/C-73, Folder 11: *To Card. Spellman, N. Amer. Coll.*

[112] Vatican December 2, 1947, Burns to O'Connor, KC, *Enrico Galeazzi Papers*, *NAC Correspondence*, Box 29, File 11.

of the summer agreement with Propaganda. O'Connor included six documents to support the American position.[113] The first was the October 1, 1944 letter from Silvestri to the Propaganda, accompanying a check to the Propaganda for 134,388.50 lire [$1,275,000] in payment of back taxes [at an annual rate of 3.5% of the property value of the Umiltà], insurance premiums owed by the College, as well as taxes on the salaries of dependent workers, up to December 31, 1943. Silvestri reminded the Propaganda that the College would not pay the property taxes due on the College for the war years during which the Umiltà property had been controlled by the Italian State, and for which the Propaganda had received a rental payment from the Italian government.

The whole question of back taxes was a sore point for the Americans, since the Americans paid for major repair work at the College during the war, especially in 1941when part of the roof collapsed.[114] Likewise, the Americans were unhappy because during the war years, special collections for Propaganda were taken up in every parish in the United States. Receiving millions of American dollars during each war year, ". . . it would seem that Propaganda was very munificently recompensed for the monies it may have expended for the American College", wrote one archbishop to Spellman.[115]

The second of O'Connor's documents included in his report to the Propaganda was the October 3, 1944 letter from the Propaganda general secretary, Monsignor Celso Costantini, answering Silvestri's letter and acknowledging receipt of the check and notifying that all debts to the Propaganda by the College were satisfied. Offering a reminder that the College could begin paying future Italian government taxes by sending them to the Propaganda on a monthly basis, Costantini also confirmed that the College had an additional 69,800 lire [approximately $600,000] accredited to its Vatican account from the Congregation from various notes and investments

---

[113] Rome January 25, 1948 "Relazione del Rettore del Collegio Americano del Nord," CUA, *O'Connor Papers*, Box 44: *NAC.*

[114] Rome April 12, 1941, Bp. Ralph Hayes to Spellman, NYC, Box S/C-73, Folder 1: *To Card. Spellman, N. Amer.Coll.*

[115] Milwaukee April 15, 1941, Abp. Moses E. Kiley [NAC 1911] to Spellman, NYC, Box S/C-73, Folder 1: *To Card. Spellman, N. Amer. Coll.*

held by the Propaganda during the years, from Monsignor Kennedy's time in 1906, which had come due on January 1, 1945.

The third document was O'Connor's July 25, 1947 *Memorandum for Cardinal Spellman and Board of Trustees*, mentioned above. The fourth, the October 13, 1947 letter from Cardinal Fumasoni-Biondi to O'Connor, as mentioned above, asking the Rector to outline precisely the questions of the American bishops about the College properties. The fifth document was the October 17, 1947 response to the Cardinal by Silvestri, telling the Cardinal Prefect that the process was being held up by the architect of the Propaganda, Signore Busiri [whose relative had been Bedini's architect when the College first opened]. The final document attached was the November 3, 1947 letter by Monsignor Burns responding in O'Connor's name to Fumasoni-Biondi's of October 17th.

As the paperwork grew, the question dragged on for months, with no result. O'Connor had another meeting with Fumasoni-Biondi in late April 1948, during which he asked the Prefect of the Propaganda the status of the question of property titles. O'Connor reported the Cardinal's response that "as far as he was concerned he was anxious to conclude the whole matter and most willing to help in any way." But, the Prefect continued, both Monsignor Costantini and Prince Pacelli had questions, of which he was unclear. Giving no further information, and repeating three more times that he was "most anxious to conclude the affair," Fumasoni-Biondi agreed with O'Connor that the lawyers should begin meeting once again on the subject.[116]

But the College lawyer knew what Prince Pacelli's objections were, since he had repeated them numerous times during their discussions: the value of the Janiculum land jointly owned by the Propaganda and the Americans was worth far less than the value of the land at the Via dell'Umiltà and the Palazzo Orsini that stood atop that land, both technically owned by the Propaganda. If a land swap was to be made, the Propaganda wanted the cash value of the Umiltà

---

[116]   Rome April 23, 1948 O'Connor "Memorandum of Meeting with Cardinal Fumasoni-Biondi", CUA, *O'Connor Papers*, Box 42: *NAC subfiles*.

property from the Americans, plus the title to the commonly-held Janiculum property.[117]

There was another aspect to these negotiations that caused concern for the Americans and the Pope. Even if the Propaganda appeared to be working solely for its own financial interests, the importance of the developing Cold War between the United States and the Soviet Union affected even these local Roman questions. Following the 1947 Communist coup in Czechoslovakia, the United States became more wary of Soviet interests throughout Europe, and especially in Italy. The leader of the *Partito Communista Italiana* was Palmiro Togliatti, who boasted that Italy's Communist Party was the largest in Europe and unlike all others, welcomed intellectuals, and promised to lessen the Soviet influence in the Italian Communist Party and in Italian politics. While vastly popular, the weakness of the party was that so many of its leaders had willingly embraced Mussolini's Fascist government before and during the war.[118]

Both the United States and the Vatican saw the danger. Alcide De Gasperi, the founder of the Christian Democratic Party and Prime Minister, had spread the word that his party would work to defeat Communist influence in Italy, if the Christian Democrats could win the 1948 General Election.[119] He had secured a small American loan to Italy in 1947, which he touted as an American vote of confidence in his government. He was helped in America by Henry Luce, publisher of *Time Magazine*, whose wife, Clare Booth Luce, would become the United States Ambassador to Italy in 1953.[120] De Gasperi and Clare Booth Luce were all fervent Catholics, friends of Galeazzi,

---

[117] Rome January 20, 1948, Silvestri to Galeazzi, KC, *Enrico Galeazzi Papers*, No. Amer. Coll., *Corresp. with the Rector*, Box 50, File 2.

[118] Jody, Tony, *Postwar: A History of Europe since 1945*, London 2006, pp 207-208.

[119] De Gasperi was the founder and head of the Christian Democratic Party and Prime Minister for eight successive coalition governments. He was strongly supported by the United States, especially during the 1948 general election that put him and the Christian Democratic Party in power, soundly defeating the Communist Party in Italy, then the largest in Europe, outside the Soviet Union.

[120] Henry Luce put DeGasperi on the front cover of the April 19, 1948 number of *Time Magazine*, showing DeGasperi's portrait in front of a map of Italy in the grip of a giant red octopus, with the by-line: "Can he cut the red tentacles?" It was published immediately before the 1948 Italian general elections.

supporters of Pius XII, and friends of the American College in Rome. The United States poured millions of dollars into the 1948 election, and secured the victory for the Christian Democrats. It would be De Gasperi, the Vatican and the United States, that would push forward Italian industrial growth and serious agrarian reform throughout Italy, resulting in the "Italian miracle" post-war recovery, while keeping the Communists at bay.

Another possible reason for the delays and difficulties was Cardinal Fumasoni-Biondi himself. While he once had been the Apostolic Delegate to the United States (1922-1933), he strongly believed the American government and American churchmen should have little influence in the rebuilding of post-war Italy. There were many disquieted by the enormous American political and ecclesiastical influence in the world.[121] And, while he agreed with the Pope that the Communist party should not dominate Italian politics, he disagreed with the Pope and with the Americans about how that should be affected. He held that elections, freed from any outside influences, either by the United States or by the Vatican, would result in the natural defeat of the *Partita Communista Italiana*. In fact, he and a few others in the Roman Curia held that a Catholic

---

[121] NYC, Spellman Diaries, vol. 23: The American bishops were very much involved with efforts by the Vatican and the United States during and after World War II to rebuild Italy and Europe, while continuing to support the usual pastoral and missionary efforts of the Church. Archbishop Spellman is a good example of such activity, which most people would not expect of Catholic bishops. The following entries from his diary give a taste of his involvement: August 7, 1945, "First atomic bombs Hiroshima, Japan." August 8, 1945: "Russia declares war on Japan. Henry Luce + Joe Kennedy came to see me to ask if I would ask President Truman for 5 or 6 days truce to give Japan 'a chance to surrender.'" August 10: "Japan offers to surrender under terms of Potsdam. Worked frantically all day + took train to Washington." August 11: "John L. Sullivan accompanied me to President Truman. It was an historic meeting. Secretary of State Byrnes came in with document to be sent to Japan accepting proviso to retain Emperor + President read it to me + Sens. Forestal + Hannegan, Sec. James Byrnes very nice to me too + Leo Crowley Flew back to N.Y. + prepared broadcast for V.J. day. President at Mass in St. Patrick's." Following the war, most cardinals and bishops worked to send food, medical and construction supplies and funds around the world to help post-war reconstruction.

Communist party should be allowed to exist, and that a free flow of the democratic process would result in the best possible government in Italy.[122]

Pius XII disagreed wholeheartedly with this naïve approach, as did the American government, the American bishops, and Alcide De Gasperi. Anything helpful to the Vatican/American efforts to defeat Communism in post-war Italy should be done. If the *Partita Communista Italiana* won in local and national elections, everyone knew that such a victory would have disastrous effects. One such effect could be the halting of the construction project of the American seminary in Rome, despite the fact that it would employ hundreds of Italian workers and inject millions of dollars into the Italian economy. Likewise, the successful construction of the seminary could be used as a sign of the benefits to be had of the united Vatican/American efforts and a Communist defeat. Neither the Vatican nor the American government could run the risk of a possible Communist victory, especially in view of the then recent Soviet advances into Eastern Europe and attacks against the Catholic Church.[123] None of this went unnoticed by those working for the new College, either in Rome, the Vatican, or in the United States.[124]

---

[122] Kent, Peter, *The Lonely Cold War of Pope Pius XII: The Roman Catholic Church and the Division of Europe, 1943-1950*, Montreal, 2002, p 28, ff.

[123] Fogarty, Gerald, *The Vatican and the American Hierarchy From 1870 to 1965*, Stuttgart, 1982, pp 315-346:details the American Church's efforts to co-operate with the American government to intervene in the Italian general and local elections of 1948, 1953 and 1958, as well as acting to benefit the Holy See's humanitarian work and political positions around the world. Prior to the 1948 Italian general election, Cicognani and Spellman both sent circular letters to American bishops in whose dioceses were large Italian communities, and to pastors of Italian national parishes, instructing them to encourage their Italian-American parishioners to write their relatives in Italy that they should vote against the communists.

[124] The Communist influence would come into play also in O'Connor's negotiations with the Italian government about funding the Janiculum construction project by the use of "blocked lire" owned by American film corporations, which negotiations were going on at the same time in 1948, which will be discussed in greater detail below.

O'Connor made his report to the Executive Committee cardinals during the June 24, 1948 meeting at St. Charles Seminary outside Philadelphia. He had just received word from his Vice Rector, Monsignor Burns, that the property matters had been presented during the June 14th plenary meeting of the Propaganda. But there were no results. What was understood by the Americans to be stalling on the part of the Propaganda Fide officials led to a unanimous decision by the Executive Board that Cardinal Dougherty, President of the Board, would write the Holy Father if delays continued, "asking his intervention to obtain a decision in this matter."[125]

O'Connor filled in the details of the heated Philadelphia meeting to Count Galeazzi, including his own suggested solution:

> Some members of the Board wished to address a letter by airmail to the Holy Father immediately, but accepted my opinion that, in view of the fact that the matter was under consideration, it might be better for me to bring the letter personally to Rome when I could present it if the circumstances warrant. This letter authorizes the presentation of a memorandum previously prepared for the desk of the Holy Father before I left Rome.[126]

He continued that the bishops were very concerned that any further delay by Propaganda might undermine the entire seminary construction project, and render fund raising efforts impossible, since no one would give money to build a huge seminary on land owned by someone else—the Propaganda.

---

[125] June 24, 1948" Minutes of the Board Meeting, St. Charles Seminary, Overbrook", NYC, Box S/C-73, Folder 12: *To Card. Spellman, N. Amer. Coll.*

[126] Scranton June 25, 1948, O'Connor to Galeazzi, KC, *Enrico Galeazzi Papers, N. Amer. Coll, Most Rev. Martin J. O'Connor, Corresp. Jan-Sept, 1948*, Box 30, File 8.

O'Connor then mentioned the two telegrams he sent Galeazzi on the same day, by way of the Vatican telegraph office, with references to the subject matter sufficiently clear that "unofficial" reports and rumors might be spread around the Vatican, that something important was about to happen. The hope was that these rumors might hasten a decision, so Dougherty's letter to the Pope might not be needed. To make sure everyone knew, O'Connor sent two copies of each telegram at various times during the day:

> Meeting today satisfactory STOP. I reported simply matter presented Congregation and under consideration STOP. Will write STOP. Please do not proceed excavations until you hear from me on return will bear letter from committee to highest authority to be presented only if necessary.

His second telegram filled in the blanks of the first:

> Supplementing Philadelphia message STOP. Letter previously mentioned signed by Dougherty for committee authorizes me to present memorandum prepared before Rome departure and urges personal intervention for happy conclusion in matter. Presentation left to my discretion according to circumstances.[127]

Everyone in the Vatican knew O'Connor and Galeazzi were working on the new American seminary, and, since there are no secrets in the Vatican, everyone knew about the question of property titles and the Propaganda's delay. To emphasize his hope that Galeazzi might use his influence in the Vatican, the Rector added:

> I sent you two cables, one from Philadelphia and one from Washington, so that you might be informed in

---

[127] Cables Scranton June 25, 1948: Four telegrams from O'Connor to Galeazzi, KC, *Enrico Galeazzi Papers*, above ref.

order to be better able to judge the situation and to take any necessary steps. It would be a blessing if this matter were settled before my return [to Rome, carrying Dougherty's letter to the pope] and that I could so notify the Episcopal Committee after my arrival.[128]

But any hoped-for solution without presenting Dougherty's letter and his extraordinary appeal to the Pope never materialized.

Bishop O'Connor, therefore, presented Cardinal Dougherty's letter to Pope Pius XII in a private audience on July 25, 1948. Accompanying the letter was O'Connor's memorandum concerning the two legal questions: the negotiations for the Umiltà property title that had continued between the Propaganda Fide and the American bishops for nearly the entire history of the College, and that of the Janiculum property, "which the American bishops purchased twenty-five years ago, at the request of the Holy See"; the need to draw a new boundary line on the Janiculum clarifying the Propaganda property and that of the College, and thereby arrive at an agreement for a driveway for the American property. All for which the Americans were ready and willing to cede their rights to that portion of the Janiculum property commonly held by both institutions, ". . . which adjustment would also obviously benefit Propaganda." Dougherty's letter continued:

It is the unanimous decision of the Episcopal Administrative Committee that the Rector present to Your Holiness the facts of the memorandum as it is our belief that further delay on the part of the Sacred Congregation [de Propaganda Fide] will have serious effect upon the program for the erection of the new

---

Seminary on the Janiculum Hill, for which we are now engaged in collecting more than $3,000,000.[129]

The Rector dutifully telegrammed back to the Cardinal Dougherty:

> Presented your letter STOP. Very successful audience STOP. Propaganda advised me yesterday they had communicated to Your Eminence favorable reply on the two legal questions STOP. Hope to have rescript from congregation this coming week when formalities will be concluded.[130]

Cardinal Fumasoni-Biondi formally notified Cardinal Dougherty on July 30th that the Pope had received and read Dougherty's letter and O'Connor's memorandum, and approved the decisions the Americans requested. "Please communicate these decisions to the American Bishops", was the official, terse announcement.[131] In the rescript dated July 26th sent to Dougherty, the secretary of the Propaganda clearly stated that the Pope granted everything requested by the American bishops: transfer of the title of ownership of the Umiltà property and building to them;[132] the ceding of the jointly owned property on the Janiculum to Propaganda; and the agreement by Propaganda to permit the driveway needed by the College; as

---

[129] Philadelphia June 28, 1948, Cardinal Dougherty to Pope Pius XII, CUA, *O'Connor Papers*, Box 42, Folder: *NAC subfiles*.

[130] Cable, Rome July 26, 1948 O'Connor to Dougherty, CUA, *O'Connor Papers*, Box 42, Folder: *Propagation of the Faith*.

[131] Vatican July 30, 1948, Fumasoni-Biondi to Dougherty, CUA, *O'Connor Papers*, Box 42, Folder: *NAC subfiles*.

[132] Vatican July 26, 1948, *Ex Audientia Summi Pontificis Pii Div. Prov. Papae XII*, Prot. N. 3098/1948, CUA, *O'Connor Papers*, Box 23, *Misc. Corresp*, Folder: *Corresp: Washington 1973*: "1. Sacra Congregatio de Propaganda Fide suum plenae et absolutae proprietatis jus memoratum Aedium, jam a multis annis Collegio Sacrorum alumnis Statuum Foedertatorum Americae Septemptrionalis insitutendis in usuam ad beneplacitum Sanctae Sedis concessarum, in idem Collegium transfert".

well as the assurance that Propaganda would not interfere with the construction of the Americans' new seminary.[133]

O'Connor wrote Dougherty in mid-August, sending a copy of the official printed papal rescript to him, along with his own report of events. The Rector told the Archbishop of Philadelphia that he was received in private audience by the Pope on July 25th, and the Pope told him:

> From a strictly juridical point of view, Propaganda has presented its evidence concerning its rights. However, this point of view is superseded by the honor so well deserved [*doveroso omaggio*] by the Episcopate of the United States.[134]

The following day, O'Connor went to the Propaganda and met with Costantini. He was given a copy of the rescript, but O'Connor requested that further written clarifications be made to avoid future misunderstandings regarding the Umiltà buildings, including those portions of the building presently leased by the Propaganda to various businesses, which were providing the Congregation with rental income. Likewise, he requested that an authentic site map of the Janiculum properties be drawn up and agreed to by the College and Propaganda lawyers. He also requested that the words of Pius to O'Connor during the audience—*doveroso omaggio*—regarding the American bishops be included in the final form of the rescript.[135] On Saturday, August 7th, Silvestri received the amended rescript from

---

133 Prot. 3098/1948 *Ex Audientia Summi Pontificis Pii Div. Prov. Papae XII July 26, 1948*, NAC, *NAC Construction*, #224. Rome August 13, 1948, O'Connor to Galeazzi, CUA, *O'Connor Papers*, Box 42: *NAC*, Folder: *Propagation of the Faith*. O'Connor attached a personal note card to the printed copy of the rescript, telling Galeazzi, "All is peaceful!"

134 Rome August 13, 1948, O'Connor to Dougherty, KC, *Enrico Galeazzi Papers, Card. Spellman Correspondence, Box 80*, File 1.

135 Vatican August 15, 1948, Galeazzi to O'Connor, CUA, *O'Connor Papers*, Box 42: *Propagation of the Faith*: "I have spoken to Msgr. Burns about the future use of this 'so well deserved' [*un doveroso omaggio all'Episcopato degli Stati Uniti*] document. Renewed congratulations!"

Costantini, which included O'Connor's clarifications and site map, signed by Costantini, himself. Prince Carlo Pacelli, representing the Propaganda, and the College lawyer, Francesco Silvestri, were to draw up the formal and final contracts within six weeks. The next day, Sunday, August 8th, O'Connor delivered to the Undersecretary of State, Monsignor Giovanni Montini, a letter of thanks to the Holy Father.

Dougherty responded thanking the Rector for his efforts and congratulated him on the successful outcome. The Cardinal sent copies of the papal rescript to all the American bishops; likewise, he sent copies of O'Connor's letters to himself to the members of the Episcopal Board. He wrote O'Connor:

> You may now meritoriously be considered the second
> founder of the American College, Rome.[136]

The Rector answered, "May I also thank Your Eminence . . . it is your interest and support that has [sic] helped me so effectively." [137]

In their June 24, 1948 meeting, the Episcopal Board of the College had given O'Connor permission to secure bids for borings and excavation work to begin for the Janiculum project "if in his opinion negotiations with Propaganda were satisfactorily concluded."[138] Since the Holy Father had granted the rescript just one month later, it seemed that the negotiations were satisfactorily concluded, except for the formalities, which the Rector told the Episcopal Board would be completed by January 1949. Accordingly, O'Connor signed contracts for the excavation work, and [unofficially] broke ground for the Janiculum project on October 17, 1948, the feast of Saint Margaret Mary Alacoque. He also asked the bishops' authorization

---

[136] Philadelphia August 21, 1948, Dougherty to O'Connor, CUA, *O'Connor Papers*, Box 42: *NAC subfiles*.

[137] Rome August 26, 1948, O'Connor to Dougherty, CUA, *O'Connor Papers*, Box 42: *NAC subfiles*.

[138] "Rector's Report, North American College, October 24, 1948", CUA, *O'Connor Papers*, Box 44: *NAC*, Folder: *Rector's Reports*.

so he could "take all necessary steps leading to a most practical solution of the problems", in reference to the Umiltà buildings.[139]

There was, however, one other legal knot: the fact that the formal legal execution of the Pope's decision about the Umiltà property was not merely dependent upon the Vatican. Since the Umiltà property was not extra-territorial, it was subject to the laws of Italy and the City of Rome for title transfer, construction work and renovation of historical buildings.[140] Taxes to the Italian government continued to be paid on the Umiltà property, as well, by the Americans. The continued irritation in the relationship between the College and Propaganda officials was partially the result of the continued insistence by Propaganda that the Americans pay the back taxes due for the war years, even though the Umiltà had been confiscated by the Mussolini Government, as seen above, and the Propaganda had pocketed the rental payments from the Italian government.

Likewise, there was a third property torment afflicting the progress of the re-opening of the College, and it now came into play: the Villa Santa Caterina in Castel Gandolfo, which was not extra-territorial. It was owned outright by the American College, but subject to the laws of Italy and of Castel Gandolfo—whose citizens were soon to hand the local Communist party a victory in local elections. The government officials had already asked the College for money in exchange for their taking into consideration the American bishops' requests about roads, reconstruction of an historic building, and the re-opening of the Villa for student use.[141]

---

[139] New York November 12, 1948, O'Connor to Silvestri, NAC, *Collegio Americano, Corris. Rettori, Card. Spellman—M.C. Geough* [sic].

[140] Rome October 8, 1951, Silvestri to Galeazzi, CUA, *O'Connor Papers*, Box 42: *Propagation of the Faith*.

[141] Rome October 1, 1947, "Report of His Excellency Monsignor Martin J. O'Connor, Rector of the North American College in Rome, on work done in Accordance with the Directives of the Episcopal Committee", NYC, Box S/C-73, Folder 10: *To Card. Spellman, N. Amer. Coll.* One of O'Connor's first tasks was to purchase from Castel Gandolfo the road dividing the Villa from the other parcel of land owned by the College known as the *Pocaterra*, in order to unite the properties. This was never accomplished.

A full report of the history of the College properties, including excerpts of legal documents and opinions in English, was sent to the College Board on August 3rd, as well as the complete documentation prepared as a formal memorandum in Italian on October 31, 1948, to conclude the legal meetings prior to the "formalities" concerning the actual implementation of the Pope's rescript.[142]

But the Propaganda once again dragged its feet. Rescript or no rescript, a tangle of questions developed on the Propaganda side about what actual and legal form the Pope's decision should take regarding the Umiltà property, especially when dealing with the Italian government.

Based upon Silvestri's clear legal observations, Galeazzi's political connections in Rome and insights into the Vatican, O'Connor suggested that the Americana bishops scrap the two possible solutions then being suggested by Propaganda regarding the Palazzo Orsini on the Via dell'Umiltà: the Americans should neither purchase the property nor should they accept it as a donation from the Propaganda Fide. The reason was the exorbitant taxes to the Italian government that the Americans could expect to pay based upon the estimated property value: 12% of the total property value if sold to the Americans; 80% of the total property value if the Propaganda donated the property to the Americans! Such taxes concomitant with either solution would be too astronomical for the Americans, already struggling to fund the seminary construction projects; and the Propaganda refused to lift a hand to pay any of it.

Silvestri, Galeazzi and O'Connor offered two possible alternative solutions, which might solve both property questions of the Umiltà and Castel Gandolfo. The first suggested that during the 1901 purchase of the Palazzo Tomba portion of the Umiltà property, the Italian government had recognized the "juridic personality" of the American College as having existed since its founding in 1859 by the then-legitimate papal government. That being so, the College

---

[142] *Memorandum per l'esecuzione del Rescritto di Sua Santita Pio XII in data 28 luglio 1948 e per la rettificazione delle intestazioni delle attuali proprieta del Collegio Americano del Nord.* CUA, *O'Connor Papers*, Box 43: *NAC subfiles*, Folder: *Rescript of Pope Pius XII*.

could simply request that the Italian government officially recognize that the American bishops actually owned the Palazzo Orsini they had occupied and funded for nearly a century, which had been given them by the Propaganda in perpetuity, *ad beneplacitum Sanctae Sedis*.

The second suggested solution was to seek recognition of the College as a juridic person *ex novo*, according to the procedural norms established in Italian law, which recognition would begin now, in 1948, taking no account of the earlier recognition. This could allow that the American civil corporation, *The American College of the Roman Catholic Church of the United States*, chartered in Maryland, be the *Intestataria Figurativa* of the Palazzo Orsini, as it was already of the Villas Santa Caterina in Castel Gandolfo and of the Palazzo Tomba portion of the Umiltà, as recognized by the Italian government of April 24, 1924. The American civil corporation already held and used the Palazzo Orsini portion of the Umiltà property, the Italian government had accepted payment of property taxes on it from the American bishops for decades, and American bishops had invested heavily in capital projects there for nearly a century. So, as Silvestri narrated, according to article 29 of the 1929 Concordat between the Holy See and Italy, there would be no property transfer taxes to the Italian government resulting from the papal rescript, because there would be no property transfer to tax.[143] Neither Kealy nor O'Connor could have foreseen or imagined this. And only by Silvestri's genius, and Galeazzi's political influence could they pull it off.

By November, the lawyers were still in discussions. The Pope had demonstrated his appreciation of the Americans by his decision in favor of their position about the property title, as clearly demonstrated in his rescript. But, while that rescript instructed that

---

[143] *Memorandum per esecuzione del Rescritto. . .* , pp. 14-16; 27-28. CUA, *O'Connor Papers*, Box 43: *NAC subfiles*, Folder: *Rescript of Pope Pius XII*. Detroit February 6, 1953, Mooney to Spellman, NYC, Box S/C-74, Folder 2: *To Card. Spellman, N. Amer. Coll*: "Moreover, I recall that in 1924 when Monsignor O'Hern transferred the Tombola Palace to the College Corporation, the College lawyer at that time got a considerable reduction in taxes on the plea of reciprocity—that property owned by Italians in Maryland and used for religious purposes would enjoy tax exemption."

the title be given to the American bishops, it did not determine when that might take place, or by what legal form that transfer should be realized. The Pope moved on to other more urgent matters of the Universal Church, and the papal decision was submitted to the usual Vatican bureaucratic machinery.

A paper chase now began, with Silvestri insisting that the property transfer be registered in the Vatican City State as an immediate practical solution. This, in turn, led to Propaganda requests to the College lawyer to approach Italian authorities to begin the legal process with the Italian government for the Umiltà property as well, to prepare necessary American bishops' authorizations for the transfer of the Janiculum property. He was also to prepare the documentation required by the Vatican to secure a power of attorney for O'Connor to affect the transfer, and to write Spellman asking for written authorization and for a copy of the College by-laws.[144] The Episcopal Board granted the authorizations during their November 15th, 1948 meeting.[145] The Janiculum agreements were finally completed, but the battle for the Umiltà property continued for years, even while vast sums of American dollars were spent on its restoration. At the same time, O'Connor continued working to secure the property transfer under Italian law, and to do it without paying Italian taxes.

By late 1949, the Episcopal Board instructed O'Connor to visit with the American ambassador to Italy, James Clement Dunn, asking that he write in support of the property transfer and that it be recognized by the Italian government.[146] Dunn instructed Lionel Summers, the legal counsel of the American Embassy, to find a solution to the difficulty, and a meeting with Francesco Silvestri was arranged to discuss the matter. It was decided to prepare two documents: a memorandum in O'Connor's name to Summers, outlining the property question; and a letter dated February 2,

---

[144] Scranton December 3, 1948, O'Connor to Msgr. John Maguire, CUA, *O'Connor Papers*, Box 25: *Misc. Corresp.*

[145] Scranton December 3, 1948, O'Connor to Burns, CUA, *O'Connor Papers*, Box 36, Folder: *Burns.*

[146] New York January 18, 1950, Spellman to O'Connor, NYC, Box S/C-74, Folder 7: *To Card. Spellman, N. Amer. Coll.*

1950 from Silvestri to Summers, calling attention to the reasons that determined the original registration, and explaining why this was never changed during all the years the Americans occupied the Umiltà property. Silvestri and O'Connor prepared them.

On February 6, 1950, the American ambassador addressed a *Nota Verbale* to the Italian Minister of Foreign Affairs, asking that "careful attention be given to the views of Avvocato Silvestri as a favorable solution to the problem which is of prime importance to the College." In the meantime, O'Connor suggested that Spellman write Alberto Tarchiani, the Italian Ambassador to the United States, to secure his support as well.[147] Spellman wrote the Ambassador on March 4th, and received a positive albeit Italianate response dated March 10th, Tarchiani assuring the Cardinal that he would "warmly recommend that the Ministry of Finance be invited to consider the possibility of having the question settled along the lines you have indicated."[148]

During a visit to Rome, Cardinal Stritch met with Cardinal Fumasoni-Biondi and other Propaganda officials to discuss the registration of the papal rescript in the Vatican, and was informed that the Propaganda refused to register any transfer with the Italian government. The discussion centered around Costantini's insistence that the reason why the Propaganda refused to sign a contract about the transfer of property ownership was the same reason they refused to sign a document for the sale of the property: Costantini wanted to affect the Pope's rescript by a simple contract that would reflect the actual and daily juridic situation of the property and building known as the Palazzo Orsini; in other words, a simple act of donation, as the Pope intended. The problem was that such a legal act of donation to an American civil corporation, which the North American College was, would bring with it an exceptionally onerous registration tax with the Italian government. Here, Stritch repeated the idea that the solution to the problem might be with a canonical contract by which

---

[147]   Rome February 21, 1950, O'Connor to Spellman, NYC, Box S/C-74, Folder 7: *To Card. Spellman, N. Amer. Coll.*

[148]   Washington, D.C. March 10, 1950, Alberto Tarchiani to Spellman, NYC, Box S/C-74, Folder 7: *To Card. Spellman, N. Amer. Coll.*

the Propaganda might solemnly declare that the property used by the College already belonged to the College, at least by long use; and that the Propaganda "was ready at any time to do whatever the American Bishops might request." Both Stritch and Costantini expressed that such an "act of donation in favor of the Pontifical North American College" might work, especially "since the College was already recognized as a moral entity with a juridic personality" by Italian law.[149] Stritch reported this as an *agreement*, which would later cause misunderstandings.

Just as the Italian government appeared to be prepared to recognize the title transfer of the Umiltà property to the College, the Propaganda let loose a time bomb. The Propaganda informed the College lawyer that Costantini had developed a new qualm concerning the Congregation's ability to give over the property title to the Umiltà, because the wording of the Pope's rescript did not exactly mirror the wording of an earlier agreement between the Propaganda and the American College. Likewise, the secretary of the Congregation believed a formal written agreement transferring the property title would be contrary to the spirit of the Holy Father's wishes as expressed in the July 26, 1948 rescript, which by itself was a juridical act.[150]

Silvestri and Galeazzi were wild, writing to Spellman that this was "*una viva sorpresa*", especially considering the numerous meetings and conversations with Propaganda officials and the guarantees received:

> The Rescript IS an internal act: so, whether the agreement takes one form or another, it expresses

---

[149] "Report of the Rector of the North American College in Rome to The Episcopal Administrative Committee for the Hierarchy of the United States, November, 1950", *Relazione indicativa del Lavoro di Consultenza Legale ed Amminstrativa svolto dall'Av. Francesco Silvestri dal 1 Gennaio al 30 Settembre 1950, per la tutela degli interessi del Pontificio Collegio Americano del Nord*, p. 11, CUA, *O'Connor Papers*, Box 44: *NAC*, Folder: *Report Board of Trustees (1950)*.

[150] Rome July 19, 1950, Propaganda Fide, Prot. N. 896, to Silvestri, KC, *Enrico Galeazzi Papers, Card. Spellman Corresp., Prop. Fide*, Box 80, File 1.

the will of the Holy Father, and does not violate the spirit of the Rescript, since, as repeatedly stated, it is a mutual statement defining the relationship between the two institutions.[151]

Likewise, there was a type of corporate game playing going on, even in Rome. Members of the Curia sometimes thought they could do as they pleased. In this case, either slowly taking control of ecclesiastical lands owned by the American bishops, or encroaching on American land simply by using their charm, hinting at possible career advancement in exchange for American co-operation, or by simple bullying. A prime example of this was the building of the children's Hospital of Bambino Gesu next to the College on the Janiculum. Plans were made to expand the hospital, and some Vatican officials simply presumed they could expand the hospital and build on the College sports field! That never happened because the College Rector and Board refused, once they learned of the plans.[152] Joking about the hospital's interest in the College land, O'Connor wrote Galeazzi, counseling him to take some rest, because ". . . we would like you present for the [College] dedication and when we take over Bambino Gesu Hospital in 1965!!"[153]

Spellman notified Stritch that he thought ". . . the Propaganda is manufacturing difficulties, but I agree with Your Eminence in accepting its proposal as a practical but not entirely satisfactory solution."[154] After further meetings, the Americans agreed to bring the Propaganda proposal to the Episcopal Board the following November.

---

[151] Vatican n.d., but pinned to the above July 19, 1950 Propaganda document to Silvestri, "PRO-MEMORIA", KC, *Enrico Galeazzi Papers, Spellman Corresp., Propaganda Fide*, Box 80, File 1.

[152] New York, Interview of Edward Cardinal Egan by the author, April 23, 2012.

[153] Rome March 16, 1951, O'Connor to Galeazzi, KC, *Enrico Galeazzi Papers, North Amer. Coll, Correspondence Martin J. O'Connor, 1950-1951*, Box 30, File 11.

[154] New York August 28, 1950, Spellman to Cardinal Stritch, NYC, Box S/C-74, Folder 7: *To Card. Spellman, N. Amer. Coll.*

During that meeting, Cardinal Spellman moved that the Propaganda proposal be accepted, and this was seconded by Archbishop Ritter. The minutes recorded that:

> The title to this property [Palazzo Orsini on the Via dell'Umiltà] will remain in the name of Propaganda. Propaganda will issue a solemn declaration stating that its holding the title is a fiction of law and that the real owners are the American bishops. In the document Propaganda will state that the American Bishops have every right of ownership, including the right to sell the property and that Propaganda, as far as legal requirements demand, would act without question according to the decision of the American Bishops. Propaganda would ask the Holy Father to approve the solemn document.[155]

The proposal passed unanimously, and Propaganda was informed of the decision with a request to proceed with the plan.

But, once again, nothing happened. While they waited for action from the Propaganda, O'Connor and his team turned their attention to the other aspects of the project: questions of funding for renovation of old buildings and for new construction; negotiations with the Italian government for blocked lire;[156] architectural designs and construction problems of the new seminary; the refurbishing of the Villa and the Umiltà; the drafting of a new constitution for the College; the day-to-day operation of the College and of the graduate priest house, which had both re-opened with new seminarians and student priests; the recruitment of new seminarians for the subsequent academic years; operational deficits; and the newly opened American Visitors Office to the Vatican during the 1950 Holy Year, housed at

---

[155] Scranton December 9, 1950, O'Connor to Galeazzi, KC, *Enrico Galeazzi Papers, North Amer. Coll, Financial management*, Box 13, File 8.

[156] "Rector's Report, North American College, April 2, 1951": *Rector's Note*, p 14, CUA, *O'Connor Papers*, Box 44: *NAC*, Folder: *Rector's Report (April 1951)*.

the Umiltà property, and the reception of members of the American hierarchy and laity in Rome.[157]

On July 7, 1951, O'Connor wrote once again to Propaganda, asking the status of the title question. But no substantive response was ever given him, other than a July 10th note acknowledging the reception of his letter. So, on September 6th, the Rector requested a meeting with Prince Carlo Pacelli, the nephew of the Pope and the Propaganda lawyer. During the meeting, O'Connor brought up the earlier meeting of Cardinals Stritch and Fumasoni-Biondi, when it was agreed that a temporary solution to the problem might be a simple canonical one concerning the Umiltà property, as subsequently ratified by the Episcopal Board during their November 1950 meeting.

While this was being digested, and following the August *ferie*, the Italian government issued a formal decree that, "because of their historic and artistic value, the Palazzo Orsini and chapel were of notable national importance", and notified the College—and not the Propaganda—that its buildings had been declared a national monument.[158] O'Connor decided not to inform Propaganda of this decree, telling Burns to write O'Connor's opinion to Silvestri "that it is prudent to consider the transfer of the Orsini Palace as already having come about by the Rescript of His Holiness."[159] O'Connor understood that the property was immediately theirs from the moment the Pope issued his rescript, and Propaganda need no longer be informed about College business. It was now solely an American concern.

---

[157] "Rector's Report North American College, November 14, 1951", *Legal Report*, p. 49, CUA, *O'Connor Papers*, Box 44: *NAC*, Folder: *Rector's Reports*: O'Connor furnished details: from January 1-October 1, 1951: 11,543 American pilgrims had obtained papal audiences through the College; 3,615 letters were answered by the Rector concerning the seminary, the construction work and the College Audience Office.

[158] Rome October 8, 1951, Burns to Silvestri, CUA, *O'Connor Papers*, Box 42, Folder: *Propagation of the Faith*: The positive effect of this decree was that the Umiltà property would be safe from any future changes of the zoning ordinances by the City of Rome.

[159] Rome October 8, 1951, Burns to Silvestri, CUA, *O'Connor Papers*, Box 42, Folder: *Propagation of the Faith*.

The lawyers for Propaganda responded to O'Connor's July 7th letter on September 19, 1951.[160] But the response was not relayed by Cardinal Fumasoni-Biondi to O'Connor until October 15th, assuring the Rector that "the offices of this Holy Congregation are poised for the final steps of this process, in order to arrive at a final definition of the relationship between the North American College and Propaganda Fide."[161]

Pacelli thought the papal rescript of July 26, 1948 dealt with an exchange of title and rights over property of both the Propaganda and the American College. But these rights were somehow superseded by the Pope's own statement that the Americans' wishes be granted because of the *"doveroso omaggio all'Episcopato degli Stati Uniti."* The task was to interpret and apply canon 1529 of the 1917 Code of Canon Law, in order to make this grant by the Holy Father effective under Italian civil law.[162] However, since this was an exchange of properties, the common-held Janiculum property in exchange for the Umiltà Palazzo Orsini, no civil authorization would be necessary under Italian law. When Cardinal Stritch met with Cardinal Fumasoni-Biondi, Pacelli continued:

> they had agreed [*avevano convenuto*] to limit themselves, for the moment, to the drawing up of a canonical provision by which the Sacred Congregation would remain the civilly registered owner [*intestataria civile dell'immobile*] of the property known as the Palazzo Orsini, while solemnly recognizing that the property belonged [*la proprieta*

---

160   Roma September 19, 1951, Carlo & Giulio Pacelli to O'Connor, CUA, *O'Connor Papers*, Box 42, Folder: *Propagation of the Faith*.

161   Rome October 15, 1951, Prot. No. 2639, Fumasoni-Biondi to O'Connor, CUA, *O'Connor Papers*, Box 42, Folder: *Propagation of the Faith*.

162   Canon 1529 basically stated that the law of the particular territory in effect at the time the contract was entered into was recognized as canonically binding, with some qualifications, unless contrary to natural or divine law. [cf *The Code of Canon Law, A Text and Commentary*, ed. Corden, James, Green, Thomas, Heintschel, Donald, New York, 1985, p 878.]

spetta] to the American bishops, who could, if and when they determined, sell the property itself.

Prince Pacelli concluded by saying he thought that, in light of the interests of the American bishops, and the agreements [*le intese*] recently exchanged between Cardinals Stritch and Fumasoni-Biondi, and especially considering the very heavy financial burdens that would result from a civil act of registration according to the laws of Italy, "the solution of simple notarized acts in the Vatican would be temporarily sufficient."[163] Precisely what Silvestri, Galeazzi, O'Connor, and the American bishops had been proposing since 1948.

Monsignor Burns immediately sent copies of the original documents to O'Connor, shared the Pacelli opinion with Galeazzi and Silvestri, and began preparing a response, completed on November 3rd. In that response, employing the thoughts of O'Connor and Galeazzi, and prepared by Silvestri,[164] Burns asked Fumasoni-Biondi if he agreed with Pacelli's suggested solution of a notarized act in the Vatican concerning the Umiltà property, ". . . and if you would authorize that which Pacelli proposes along with an accurate re-examination of the drafts of those acts that had been prepared already for some time."[165] O'Connor sent all these documents to Stritch with the comment:

> it seems to me that the suggestion in my report would still be acceptable; namely, that we do not press too hastily the decision, but that we try to secure agreement on the arrangement understood

---

163 It was this final paragraph that O'Connor and Silvestri underlined that caught the attention of the American bishops as they pondered how to conclude this aspect of the work.

164 Rome November 6, 1951, O'Connor to Stritch, CUA, *O'Connor Papers*, Box 42, Folder: *NAC subfile*.

165 Rome November 3, 1951, Burns to Fumasoni-Biondi, CUA, *O'Connor Papers*, Box 42, Folder: *Propagation of the Faith*.

and proposed by Propaganda on the occasion of your visit.[166]

In his November 14, 1951 report to the Episcopal Board, O'Connor outlined the financial status, the progress of the construction projects, and the present state of negotiations with the Propaganda about the Palazzo Orsini. Because the Umiltà property had been designated a national monument by the Italian government on July 11, 1951, the first effect was that no zoning ordinances could affect the buildings, such as had threatened them in the late 1930's, when a new street was decreed to be cut directly through the property, destroying the College buildings.[167]

Despite numerous meetings and discussions with Propaganda, no agreement had been reached. The Rector expressed his opinion that "some settlement can be reached this year concerning the question first proposed to Propaganda in December, 1946, but there is no need for haste. A solution that satisfies all parties is desirable." It had taken so long, and there seemed some unstated reason why Propaganda continued to block this title transfer, O'Connor rightly thought that instead of rushing now, simply to conclude the matter, possibly making a hasty decision that might be regretted in the future, it would be better to fashion an agreement most advantageous to the College,

---

[166] Rome November 6, 1951, O'Connor to Stritch, CUA, *O'Connor Papers*, Box 42, Folder: *NAC subfile*. The "visit" referred to Stritch's 1950 visit to Rome and his meeting with Fumasoni-Biondi.

[167] "Rector's Report North American College, November 14, 1951": *Legal Report*, p. 33, CUA, *O'Connor Papers*, Box 44: *NAC*, Folder: *Rector's Reports*. The effects of the Italian decree were that demolition, restoration of any artwork or fixtures, especially in the chapel, or modification of the buildings in any substantive manner, could not be done without the express approval of the Italian government. Silvestri had assisted Monsignor Hayes in 1939 in formulating the College protest of the Roman plan to cut a street through the Umiltà property, and provided the Italian government with the precise arguments for the preservation of the Palazzo Orsini as an artistic and historical treasure that the government used now. Silvestri stressed that, since the present work on the Umiltà pre-dated this decree, the work could continue without difficulty, except concerning the chapel and refectory.

and to understand what actually was going on.[168] The Episcopal Board of the College accepted O'Connor's recommendations "without question."[169]

As another New Year wore on, there still was no word from Propaganda about the process to be adopted by which the Pope's 1948 rescript would be realized. On April 23, 1952, O'Connor met with Fumasoni-Biondi once again, and brought up the subject, saying that following Cardinal Stritch's 1950 meeting with the Prefect, the College referred the Propaganda's suggested proposal to Silvestri, "namely to draw a canonical document showing that the property was to all effects and purposes that of the American Bishops." O'Connor asked further questions about Costantini's objections and the position of Prince Carlo Pacelli, which the Prefect said he did not understand. Finally, O'Connor asked if he should send Silvestri to reopen discussions with the Propaganda representatives, stating that Spellman and the American bishops wanted a solution, and the Prefect agreed.[170]

Meeting with Silvestri, Galeazzi and Burns during the spring and summer, O'Connor instructed them to contact Stritch, since he had arrived at the agreement with Fumasoni-Biondi during his 1950 meeting. So, on August 1, 1952, Burns wrote the Cardinal Archbishop of Chicago, relating the torturous history of the negotiations, and asked Stritch to give his opinion and guidance. Stritch answered on August 11th, after consulting with Cardinal Mooney, suggesting that the matter be decided by the Americans at the November meeting of the Episcopal Board, and that O'Connor incorporate the full proposal in his report.

Stritch then clarified an important point: during his 1950 meeting with Fumasoni-Biondi, no agreement had ever been reached! Stritch went on that, contrary to common opinion, he had been asked to

---

[168] "Rector's Report North American College, November 14, 1951": *Legal Report*, p. 26, CUA, *O'Connor Papers*, Box 44: *NAC*, Folder: *Rector's Reports*.

[169] Scranton November 20, 1951, O'Connor to Galeazzi, KC, *Enrico Galeazzi Papers, No. Amer. Coll, Financial Management*, Box 13, File 8.

[170] Memorandum, April 23, 1952, O'Connor to Spellman, CUA, *O'Connor Papers*, Box 44, Folder: *Propagation of the Faith*.

relay Constantini's proposal to the Episcopal Board, which he did. But, he continued, "I had no authority to enter into an agreement, and I did not enter into an agreement in the matter."[171]

With no further input from Propaganda, O'Connor and his team decided to take the matter into their own hands. Galeazzi met with various Vatican officials unofficially, while Silvestri re-opened discussions with the Italian government, unofficially. By October, the Rector's report was completed, including Silvestri's legal report with a two page brief history of the frustrating negotiations with Propaganda, and Stritch's correction about the 1950 "agreement" with Propaganda. Along with this, the Rector included his own recommendation to the committee: Since the Propaganda is unwilling to draw up either a legal contract or an agreement to be notarized in Vatican City for the title transfer, the American bishops should determine the means of implementing the Pope's generous action by executing the papal rescript themselves. Since the rescript was granted to the Americans and not the Propaganda, the American bishops should draw up a document relating the contents of the papal rescript, and have it notarized in the Vatican, and then they should register the property transfer with the Italian government, and pay the taxes, hoping for the lowest possible rate [which looked to be at least 7 million lire, approximately $6 million], "granting to the Rector ample discretionary authority to make the decisions necessary to bring this timeworn matter to an happy conclusion."[172]

In other words, the Americans would do an end run around the Propaganda officials, even if it meant paying the enormous Italian taxes, and the Propaganda would have to content itself with the Janiculum property, receiving nothing for the Umiltà land or building. And that is precisely what they did.

The Propaganda complained to Burns two weeks later that they had heard nothing from the College since April 1952 concerning the Umiltà property. Burns sent the letter to Silvestri, who suggested

---

[171] Chicago August 11, 1952, Stritch to Burns, CUA, *O'Connor Papers*, Box 44: NAC, Folder: *Propagation of the Faith*.

[172] "Report of the Rector, November 12, 1952", p. 8. CUA, *O'Connor Papers*, Box 44: *NAC*, Folder: *Rector's Reports*.

that he not respond until December. When December arrived, Burns answered, by simply acknowledging receipt of the Propaganda letter and to lament that the Rector was absent from Rome, in the United States for the annual bishops' meeting.[173]

The motion was approved by the American bishops, and by January 1953 the ecclesiastical title for the Umiltà property had passed from the Propaganda to the American College, and Silvestri continued negotiating with the Italian authorities for the civil title to the Palazzo Orsini, as well as some agreement about taxes.[174] Eventually, the College paid $23,000.00 [$200,579.00] in taxes to the City of Rome. As Spellman wrote Mooney, "It was the opinion of all in Rome that it would be better to finalize this matter."[175]

While all this occurred, there were many other pieces of the puzzle to build a new American seminary in Rome that occupied all concerned, not the least of which were securing sufficient funding, and the actual construction of the new building on the Janiculum Hill. To understand how those pieces came together, we must return to the 1947 Episcopal Board meeting and see the course decided upon by the American bishops.

[173] Rome December 4, 1952, Burns to Propaganda, CUA, *O'Connor Papers*, Box 44: *NAC*, Folder: *Propagation of the Faith*.

[174] New York, January 22, 1953, Spellman to College Board Members, NYC, Box S/C-74, Folder 2: *To Card. Spellman, N. Amer. Coll.* New York July 31, 1953, MaGuire to Spellman, CUA, *O'Connor Papers*; NAC Subfiles, Folder: *NAC*.

[175] New York February 20, 1953, Spellman to Mooney, NYC, Box S/C-74, Folder 2: *To Card. Spellman, N. Amer. Coll.*

Chapter 4

Funding a Seminary

> *"During these past two years of work, I have had the opportunity to admire the extraordinary diligence, exceptional zeal and great ability of the Rector so that all difficulties and challenges are brought to the best solution, and I believe that shortly all would have failed without his tireless efforts. I have also felt that he has absolute trust in your help, knowing strongly that you love the College, and that you have always and without hesitation supported the plans for the immediate construction of its new home."*
> —Count Galeazzi to Cardinal Spellman, 1948

The Episcopal Board met on April 24, 1947 at Saint Charles Seminary, Overbrook, Pennsylvania, moving the rehabilitation and construction plans one step closer to realization. It was urgent that decisions be made, especially since the bishops hoped to re-open the College at the Castel Gandolfo property in October 1947.[176]

O'Connor immediately informed his team of the decisions and asked them to begin implementing them.[177] The Rector had full

---

[176] Rome November 29, 1946, Silvestri to Spellman, NAC, *Coll. Amer., Corrisp. Rettori, Card. Spellman—M. C. Geough* [sic]. New York November 30, 1946, Spellman to Galeazzi, NYC, Box S/C-73, Folder 6: *To Card. Spellman, N. Amer. Coll.*

[177] N.p. April 26, 1947, O'Connor to Burns, CUA, *O'Connor Papers*, Box 36: *Rel. Org/Priests, Folder: Burns, Msgr. Richard F*; Scranton May 29, 1947, O'Connor to Galeazzi, KC, *Enrico Galeazzi Papers*, Box 30, File 7: *No. Amer. Coll., MJ O'Connor Corresp, 1947*; Scranton May 29, 1947, O'Connor to Silvestri, NAC, *Coll. Amer, Corrisp. Rettori, Card. Spellman—M.C. Geough* [sic].

faith in his Roman team. And, while he continued his work in the States, he instructed Father Joseph Lacy, the new College Business Manager, that, "Because of my lack of familiarity with conditions, be guided by what Father Burns and yourself think best", concerning the immediate studies and work projects in Rome.[178]

O'Connor also phoned Monsignor John J. Maguire, Vice Chancellor of the Archdiocese of New York, and asked for the transfer of the $120,000 [$1,238,125.56] needed for repairs on the College buildings. Maguire prepared a memorandum outlining the College financial situation for Cardinal Spellman, who was the treasurer of the Episcopal Board. The amount requested by the Rector could be had by releasing some of the College's assets, Maguire wrote. The balance in the Rector's account totaled $8,577.81 [$88,503.38]; investment income accumulated since the close of the College totaled $86,168.40 [$889,060.82]; income recently received by the College from the Gormully estate totaled $20,437.78 [$210,871.15]. The balance needed by O'Connor "will be realized from income before the Rector will have need of it." That left only $27,500 [$283,737.11] as "not too large a cushion" against possible depreciation of investments.[179]

Maguire supplied his boss with only the basic numbers. The estimated cost for the new seminary on the Janiculum hill was a whopping $2,740,000 [$28,270,533.63].[180] However, since the estimated construction period was three years, and both costs and

---

[178] N.p. May 24, 1947, O'Connor to Lacy, CUA, *O'Connor Papers*, Box 25: *Misc & Unfiled Corresp*, Folder 11.

[179] New York May 29, 1947, Maguire "Memorandum to His Eminence Re: North American College", NYC, Box S/C-73, Folder 9: *To Card. Spellman, N. Amer. Coll.*

[180] Washington, D.C. May 12, 1948, O'Connor's "Address to the Alumni Association of the North American College in Rome at the Meeting in Washington's Mayflower Hotel", KC, *Enrico Galeazzi Papers, N. Amer. Coll, Alumni Assoc., Form letters, articles, addresses, 1948, 1950-51, undated,* Box 29, File 19. O'Connor reported Galeazzi's figures: The estimated construction cost for approximately 300 students would be 57 cents per cubic foot; the building volume estimate was 4,500,000 cubic feet; unit cost per student, $8,600; total cost in dollars for the buildings, walks, gardens and athletic grounds: $2,740,000. The total area of ground available was 47,000

exchange rates would fluctuate, a budget for at least $3,000,000 [$30,953.139.01] was suggested. The building was "simple in design, ecclesiastical and Roman." The Umiltà works would be put out for bid, and contracts for the Villa would be given to the winner of the Umiltà project. The Villa Santa Caterina rehabilitation for year-round occupancy would cost approximately $200,000 [$2,063,542.60], not including the cost of a heating system, laundry equipment or furnishings to accommodate 100 students, faculty, religious Sisters and domestic staff. The repairs and upkeep of the extensive, important gardens and rare tree collection would be another large expenditure, but necessary because of the quality of the collection itself: the trees alone were valued at 16 million lire [nearly $12 million]. He outlined the legal negotiations with the Commune of Castel Gandolfo, which were not progressing well. The College mausoleum at Campo Verano was being repaired at a cost of $900.00 [$9,285.94], and would be completed by December 1, 1947.

The architectural fees were 5% of the cost of the work for the Umiltà project, which included the bookkeeping and work oversight. The same 5% would be applied for the Janiculum project, but a separate work superintendent and bookkeeper would be engaged, since that project was so large and complex. The final College property, the Casa San Giovanni on the Janiculum site that had been serving as the post-graduate house, would be self-supporting by October 15th, with an earlier expenditure of $25,000 [$257,942.83] for repairs and updating of the facility.

There in a nut shell were the basics: few funds to finance much construction, to be accomplished simultaneously while running a seminary in post-war Rome, and local decisions about these Roman projects to be made 3,000 miles away in New York.

O'Connor remained in the United States until late June, addressing the alumni meeting in Chicago in May, to secure their support for the new College. He then traveled across the country, meeting with bishops, alumni, and donors, visiting American

---

square meters, or about 12 acres; the new building was to occupy 7,000 square meters or less than 1/7th of the total available area.

seminaries, studying their programs and facilities. He also purchased equipment needed at the Casa San Giovanni, everything from a commercial ice box to automobile tires and replacement parts for the College Chrysler, all obtained through the War Relief Services. In his correspondence to members of his Roman team, O'Connor frequently reminded them to complete the repair work below budget, or at least to remain within the budget established by the Episcopal Board and Monsignor Maguire.[181] During the summer months, the team worked to complete the repairs, to make some progress in the title negotiations with the Propaganda, and, most importantly, to complete the preliminary designs for the Umiltà rehabilitation, which the Rector wanted to present at the upcoming bishops' meetings in October.[182]

In preparation for these important presentations, Galeazzi prepared drawings and a 28-page report on the Umiltà building restoration, including the measurements and studies made by his team of technical assistants, and based on his numerous inspection visits with Silvestri. The buildings were in very bad shape, with roofs, terraces, flooring, doors and window casements all in need of replacement; the plumbing, heating and electric systems "useless." Even in 1940, both men remembered, the buildings were in terrible condition, and were "entirely inadequate to the needs of a modern college. The severe war years have completed the devastation."[183]

Galeazzi also prepared a study of the Janiculum property and made his recommendations to Bishop O'Connor to relay to the Episcopal Board. The property, measuring twelve acres, was occupied by a collection of ramshackle buildings and cottages of the former mental hospital of Santa Maria della Pieta. These would all be demolished, except for the Villa Gabrielli, to be renovated to serve as the temporary home of the priest graduate house.

[181] N.p. June 18, 1948, O'Connor to Burns, CUA, *O'Connor Papers*, Box 36: *Rel. Org/Priests Corr*, Folder: *Burns, Msgr. Richard K.*
[182] Rome September 16, 1947, O'Connor to Joseph Cardinal Pizzardo, KC, *Enrico Galeazzi Papers, Card. Spellman Corresp., 1947-1955*, Box 80, File 1.
[183] Vatican September 29, 1947, Galeazzi: "Pontificio Collegio Americano del Nord Progetto di Restauro del Fabricato di via dell'Umiltà, in Roma", NYC, Box S/C-73, Folder 7: *To Card. Spellman, N. Amer. Coll.*

In Galeazzi's opinion, after considering its superb view of Saint Peter's Basilica, the most impressive aspect of the property was the avenue of ancient Roman pine trees, which the architect took into consideration as he designed the building. The height of the new seminary "has accordingly been limited in keeping with the very beautiful wooded area which frames the view of this land, as seen from the Vatican."[184]

The first design produced by Galeazzi, consisted of a group of three five-story buildings forming the letter "Z".[185] Galeazzi believed the design reflected Roman ecclesiastical architecture, and capitalized "upon the concept of maximum enjoyment afforded by the vista of the cupola of Saint Peter's through the avenue of pines." The lower portion of the walls was to be covered in Roman Travertine, and the upper stories of simple colored stucco. The building would be topped by a campanile, and roofed terraces, and the ecclesiastic character of the building emphasized by numerous interior archways.[186] The new seminary would cover 7,000 cubic meters of the 47,000 cubic meters of land owned by the College, and might be completed within three years of the construction starting date.[187]

By the fall, O'Connor was in the States preparing for the upcoming bishops' meeting, which had been postponed until November 10th, since Cardinals Mooney and Stritch could not be present earlier. Knowing that time was short and the repair work load immense, O'Connor approached Cardinals Dougherty and Spellman before the bishops' meeting to secure their approval that Galeazzi might

---

[184] Vatican October 1, 1947, Galeazzi Report, "The New Site of the Pontifical North American College on the Janiculum Hill in Rome", p. 4, CUA, *O'Connor Papers*, Box 44: *NAC*.

[185] Galeazzi Report, p. 5, CUA, in above ref.

[186] This original plan proved improbable, for a variety of features: student showers on the ground floor near the laundry, a full combined gymnasium/auditorium half below ground level, an infirmary on the 4th floor with a 5th floor "isolation ward", huge covered terraces providing "ample space for recreation on rainy days", and no basement areas.

[187] Galeazzi listed those who assisted in his design: Nello Ena, architect, Mario Bedini, engineer and architect, and Costantino Mazzoleni, designer.

move ahead. Because building materials, especially steel, were scarce commodities in Italy, the Rector cabled Galeazzi: "After consultation with Cardinals Dougherty and Spellman authorize your purchase of 100 tons steel."[188] The absent Cardinals were not pleased that the decisions were made without them, so Spellman confirmed the authorization one week later, cabling his apology to Galeazzi, "I take responsibility for authorizing you to proceed proposed work on Umiltà Property."[189] After receiving Spellman's permission, so as to lose no time,[190] O'Connor sent another cable to Galeazzi the same day: "To have time suggest you request bids from necessary firms and contractors but do not advise this procedure if it entails obligation of actually proceeding with work Via dell'Umiltà without approval of our board. Please acknowledge."[191]

As November 10th drew nearer, and even while he was urging work to commence, the Rector began worrying about the bishops' approval of his plans, with word from Rome that the Propaganda title negotiations continued slowly; that the Umiltà was still inhabited by Italian social workers; that building materials in Rome were scarce; and that there were workers' strikes in the city.[192] He wrote his Vice Rector: "As I see it, at the present time, it look [sic] as though the future college and appropriation for it will require more effort. I hope that I will be able to have the approval of the complete program, but I am not too certain."[193]

---

[188] N.p. October 18, 1947, O'Connor to Galeazzi, CUA, *O'Connor Papers*, Box 36: *O'Connor Rel. Org/Priests Corr. Folder: Burns, Msgr. Richard K.*

[189] New York October 22, 1947, Spellman to Galeazzi, KC, *Enrico Galeazzi Papers, N. Amer. Coll. Corresp, Most Rev. Martin J. O'Connor, 1947*, Box 29, File 11.

[190] Scranton October 21, 1947, O'Connor to Burns, CUA, *O'Connor Papers*, Box 36: *Rel. Org/Priests Corr. Folder: Burns, Msgr. Richard K.*

[191] Cable, Scranton October 22, 1947, O'Connor to Galeazzi, KC, *Enrico Galeazzi Papers, N. Amer. Coll. Corresp, Most Rev. Martin J. O'Connor, 1947*, Box 29, File 1.

[192] Rome November 4, 1947, Silvestri to O'Connor, NAC, *Coll. Amer. Corris. Rettori, Card. Spellman—M.C. Geough* [sic].

[193] Scranton November 2, 1947, O'Connor to Burns, CUA, *O'Connor Papers*, Box 36: *Rel. Org/Priests Corr.*, Folder: *Burns, Msgr. Richard K.*

Burns answered the Rector, giving a brief report showing some progress, and encouraged him, priest-to-priest:

> We are praying for your success, or that God's will be done, on November 10th; but we cannot but hope that God's will and ours are the same. Take good care of yourself, and after the meeting be sure to get the rest you need—and so well deserve.[194]

During the meeting of the Episcopal Board at St. Charles Seminary outside Philadelphia, the Rector made his report about the progress he and his team had made to implement the bishops' directives of April 24, 1947.[195] There had been thirteen seminarian applications received for the first theology class and three for first philosophy, as a result of O'Connor's August 8th letter and copy of the Gregorian University catalogue he sent to every bishop ordinary in the country. The architectural studies revealed the bad state of the Umiltà buildings, with an estimated cost for repairs and furniture of $550,000 [$5,674,742.15]. There were serious questions about the foundations, and doubts about the structural stability of the buildings, which would require further investigations.

In view of the future negotiations to be entered into by the College and the City of Rome for the Umiltà property title, funding, building permits, and permissions for restoring the historic seminary buildings, Galeazzi and Silvestri urged the Rector to downplay the damage caused by the "several thousand boys" who had used the Umiltà during the war. O'Connor did so in his report, suggesting

---

[194] Rome November 5, 1947, Burns to O'Connor, CUA, *O'Connor Papers*, Box 36: *Rel. Org/Priests Corr.*, Folder: *Burns, Msgr. Richard K*. Throughout the correspondence between O'Connor and his team, there is an obvious and shared strong faith, a love for the priesthood, and a devotion to the College as a project well worth their combined efforts.

[195] Rome October 1, 1947, "Report of His Excellency Monsignor Martin J. O'Connor, Rector of the North American College in Rome, on Work done in Accordance with the Directives of the Episcopal Committee", NYC, Box S/C-73, Folder 10: *To Card. Spellman, N. Amer. Coll.*

that the bishops not demand too high a compensation from the Italian government.

Prior to the meeting, the Rector sent the bishops a memorandum about the College finances in which he made his own suggestions. He reminded the bishops that the North American College was established by the Popes and committed to the care of the bishops of the United States, and as such, was a national obligation of the American Hierarchy.

Reporting about the title negotiations with the Propaganda, O'Connor told the committee that Cardinal Fumasoni-Biondi preferred to maintain title to the Umiltà. The Cardinal Prefect told the Rector that this should prove no difficulty for the American bishops, since they enjoyed perpetual use of the property since 1862, *ad beneplacitum Sanctae Sedis*, and that the bishops could begin the restoration work on the building, even without possessing the property title.[196] But it did present a problem, for the bishops feared American Catholics would give no money to a large construction project to be built on land in a foreign country that Americans did not own.

Because the Board felt uneasy that work could not be completed by the fall of 1947, they decided to postpone the re-opening of the College until the fall of 1948. They also decided that new students should be accepted only from those dioceses with educational burses for the College, assuring that the tuition would be paid. It was estimated that the annual cost for room and board per student would be $750.00 [$7,738.28]. This decision would plague the Rector for years, because tuition never covered the College's basic operational expenses. And, despite his annual reminders of the growing operational deficit, the bishops annually chose to disregard his warnings.

---

[196] Vatican March 13, 1950, Galeazzi to O'Connor, KC, *Enrico Galeazzi Papers, No. Amer. Coll. Corresp Msgr. Martin J. O'Connor, 1949-1951*, Box 29, File 21: Restoration work on the Umiltà actually began in December 1947, and the first portion of the building, the Palazzo Tomba, was completed in February 1949, the students took possession of the renovated portion by March. The gardens were completed in November.

O'Connor also presented the report by the New York architect, Thomas A. Kelly to the bishops, which stated that the primary project was the renovation of the Umiltà property, "with alterations and additions."[197] Kelly reminded the bishops that if the College were to re-open in the fall of 1948 as hoped, they would have to make a decision soon. Even though Kelly had never seen the Umiltà buildings, nor even been to Rome, he expressed concerns about spending $550,000 on a decrepit building with unsound foundations and inadequate space. Kelly preferred to level the Umiltà and build a new, eight-story seminary on the property, although he noted, "It may be that the historical and spiritual values attached to the old building would make its retention mandatory".[198]

O'Connor also suggested the establishment of a permanent office in the United States, *The Executive Secretariat of the Reconstruction and Building Program for the North American College*, to publicize the College as a national and pontifical institution in Rome for Americans, and "to keep the issue constantly alive by personal contact with the Hierarchy." O'Connor knew that cheerleading this project was essential,[199] otherwise the bishops would become distracted by their own massive diocesan construction projects as well as national Catholic projects, such as the construction of the National Shrine of the Immaculate Conception in Washington, D.C. [200] Monsignor

---

[197] Kelly, *Report to Bishop O'Connor on the following Two Construction Projects for the North American College in Rome, October 31, 1947*, CUA, *O'Connor Papers*, Box 47, Folder: *Galeazzi Proposals and Estimates, 1947-50*.

[198] Ibid, Kelly included estimated costs for the renovation of the Umiltà: 55 cents per cubic foot, including 10% allowance for furnishing; for the new College construction on the Janiculum, 58 cents per cubic foot.

[199] N.p. November 22, 1947, O'Connor to Burns, CUA, *O'Connor Papers*, Box 36: *Rel. Org/Priests Corr.*, Folder: *Burns, Msgr. Richard K*: "I went to Chicago for the Church Extension meeting and had an opportunity to meet some of the one hundred and three bishops who were there."

[200] Scranton November 14, 1947, O'Connor to Galeazzi, KC, *Enrico Galeazzi Papers, No. Amer. College, Most Rev. Martin J. O'Connor Corresp, 1947*, Box 30, File 7.

John J. Russell [NAC 1923], Pastor of Saint Patrick's Parish in Washington, D.C., was chosen to head the new office.[201]

O'Connor cabled Galeazzi the results of the meeting, "Entire program old building and new seminary approved by committee and hierarchy."[202] Later the same day, after he returned to Scranton, the Rector sent a second cable, "You must be pleased, insofar as all our plans for the old college building [Umiltà] have been approved with the exception of some minor changes."[203]

Not everyone was so happy with the decisions. Spellman responded to reflections by his friend Monsignor Kealy about the College Board's decisions, commenting, "as you know, [the decisions] were a complete reversal of the conclusions reached at our meeting in Rome" following the February 1946 consistory, which included the purchase of the Villa Abamalek.[204] Likewise, some bishops were not convinced that the project should move forward because of the College had only $268,000 [$3,162,193.85] on hand.[205]

The bishops approved that funding for the entire rehabilitation of the College buildings would come from the monies pledged in 1939 as quotas from each American diocese, and each diocese

---

[201] New York December 17, 1947, Spellman to Russell, NYC, Box S/C-73, Folder 13: *To Card. Spellman, N. Amer. Coll.* One of the office's initial projects was a nationwide collection for Sunday, November 14, 1948, to solicit donations directly from Catholics in the pews to help fund the College. Envelopes were printed and issued to parishes, with the message, "Help the Holy Father Train American Priests. Help rebuild the North American College in Rome. The Priesthood, the Bulwark Against Communism."

[202] Cable Washington, D.C. November 14, 1947, O'Connor to Galeazzi, KC, *Enrico Galeazzi Papers, No. Amer. Coll., Corresp, Most Rev. Martin J. O'Connor*, Box 29, File 11. O'Connor made a presentation to the entire American hierarchy during their annual meeting on November 14, 1947.

[203] Cable, Scranton November 14, 1947, O'Connor to Galeazzi, KC, above ref.

[204] New York January 4, 1947, Spellman to Kealy, NYC, Box S/C-73, Folder 8: *To Card. Spellman, N. Amer. Coll.*

[205] New York November 30, 1946, Spellman to Galeazzi, KC, *Enrico Galeazzi Papers, No. Amer. Coll. Corresp., Francis Card. Spellman*, Box 30, File 16.

would be given another quota to defray the construction costs of the new seminary.[206]

The alumni were to be solicited to donate the funds for the new chapel, expected to cost $350,000 [$3,613,334.08]. Since Spellman was the Treasurer for the Episcopal Board, the task of soliciting and collecting these alumni funds and the diocesan quotas fell to him. Spellman contacted his classmates, writing:

> I have pledged the gift of the altar from the class of 1916 and I am subscribing $25,000 for this purpose. I believe that this sum of money will be ample to care for the cost but if you would care to make a contribution toward this altar I shall be pleased to include it with my own gift and any monies that will remain over and above the cost of the altar will be assigned to the chapel fund of the alumni of the College.[207]

He also wrote to bishops ordinary, reporting the financial obligation of each as determined by the bishops in their recent vote for the rebuilding of the College properties, as well as the contribution for the new construction: each bishop ordinary was to pledge a contribution equal to "fifteen times the annual offering made by the Bishops in the year 1947 for the National Catholic Welfare Conference work."[208]

Within a few months, the Holy Father himself issued a letter supporting the construction of the new College, and Spellman found himself in the unenviable position of writing bishops a second time. (The Holy Father's 1948 letter was carved in marble, and mounted above a bronze bust of the Pope Pius XII on the *piano nobile* of the new seminary. The text can be found in Appendix I). Even after

---

[206] N.p. November 12, 1947, O'Connor to Galeazzi, CUA, *O'Connor Papers*, Box 36: *Rel. Org/Priests Corr*, Folder: *Burns, Msgr. Richard K.*

[207] New York November 15, 1947, Spellman to Fr. Laurence B. Killian [NAC 1915], NYC, Box S/C-73, Folder 11: *To Card. Spellman, N. Amer. Coll.*

[208] New York November 20, 1947, Spellman circular letter to American ordinaries, NYC, Box S/C-73, Folder 11: *To Card. Spellman, N. Amer. Coll.*

the Pope's letter supporting the project, the response by American bishops was not universally positive, as seen in one letter to Spellman: "Following close upon the Holy Father's letter in the same cause, I have Your Eminence's 'summons' to the carpet for Fall River in re: the old and new American College in Rome." Bishop James E. Cassidy did send a check for $3,000 for his 1948 allocation, and a personal check for $1,000, "from my own meager means and beg Your Eminence to assure the Holy Father that I shall do everything I can, in unstinted loyalty and devotion to His Sacred Person, to further and support any project He may father . . ."[209]

Spellman's reply was brief and telling: "I fully understand and appreciate the observations in your letter and agree with them."[210]

Nevertheless, by mid-March, 1948, Spellman reported to those bishops who had not yet replied to his earlier summons, that 15 of the 23 American archdioceses and 70 of the 95 American dioceses had accepted the suggested quotas for the rehabilitation of the College buildings, and made pledges to the new College construction.[211] By April 20th, $583,482.86 [$6,020,208.69] had been collected to restore the Umiltà property; $3,023,120 [$31,191,684,54] had been pledged, of which $524,040 [$5,406,894.32] had been paid by American ordinaries for the construction of the new College. "On the whole, the response to this appeal has been most enthusiastic", Spellman wrote, and encouraged all bishops to lend a hand.[212]

The Roman team began soliciting construction bids, and contracts were signed on December 2, 1947 for the reconstruction work at the Umiltà and Castel Gandolfo properties, and work began on December 3rd.[213] But the euphoria about the new College and the

---

[209] Fall River March 19, 1948, Bishop James E. Cassidy to Spellman, NYC, Box S/C-73, Folder 13: *To Card. Spellman, N. Amer. Coll.*

[210] New York March 25, 1948, Spellman to Cassidy, NYC, in above reference.

[211] New York March 15, 1948, Spellman circular letter to American ordinaries, NYC, Box S/C-73, Folder 12: *To Card. Spellman, N. Amer. Coll.*

[212] New York May 13, 1947, Spellman circular letter to American bishops, CUA, *O'Connor Papers*, Box 44: NAC.

[213] Vatican December 2, 1947, Burns to O'Connor, KC, *Enrico Galeazzi Papers, No. Amer. Coll, Correspondence, Most Rev. Martin J. O'Connor, 1947*, Box 29, File 11: the contracts were awarded to Provera Carassi for the work.

approval of O'Connor's program by the American bishops could not buoy up the situation for long. As the allocated funds began to be spent quickly, it became apparent that diocesan and alumni contributions would go only so far. They were insufficient to fund all the construction projects.

O'Connor and his team spent the winter and spring months overseeing the reconstruction work at the Umiltà and Castel Gandolfo properties; running the graduate house of studies, refining architectural designs,[214] attending unending meetings with Propaganda officials, drawing up a rule of life for the seminary, meeting with officials of the Congregation for Seminaries and Universities, making purchases for the upcoming academic year, showing visiting bishops, alumni priests and donors the seminary properties, and attending to the endless flood of correspondence and paper work involved in all these projects.

By May 1948, O'Connor returned to Scranton, Pennsylvania to prepare for the June meeting of the bishops. As the Rector narrated to Galeazzi in a long letter, the intervening weeks were spent on the road: to Washington, D.C. for the College alumni meeting and to speak with Monsignor John Russell, now heading the new office of the Executive Secretariat for the College, and to visit with Archbishop Patrick O'Boyle, "with whom I went to school many years ago and who is very sympathetic towards the College."[215] Then to Philadelphia for two days with Cardinal Dougherty; on to Cleveland for the consecration of Bishop John Dearden, [NAC 1932] new auxiliary bishop to the Archbishop of Philadelphia, and meetings with those bishops in attendance; next to Detroit, meeting

---

[214] New York June 14, 1948, Thomas Kelly to O'Connor, CUA, *O'Connor Papers*, Box 42. O'Connor sent all designs to Kelly for comment. Kelly responded to O'Connor's May 28th letter about the chapel design for the new seminary asking: "What provisions are being made for confessionals? Is the sanctuary large enough for pontifical ceremonies and ordinations? Why not choir stalls instead of pews? Why is there no throne in the sanctuary? In the south elevation, why not eliminate the brick arches at the top, which look like the head of windows which have been bricked up?"

[215] Scranton June 4, 1948, O'Connor to Galeazzi, KC, *Enrico Galeazzi Papers, N. Amer. Coll, Corresp, Most Rev. Martin O'Connor, 1948*, Box 29, File 12.

with Cardinal Mooney; then to Chicago, meeting with Cardinal Stritch; on to St. Louis, meeting with Archbishop Joseph Ritter and Bishop John Cody [NAC 1931]; next to San Francisco to meet with Archbishop John Mitty; then to New York City and finally to Scranton. "Practically all this traveling was by air", he wrote Galeazzi, which was a post-war commercial development in 1948. He hoped to go to Baltimore to meet with Archbishop Francis Keough, and then back to Washington, D.C. for the June 24th bishops' meeting:

> Everything considered I think the trip will bring forth good fruit in a better understanding of the College and the Holy Father's mind concerning it. I am of the opinion, however, that we have much work to do to make it better understood throughout this big country where everyone is so busy and harassed with so many local problems. I hope the office of the National Executive Secretary can produce literature at least to make the college known as a national seminary in Rome according to the minds of the Popes from the Founder to the present Holy Father.

O'Connor was insistent that the American bishops be repeatedly reminded about the College projects. He decided to recommend to the committee that he send progress reports to the bishops twice each year from Rome, even after the construction was completed, since he thought it would be appropriate "and most fruitful in securing their interest." He felt it essential that the bishops continue to be interested in the seminary programs:

> because I heard some isolated sentiments to the effect that there was no hope to get this building started within ten years, but none of this conversation came from the Trustees. But it could be possible that after 24 years of vacillation there might be some lack of confidence yet. If therefore we proceed at once and show the bishops of the country as well as the people

that something is being done, I feel that it will make the collection of the money all the easier.

O'Connor ended his letter to Galeazzi:

I am certain that those few bishops who do not understand will give every measure of cooperation as soon as we continue good propaganda. However, the issue must be kept alive 12 months of the year, because if it dies, quick burial will be a natural consequence.[216]

Prior to the bishops' June meeting, O'Connor expressed his concerns about seminary tuition and finances to Monsignor Maguire, and Maguire relayed them to Spellman. The tuition was unrealistically low, especially with the devaluation of the lire and the fluctuation of the exchange rate for dollars, so that the present annual tuition would never cover costs. O'Connor suggested an annual tuition of $1,900 [$18,139.48] per student would be more realistic, on the basis of an enrollment of 26 students. With 50 students, the per capita costs might come down to $1,200 [$11,456.51]; with 100, perhaps $1,000 [$9,547.10]. Since the costs could not be lowered, and bishops might balk at such high annual tuitions, "the difficulty is one of bringing up revenue at the disposal of the Rector into line with operating costs."[217]

---

[216] O'Connor also sent three cables to Galeazzi: Scranton May 21, 1948, O'Connor to Galeazzi: "I think it advisable to recommend trustees to break ground new seminary earlier than next year"; Scranton May 29, 1948, O'Connor to Galeazzi: "Need artist's color drawing of new seminary chapel for St. Charles meeting"; Philadelphia June 3, 1948, O'Connor to Galeazzi: "Send more photos of work on Umiltà; Villa photos were effective: send to St. Charles [Seminary]", KC, *Enrico Galeazzi Papers, No. Amer. Coll., Corresp., Most Rev. Martin O'Connor, 1948*, Box 29, File 12.

[217] New York June 21, 1948, Maguire "Memorandum for His Eminence Re: North American College", NYC, Box S/C-73, Folder 12: *To Card. Spellman, N. Amer. Coll.*

Maguire relayed O'Connor's information to Spellman, telling him the difficulty was that bishops had already been informed of the annual tuition for each student, and on that basis many made commitments for between four and six years of study for each student. Poorer dioceses might be reluctant to send students if they were told of a tuition increase at the last moment, so the student makeup might be restricted to only larger dioceses that could afford the increased tuition, instead of representing the entire country, as hoped. To establish an endowment might prove impossible, especially after pledging $3,000,000 for the new college building. Likewise, dioceses might not appreciate another fund drive, and another annual appropriation from the hierarchy would not obtain a favorable response.

Solutions to the financial problems were discussed and decided during the June 24th Episcopal Board meeting at Saint Charles Seminary outside Philadelphia. Spellman was the force behind the motions, and all were carried unanimously. First, O'Connor was to inquire of the Italian government for a license to purchase blocked lire from various American film companies in Italy. These lire were funds owned by American corporations abroad that were destined exclusively for a specific purpose to be spent in Italy, and which were blocked from export by the Italian government after the war. Desperate for foreign money and work for its people, the Italian government froze all foreign-owned corporate funds then in Italy. It was hoped that the purchase of blocked lire at a better exchange rate than the market offered, might be of assistance in funding the new seminary. The bishops decided that Spellman would advise the Rector "on the mechanics of this procedure".[218]

In the 1940's, Hollywood was big business, and exercised an immense influence on audiences. It was only a matter of time until the Church and Hollywood came face to face, once the Church understood the power of the movies to form minds and hearts. The Legion of Decency was organized by American bishops in 1934

---

[218] Philadelphia June 24, 1948, Minutes of the Meeting of the Episcopal Board of the North American College, St. Charles Seminary, Overbrook. NYC, Box S/C-73, Folder 12: *To Card. Spellman, N. Amer. Coll.*

to provide a moral guide to the faithful concerning feature length movies. It was so effective that Pope Pius XI praised it in his July 29, 1936 encyclical, *Vigilanti Cura*, on the relationship of the motion picture industry and the faithful. Soon after, the Italian version of the Legion of Decency appeared, known as the *Centro Cattolico Cinematografico*. Following the war, the Vatican was very eager to employ that power to shore up its own role in the forming of Italian society, culture, and politics, especially as the potential political threat of Communism grew in post-war Italy.

After the war, the Vatican was even more convinced about the possibility of using the cinema companies to spread the Church's message by influencing the content of the movies, and exercising its influence in the market itself. During the 1950's alone, more than 5,000 parish movie houses opened throughout Italy, and the Church controlled the movies shown in all parish theaters. The fight for the soul of Italy was at stake, especially as the influence of the Communist party grew among the working class in various eastern and western European countries. Pius XII issued his own encyclical in 1957 about the cinema, *Miranda Prorsus*, addressing his remarks to representatives of Hollywood, Cine Citta, and other developing European centers of cinematography.

Likewise, following the war, there were numerous film and recording proposals made involving the Vatican. In the spring of 1946, Richard Morros, producer of the 1948 movie *Inner Sanctum*, had been in contact with Spellman, who sent him on to Galeazzi, to record the Sistine Choir.[219] There was more that Morros wanted, as Galeazzi explained to Spellman in the late summer. The producer asked Galeazzi if he could arrange with the Vatican Bank an exchange of blocked lire for American dollars. A few days later, it was Spellman's turn to write Galeazzi, informing him of a possible film about the Vatican in Technicolor with the guarantee of $100,000

---

[219]   n.p. June 27, 1946, Galeazzi to Spellman, NYC, S/C-20: *To Card. Spellman from Count Galeazzi*, Folder 11: Galeazzi attached the original letter [April 20, 1946] from Morros to himself, offering 2% of the proceeds from the record sales to the Vatican, and asking for a license to use the recordings for movies, offering the Vatican 35% of the proceeds, to be worked out through the Archdiocese of New York.

for any charity that the Holy Father may designate. "The company that is interested would give to the charity designated by the Holy Father 25% of the gross receipts", in exchange for exclusive film rights. This was another proposed means of disposing of blocked lire in Italy by the film companies.[220] These were rejected by the Vatican.

Even Bishop O'Connor was contacted and given the name of Thomas Mulrooney who was associated with United Artists Motion Pictures, who:

> asked me to arrange, if possible, an appointment with you, that he might discuss some problems and plans of the Church in relation to Motion Pictures, etc. he seems to have good connections in the industry, and is anxious to see you with some information and leads that may help you in your work in Pictures.[221]

In a memorandum to Spellman, Monsignor Maguire suggested he write to the Italian ambassador to the United States, alerting him to the bishops' efforts in Rome, and to underscore the post-war humanitarian help the American hierarchy and lay Catholics were giving Italy, hinting that the Italian government might wish to repay that generosity by granting the needed government license for the blocked lire deal. Maguire wrote the draft for Spellman's letter to the ambassador, which stated:

> Our American Catholics have been called upon to support a vast post war building program. In addition they have been phenomenally generous in their response to the many appeals of their Bishops to provide vital relief and succour to the stricken people

[220] New York August 26, 1946, Spellman to Galeazzi, NYC, S/C-2: *To Card. Spellman from Count Galeazzi*, Folder 13.
[221] Tobyhanna, PA May 9, 1948, Fr. Aloysius Baluta [NAC 1907] to O'Connor, CUA, *O'Connor Papers*, Box 1: *O'Connor General Correspondence, B (1947-56)*.

of Europe and especially of Italy. Because of these factors it is foreseen that it will be most difficult to raise sufficient funds for the completion of their plans for a Roman seminary. It is earnestly asked that your Excellency represent this matter to your government in anticipation of a formal petition to be submitted by the Committee of American Bishops.[222]

Another possible solution to the financing of the new College construction came during the June meeting of the College Episcopal Board. Cardinal Dougherty proposed that the College would "be associated with the Catholic University of America Collection in order that proper provision may be made for operating deficits".

It is quite possible that the proposed association of the College with the Catholic University Collection will be sufficient safeguard against deficiencies resulting from the difference between the quotas accepted by the Dioceses and the amount that has been pledged and on which it is possible to borrow.[223]

And, to emphasize the importance of both the transfer of property title from the Propaganda to the American bishops, and the raising of needed construction funds, O'Connor reported that during the June bishops' meeting,

it was the observation of Cardinal Spellman that perhaps the whole plan should be revised so that the new Seminary would be built on a scale for approximately two hundred men instead of three

---

[222] Undated notes attached to the Minutes of the Bishops' June 24, 1948 Meeting, NYC, Box S/C-73: *To Card. Spellman, N. Amer. Coll*, Folder 12: this document was typed on the same stationery used by Monsignor Maguire in his memoranda to Spellman, and the pin holes in each match up, since they were once attached to each other.

[223] Rome September 4, 1948, O'Connor to Spellman, NYC, Box S/C-73, Folder 12: *To Card. Spellman, N. Amer. Coll.*

hundred men. When my opinion was asked at the meeting I favored retaining the old plans by building so as to eliminate room space for one hundred men. This might be done by not completing a large portion of the wing, but with the view toward future construction should the need arise later on.[224]

This was what the committee adopted, with Mooney, Ritter and Keough favoring "the plan for not completing rather than completely changing" the plan. Spellman gave his interpretation in his letter to Galeazzi, which stated his position, trying to impose his will over that of the other bishops:

It was decided to omit the building of one wing of about one hundred rooms at the present time because of the high cost of operating the college which cannot be defrayed by tuition alone, and also because the dioceses have pledged all that it is possible for them to contribute to this enterprise for the next ten years.[225]

That simply was not true: the foundation, framing, and exterior walls were to be built as Galeazzi and O'Connor insisted, but not completed for immediate occupancy, in accord with the bishops' decision, so that when funds became available in the future, that wing would be completed.[226]

---

[224] Scranton June 25, 1948, O'Connor to Galeazzi, KC, *Enrico Galeazzi Papers, No. Amer. Coll, Most Rev. Martin J. O'Connor Corresp, Jan-Sept 1948,* Box 30, File 8.

[225] New York July 5, 1948, Spellman to Galeazzi, NYC, Box S/C-73: *To Card Spellman, N. Amer. Coll,* Folder 12. The original in KC, *Enrico Galeazzi Papers, No. Amer. Coll Corresp Francis Card Spellman 1944, 1946-1949,* Box 30, File 16.

[226] *New York Times,* August 16, 1948, p. 19, reported this in an article entitled, "Church to Replace College in Rome": "In the new building there will at first be accommodation for 200 students. Plans call for an addition within a few years that will increase the capacity to 300."

O'Connor asked Galeazzi to study Spellman's proposed elimination of the south wing of the new seminary as a cost cutting effort. Galeazzi reported it would still be necessary to build the foundation for the wing, since the basement was planned to house all the *servizi* of the seminary, as well as to build the ground floor, which would be the common rooms for the students. The resulting savings would be only about $190,000 [$1,813,948.13].[227]

On September 13th, O'Connor wrote each member of the Episcopal Board, expressing his own opinions against Spellman's proposed downsizing of the new seminary. To support his position, the Rector attached a copy of Galeazzi's August 25th letter stating that savings would be minimal. The Board members unanimously agreed with the Rector and against Spellman. Cardinal Stritch summarized the Board's thoughts, "it is cheaper to add to a building at the time of the original construction, when the apparatus etc. is on the ground. In the long run, it would be cheaper to complete the building at this time."[228]

But their decision did nothing to lessen the financial headaches related to the construction, just as the bishops' dreams about the Catholic University Collection provided no help, as Archbishop Ritter wrote O'Connor in his response:

> In reference to the hope that you express that sufficient funds will be forthcoming from the annual collection for the Catholic University, I feel, confidentially, that you would not count too much on that . . . and I am confident that some definite decision will be made about the building which is now under construction in Rome.[229]

---

227 Vatican August 25, 1948, Galeazzi to O'Connor, CUA, *O'Connor Papers*, Box 44: *NAC*.

228 Chicago September 20, 1948, Stritch to O'Connor, CUA, *O'Connor Papers*, Box 42: *NAC subfiles*. All responses from the Board members can be found here.

229 St. Louis September 24, 1948, Ritter to O'Connor, CUA, *O'Connor Papers*, Box 42: *NAC subfiles*. O'Connor underlined the final sentence in Ritter's letter in pencil, which he customarily employed in his notations.

The Pontifical North American College formally re-opened after eight years on September 14th, 1948, the Feast of the Exaltation of the Cross—without fanfare. The Villa Santa Caterina in Castel Gandolfo was the new temporary home to the 49 *Nordamericani*. O'Connor hoped the Umiltà work would be completed by November 15th, to allow the seminary to return to its birthplace within the City walls.[230]

With so many important decisions to be made, the Rector hoped to return to the States for the November bishops' meeting, but Spellman, as Treasurer of the Board, refused permission. O'Connor wrote Cardinal Dougherty, the Board President, by-passing Spellman and his objections, asking his permission to come home for the meetings of the American bishops, the College Episcopal Board, and the College alumni in Chicago:

> Many of the questions which refer to building, finance and policy cannot adequately be covered in a brief written report. I would prefer the actual personal contact with members of the Board lest there be useless correspondence and possibly misunderstanding on what would turn out to be an important issue. Another trip to America now is not too inviting a prospect . . . I realize that traveling is expensive but the expense is much less than that liable to be incurred through a mistake that could possibly be avoided.[231]

Neither Cardinal responded, and so, O'Connor informed the Board members that he saw no need to attend the November bishops' meeting, but never mentioned that Spellman had refused to pay for his trips, even though they were for College business.[232]

---

[230] Rome September 20, 1948, O'Connor to Episcopal Board Members, CUA, *O'Connor Papers*, Box 25: *O'Connor Misc & Unfiled Corresp.*, Folder 10.
[231] Rome n.d., O'Connor to Dougherty, CUA *O'Connor Papers*, Box 44: *NAC*.
[232] Rome September 20, 1948, O'Connor to Episcopal Board Members, CUA, *O'Connor Papers*, Box 2: *O'Connor Misc & Unfiled Corresp.*, Folder 10.

He also understood that his presence might be unwanted since he opposed Spellman, who continued to insist that the new seminary be downsized because of the shortage of funding. But Spellman soon discovered how convincing the Rector's thoughts were about blocked lire and the full seminary construction plan with the Episcopal Board members, as they all supported the Rector, not Spellman, in their answers to an October 2nd note from the Archbishop of New York.[233] O'Connor had come into his own as the Rector of the College with significant recent accomplishments under his belt. Likewise, as a bishop himself, he understood that he was more than a functionary to the Archbishop of New York. This was not arrogance prompting the Rector to oppose Spellman, but merely his intention to do the best he could for the College he loved.

On October 6th, Count Galeazzi wrote his friend, Cardinal Spellman, *"Mio caro amico"*, interceding that Spellman permit O'Connor to attend the upcoming bishops' meeting in Washington, D.C. The warm friendship between the two is evident in this letter, and in many others, as is the developing friendship between the Count and the Rector, which Spellman could not ignore. In this letter, Count Galeazzi jumped into the breach developing between the two men, for the sake of the College and the Church. Galeazzi told Spellman that O'Connor had decided not to attend the November bishops' meeting, even though he thought his presence might be useful to provide exact information about the College to the Board members,

> . . . and to steer clear of any ill will that might arise, or any personal interests that might enfeeble this most important enterprise.

[233] Brighton October 5, 1948, Cushing to Spellman, NYC, Box S/C-73, Folder 13: *To Card. Spellman, N. Amer. Coll*; Omaha October 5, 1948, Abp G. T. Beran to Spellman, NYC, above ref; Detroit October 5, 1948, Mooney to Spellman, NYC, above ref; San Francisco October 6, 1948, Abp. John Mitty to Spellman, NYC, above ref; Baltimore October 6, 1948, Keough to Spellman, NYC, above ref; Chicago October 7, 1948, Stritch to Spellman, NYC, above ref; St. Louis October 7, 1948, Ritter to Spellman, NYC, above ref.

Honestly speaking, I am in full accord with the Rector's plans, because I am convinced that these [decisions in Washington] are <u>historic</u> for the future development of this institution, and that whatever need be done to insure their complete success cannot be compared with that which this enterprise merits.

During these past two years of work, I have had the opportunity to admire the extraordinary diligence, exceptional zeal and great ability of the Rector so that all difficulties and challenges are brought to the best solution, and I believe that shortly all would have failed without his tireless efforts. I have also felt that he has absolute trust in your help, knowing strongly that you love the College, and that you have always and without hesitation supported the plans for the immediate construction of its new home.

I also take the liberty to tell you, as far as my judgment might help, that his going there [to the bishops' meeting in Washington, D.C.] would be most opportune, and, if he were to suggest either to the President of the Bishops' Committee or to Yourself that he come, that you encourage his trip to Washington, to assure the best results of our initiative.[234]

Spellman wrote the Count by the end of the month:

Dear Enrico: I have your letter of October 6th giving your impression, in which all who know him share, of Bishop O'Connor's extraordinary competency and equally extraordinary zeal. I believe under his direction the work of the American College will develop to a happy fruition and through its influence

---

[234] Vatican October 6, 1948, Galeazzi to Spellman, NYC, Box S/C-73, Folder 12: *To Card. Spellman, N. Amer. Coll.*

will contribute much to the Catholic mindedness of the Church in America and I trust also to the Church in Rome and throughout the world. Personally, I think if he believes it advisable to come to America for the meeting of the Bishops that he should do so.[235]

In the midst of this wrangling, Spellman wrote O'Connor telling him that his solicitation for bids for the excavation work on the Janiculum might proceed, "but you will defer any actual signing of contracts for commitments to begin the work until we settle the question of the possibility of the use of blocked lire."[236]

O'Connor responded, cabling Spellman on October 12th, answering that he had only followed the instructions of the bishops, who, during their June 24th meeting, authorized his proceeding with the excavations and borings for the new College once the Propaganda property title matter was completed. That had been settled in July with the Pope's rescript, or so everyone thought. So, following those directives, the Rector signed a contract for excavation work on October 7th "only to take advantage of weather now and be completed in February."[237] In fact, with Board authorization of July 25th, he had already signed a contract for the general construction of the new seminary on September 26th, and work had begun on October 3rd. By the time the Board met in November, the ramshackle buildings were being demolished, the excavations completed, sewers were laid and some preliminary earthmoving for retaining walls and landscaping finished.[238]

[235] New York October 21, 1948, Spellman to Galeazzi, NYC, Box S/C-73, Folder 12: *To Card. Spellman, N. Amer. Coll.*

[236] New York October 9, 1948, Spellman to O'Connor, KC, *Enrico Galeazzi Papers, No. Amer. Coll, Most Rev. Martin J. O'Connor Corresp Oct-Dec 1948*, Box 30, File 9.

[237] Cable Rome October 12, 1948, O'Connor to Spellman, KC, *Enrico Galeazzi Papers, No. Amer. Coll., Corresp. Francis Card. Spellman 1944, 1946-1949*, Box 30, File 16.

[238] "Report of the Rector of the North American College in Rome to the Episcopal Administrative Committee for the Hierarchy of the United States, November, 1949", CUA, *O'Connor Papers*, Box 44: *NAC*, File: *Rector's Report (1949, Nov)*.

The Rector had already planned an elaborate groundbreaking ceremony for October 17th, announced it to Board members and to the Pope, and received congratulatory telegrams from them all.[239] O'Connor chose that day because the process for beatification of Margaret Mary Alacoque had begun in the chapel at the old College on the Via dell'Umiltà, and "I would like the work to begin under the patronage of the great Apostle of the Sacred Heart."[240] However, in obedience to Spellman's instructions, O'Connor cancelled the elaborate plans, and settled for two very small private ground breaking ceremonies, without any publicity. The first, the Rector completed alone. Years later, he added the following captions to photos of College events:

> Unofficial ceremony on the evening of October 17, 1948 accompanied by Mr. Primo Spaghetti, Vatican chauffeur. I broke ground in a private ceremony, unknown to anyone else, as I wished to place the program under the protection of Saint Margaret Mary Alacoque, whose Feast occurred on October 17. Mr. Spaghetti was my driver for many years until his retirement.[241]

---

[239] Cable Vatican September 10, 1948, Monsignor Giovanni Montini to O'Connor, NAC, R-14, *Martin J. O'Connor 1946-1964*, #116: In awkward English, the cable read: "The Holy Father receiving with pleasure news breaking of ground for new North American College on Janiculum Hill on Feast of Saint Margaret Mary Alacoque. Together with filial devoted homage of all assembled commends to the Sacred Hearts of Jesus and Mary the protection of this project so important for the Church and cordially imparts paternal apostolic blessing on all those in Rome in United States and Elsewhere who labor for its completion. Montini-Substitute."

[240] Rome September 28, 1948, O'Connor to Galeazzi, KC, *Enrico Galeazzi Papers, No. Amer. Coll., Most Rev. Martin J. O'Connor, Corresp, Jan-Sept 1948*, Box 30, File 8.

[241] NAC, Photo Album: "Views of the New Site of the Pontifical North American College in Rome", in Storage Bag: "Views of the Janiculum Site, 1948-1952, #187. The album was arranged by O'Connor "On the Feast of Saint Thomas Aquinas, January 28, 1976."

The next day, the second *official* ceremony took place, with Fathers Burns and Lacy, Galeazzi and Silvestri and the contractors in attendance as a photographer snapped the official photograph, while O'Connor wielded a shovel.

Spellman also wrote to Galeazzi the same day, repeating the contents of his earlier letter to O'Connor. He told the Count the reason he had opposed O'Connor's plans for an elaborate ground breaking ceremony: "because they were in open contradiction to one of the conditions which he [O'Connor] stated to me—that we could not finance the college unless we had the use of blocked lire." O'Connor had insisted on this position, in opposition to Spellman's skepticism of the project's success. Spellman begrudgingly added, "I shall be pleased to see Bishop O'Connor at the Washington meeting next month."[242]

Spellman had another reason for his strong insistence to scale back the planned College construction, as well as for opposing new means to finance the College: the upcoming negotiations with the Italian government to purchase blocked lire specifically to fund the construction of the new seminary. No construction work on the Janiculum, nor any publicity, nor any public ceremonies for a ground breaking could be permitted to proceed, Spellman thought, that might lead the Italian government to misinterpret these as signs that the Americans could complete their construction program without the Italian government license to purchase blocked lire. Spellman was a fox, who knew that the government was very keen to avoid any semblance of favoritism to the Americans or to the Church. Desperate for American money and anxious to secure the Vatican's stabilizing influence in society, the Italian government wanted to appear as if riding to the rescue to save a construction project in trouble, to raise Italian self-confidence in the government, demonstrated by its ability to provide jobs for Italians by saving the American project.

The Ministry of the Treasury had made certain demands to O'Connor in the late summer, and the Rector reported them to

---

[242] New York October 22, 1948, Spellman to Galeazzi, NYC, Box S/C-73, Folder 13: *To Card. Spellman, N. Amer. Coll.*

Spellman: funds deposited in Italy were not to be released for export; the government might consider a petition to release such funds if the monies were to be spent in Italy; in the case of the American College, if the American bishops presented a petition to the government requesting the release of the funds, "it must be accompanied by a declaration that the monies will be needed for the construction of the new Seminary in Rome and that without them the Bishops could not successfully undertake their building program."[243] This was the reality, that the College actually did not have the money to proceed with the work, and did need the help of the Italian government to proceed.

Spellman wrote O'Connor on October 9th, answering the Rector's of September 4th that carried the information about the small savings of $190,000 if one wing of the seminary was not built:

> I agree with you that this small proportionate saving would not justify us in making such an elimination. For this and other reasons, some of which I refer below, I am unable to authorize proceeding with this work under the present circumstances.
>
> Possibly if you can procure a license from the Italian Government to purchase blocked lire it may change the picture . . . . Unless the Italian Government will cooperate to the extent of permitting us to purchase up to three million dollars worth of blocked lire, I, as Treasurer, will not authorize the work to begin.[244]

---

[243] Rome August 10, 1948, O'Connor to Spellman, NYC, Box S/C-73, Folder 13: *To Card. Spellman, N. Amer. Coll.*

[244] New York October 9, 1948, Spellman to O'Connor, KC, *Enrico Galeazzi Papers, No. Amer. Coll., Most Rev. Martin J. O'Connor Corresp, Oct-Dec 1948*, Box 30, File 9. A copy of this is also in NYC, Box S/C-73, Folder 13.

Spellman continued, instructing O'Connor to:

> show this to the Treasurer of the Italian Government
> and either send me the license, inform me when it
> will be forthcoming, or I shall recommend payment
> of the architect and suspension of work until the
> money is on hand. All the more would it be foolhardy
> to proceed because the College is a deficit operation
> with the average cost per student amounting to twelve
> hundred on an average income per student of seven
> hundred dollars.

A copy was sent to Galeazzi. Spellman sent a second letter to O'Connor on the same day, writing that O'Connor's solicitation of bids for excavation work on the Janiculum:

> is satisfactory, but you will defer any actual signing
> of contracts for commitments to begin the work until
> we settle the question of the possibility of the use
> of the blocked lire in especial relationship to the
> conditions outlined in your letter of August 10th,

referring to the Italian government's earlier conditions.[245] In a cable sent that same day, Spellman wrote: ". . . until I am sure building can be paid for and until I receive license discussed your letter September fifth [sic: September 4th] unable to authorize your ground breaking ceremony."[246]

---

[245] New York, October 9, 1948, Spellman to O'Connor, KC, *Enrico Galeazzi Papers, No. Amer. Coll., Most Rev. Martin J. O'Connor Corresp, Oct-Dec 1948*, Box 30, File 9. A copy of this second letter is also in NYC, Box S/C-73, Folder 12.

[246] Cablegram October 9, 1948, Spellman to O'Connor, NYC, Box S/C-73, Folder 12: *To Card. Spellman, N. Amer. Coll.*

O'Connor cabled Spellman again on October 14th, "Procedure blocked funds using your letter of October Nine. O'Connor."[247] He followed this with a letter the next day:

> As stated in my last cable we have given up the idea of a formal ceremony before beginning the work of excavation which indeed will place us in a stronger position when presenting our position to the Italian Government. I am of the opinion also that Your Eminence's letter will be of invaluable assistance in beginning the negotiations.[248]

Spellman's answer clarified his position to the Rector:

> I have yours of October 15th, and I am pleased that you understood my position for certainly if we gave evidence of proceeding to build we could not consistently say that we would be unable to complete our project without the benefit of blocked lire. If you need any further documents I am in a position to furnish them as I have opinions in writing concurring with mine from the members of the Board of Trustees. In the meantime, while we are awaiting the license from the Italian Government to purchase these blocked lire and while I have many favorable offers, I would like to have an outline of the procedure which you have adopted up to the present together with a statement concerning the rate of exchange which you have been able to secure from the Vatican bank.[249]

---

[247] Cable October 14, 1948, O'Connor to Spellman, NYC, Box S/C-73, Folder 12: *To Card. Spellman, N. Amer. Coll.*

[248] Rome October 15, 1948, O'Connor to Spellman, NYC, Box S/C-73, Folder 13: *To Card. Spellman, N. Amer. Coll.*

[249] New York October 22, 1948, Spellman to O'Connor, NYC, Box S/C-73, Folder 13: *To Card. Spellman, N. Amer. Coll.*

Before leaving Rome for the Washington meeting, O'Connor visited Dr. Cesare Muzagora, Minister of Foreign Trade in Rome, on Saturday October 23rd to begin preliminary discussions about blocked lire. In his note of thanks for the meeting, and as a means of clarifying the understanding in writing, the Rector summed up the delicate points made by the Minister, thanking him for his:

> ready disposition to authorize the use of such lire as may be conveyed as a donation, while you have reserved for subsequent kindly consideration authorization for the use of other amounts, the equivalent of which the American Bishops would be thereafter obliged to refund to the aforementioned Corporations.[250]

The Rector continued his verbal *minuet*, assuring Muzagora that he well understood and appreciated the unique circumstances for the government's kind assistance to the North American College, which:

> would be prompted by a consideration of the peculiar site on which the buildings would be constructed; of the character of the undertaking for which these funds would be exclusively expended; and of the important factor of employment since the plan would guarantee a broad utilization of manual labor for a period of more than two years.

Soon after his arrival in New York, O'Connor met with Spellman and Maguire, later reporting everything to Galeazzi. Spellman was pre-occupied about the College finances, operational expenses of the seminary, construction costs for the new building, as well as those for the renovation of the Umiltà and Castel Gandolfo properties. By now, with only just over $3,000,000 pledged, Spellman repeated his thoughts "the whole Seminary should be reduced in size to

---

[250] Rome October 27, 1948, O'Connor to Muzagora, NYC, Box S/C-73, Folder 13: *To Card. Spellman, N. Amer. Coll.*

accommodate two hundred." And elaborated that "he [Spellman] is not in favor of the project of the House of Studies and expressed himself as in favor of selling the entire property [the Umiltà]." But, the Episcopal Board had approved the full program, and it was accepted by the entire Hierarchy. O'Connor wrote that he was opposed to both the Cardinal's propositions, "especially since I have assured every one from the Holy Father down that it was not the intention of the American Bishops to use it [Umiltà] for anything except a House of Studies."[251]

O'Connor's recollection of his meeting with Spellman was borne out in a memorandum prepared by Maguire for Spellman two days later, and in preparation for the November 15th College Episcopal Board meeting.[252] O'Connor had given Maguire a copy of his financial report for the College, which revealed a projected cost overrun of 10%, or $300,000 [$2,864,128.63] for the new College building. Since the bishops' support for the College and construction was strictly voluntary, Maguire proposed three possibilities: place the problem before the American bishops and ask them to increase their quotas by 10%; discard the present architectural plans and create new ones to within the limits of funds already pledged; abandon the idea of a post-graduate house, and sell the Umiltà property to pay for the construction of the new seminary. The first two were judged impractical, and the third problematic because of the alumni's nostalgic attachment to the Umiltà seminary, and "because of the implicit agreement made at the time of the recent conveyance of title from Propaganda that the property would not be sold." Also, $600,000 [$5,728,257.26] had already been invested in the alterations of that property, "and it is unlikely that the sale price would reflect this investment."

The question of the maintenance and operation of the College was also outlined in the Maguire memorandum. His opinion was

251 New York November 10, 1948, O'Connor to Galeazzi, KC, *Enrico Galeazzi Papers, No. Amer. Coll, Most Rev. Martin J. O'Connor Corresp, Oct-Dec 1948*, Box 30, File 9.

252 New York November 13, 1948, Maguire "Memorandum for His Eminence", KC, *Enrico Galeazzi Papers, No. Amer. Coll, Most Rev. Martin J. O'Connor Corresp, Oct-Dec 1948*, Box 30, File 9.

that the operating costs of the College were the responsibility of the diocese with students enrolled, and should be pro-rated. The present difficulty, he reminded Spellman, was due to the fluctuating exchange rate and unpredictable variations in pricing in Rome. These were beyond the control of the Rector. Likewise, there was no consideration for deficits in the budget: "Operating deficit plus carrying charges plus capital outlay are not, in present planning chargeable to any fund."

Maguire offered two further suggestions: in accord with the resolution adopted at the June 24, 1948 meeting: obtain from the bishops, from the Board of directors of The Catholic University of America, and from Rome authority to allocate from The Catholic University annual collection funds to meet the annual overall deficit of the College; or, include in the estimated annual budget of the College contingency allowances to cover all possible expenditures, including fluctuations in exchange rates and price of commodities, debt servicing, and depreciation charges. He suggested that capital expenditures might be charged to a depreciation fund. "This plan, I fear, would run the per student costs into prohibitive figures". In any event, all this had to be discussed at the upcoming bishops' meeting.

On November 17th, a special meeting of the College Board was held. The four Cardinals were present: Dougherty, Mooney, Spellman and Stritch, along with Archbishops Bergan, Cushing, Keough, Mitty, and Ritter. O'Connor reported that the first question was whether to proceed with the seminary project since the available funds were unequal to the construction costs. The decision was to wait and see if favorable rates on blocked lire might be obtained in Italy. Cardinal Spellman, O'Connor told his friend the Count:

> again expressed himself in favor of a reduction in the size of the seminary and the possible sale of the Via dell'Umiltà property, but the Board was not in favor of these suggestions nor did it put them to a vote.[253]

---

[253] Scranton November 18, 1948, O'Connor to Galeazzi, KC, *Enrico Galeazzi Papers, No. Amer. Coll, Most Rev. Martin J. O'Connor Corresp, Oct-Dec 1948*, Box 30, File 9.

More favorable evidence was given that profitable transactions might be realized regarding the blocked lire, which would cover any cost increases, as O'Connor had insisted upon repeatedly:

> In general, the atmosphere seemed favorable to proceeding with the whole plan regarding the construction and furnishing of the new seminary, including the retention of the house of studies on the Umiltà. The general opinion seemed to be that the Board and the Hierarchy were committed to the entire program.

And, O'Connor continued, a vote was taken, and the Rector was authorized to invite bids for the construction and furnishing of the new seminary, "with the right to reject all bids, the bidders themselves to have bonds or the legal equivalent." Also, a vote was taken concerning the bidding: if some of the bids on various items, including fees and contingencies, were within the purchasing power of $3,000,000 [$28,641,286.31], then the Treasurer, Cardinal Spellman, would be authorized to sign the contract. O'Connor recalled:

> It was expected that by securing a sufficient quantity of blocked lire, the purchasing power of $3,000,000 would be adequate to cover the increases in cost indicated in the latest estimate for the new seminary, especially if the contributions of the alumni were added.

The Rector was also authorized to return to the United States if a special meeting were necessary.

O'Connor wrote Galeazzi that he would return to New York to meet with Maguire to begin work on the blocked lire negotiations. He told the Count that the Board had decided to authorize Cardinals Spellman and Stritch to conduct the investigation about blocked lire in the United States, while O'Connor and his Roman team dealt with the Roman government. "The atmosphere seemed to indicate that everything was dependent upon the utilization of such funds to absorb the increase in cost and our deficits and no alternative was seriously considered", apparently including the Catholic University Collection. The Rector concluded:

> The atmosphere of both meetings was very encouraging and for the first time in two years I feel as if our entire program would be secure. I tried to effect a practical working plan for an American office but there seemed to be no enthusiasm for it on the part of the Board, although I deem it absolutely necessary for the future, especially for the security of the House of Studies.

Because $3 million[254] was the only sum that might be raised realistically during the next ten years for the new construction, Spellman reported to Galeazzi,

> I had suggested that the only way that we can face the budget proposed by the Rector would be to use blocked lire. The other alternative would be to reduce the capacity of the college to two hundred and fifty or two hundred beds. We were loathe to take this step and concentrated on getting a higher value for the American dollar than the legal exchange. It seems as if now we can obtain something between 25% and 30% more for the dollar by using blocked lire, and since this seems to be the case and as I am entering

[254] New York November 22, 1948, Circular letter, Spellman to "Your Eminence", KC, *Enrico Galeazzi Papers, No. Amer. Coll Corresp, Martin J. O'Connor, 1948*-1949; Richard Burns-1952, Box 97, File 4: Spellman reported to the Cardinals on the Executive Committee of the Episcopal Board that only $3,059,620 had been pledged to date by American archdioceses and dioceses for the new College construction; $851,834.76 of which had been paid. For the restoration of the Umiltà, a total of $605,632.86 had been received. Many dioceses had not yet made any payment of their 1938 quota, while others made only partial payments for the Umiltà project.

into direct negotiations tomorrow I feel that we may safely proceed.[255]

On December 2nd, Maguire met with bankers, lawyers and representatives of the motion picture industry in the New York offices of the Motion Pictures Association of America: Thomas Connellan, Vice President of the National City Bank, James Bohen, Assistant Vice President of the same bank, John McCarthy, Director of the International Division of the Motion Picture Association, Theodore Smith of the same Association, and John Glynn, Director of the Foreign Department of Warner Brothers.[256]

Following Maguire's introductory presentation concerning the projected costs for the new seminary, Warner Brothers took the lead. They offered an exchange rate of 830 Italian lire per dollar, which was 43% higher than the official rate of 575 lire, and 25% higher than the "free lire rate of 650." No one company could supply the entire $3,000,000 needed to cover the construction costs. But, by pooling resources of various companies, they could raise collectively a total of 2.4 billion blocked lire at a rate of 830 Lire per dollar, which would cover the estimated construction cost.

At one point, a representative of the Motion Picture Association asked if the College would take title to the entire 2 billion Lire holdings at once, but that was thought too risky.[257] Once an agreement had been reached, the College would "draw down Lire over a two or two and a half year period on a monthly basis, paying dollars at the time of each withdrawal through the National City Bank." McCarthy and Smith would present the matter to a committee representing the film industry and report the following week, and, if the report proved

---

[255] New York November 20, 1948, Spellman to Galeazzi, NY, Box S/C-73, Folder 13: *To Card. Spellman, N. Amer. Coll.*

[256] New York December 2, 1948, Maguire: "Memorandum to His Eminence", KC, *Enrico Galeazzi Papers, N. Amer. Coll, Financial management, 1946-49 & undated*, Box 13, File 7. This can also be found in NYC, Box S/C-73, Folder 13: *To Card. Spellman, N. Amer. Coll.*

[257] New York December 15, 1948, Thomas J. Connellan to Spellman, KC, *Enrico Galeazzi Papers, No. Amer. Coll, Financial Management, 1946-1948 & Undated*, Box 13, File 7.

satisfactory, immediate action would be taken to obtain a license from the Italian government.

John Glynn of Warner Brothers surprised the meeting when he informed the group that a verbal agreement had already been arrived at between Warner Brothers and Cardinal Stritch for $175,000 [$1,670,741.70] at an exchange rate of 830 lire, "on condition that the transfer be made within 60 or 90 days." Maguire, knowing nothing of this, responded, "I expressed the thought that this possibly was contingent upon our getting a commitment on the over all requirements as it would be impossible to proceed with our plans without the definite assurance of the availability of sufficient Lire for the entire project."

Spellman wrote Stritch, reporting the results of the meeting with bankers and representatives of the film industry. "It was indicated that while no individual firm would be in a position to meet our total requirements the pooled resources of the whole industry would be sufficient."[258] He continued that during the meeting:

> some confusion was caused by the fact that Monsignor Fitzgerald of your office was negotiating with individual firms in this same field. This has prejudiced our case as it has given rise to the impression that we are reduced to the bargaining stage and also that our organization lacks coherence and unity. Needless to say, it embarrasses me to be unable to explain why Monsignor Fitzgerald, without my knowledge, was present in New York on a mission which is in my proper sphere as Treasurer of the American College.

Spellman sent copies of Maguire's memorandum along with Connellan's letter to each member of the Episcopal Board, asking their opinions and their approval to move forward in seeking the Italian government's license. Once they established the rate of

---

[258] New York December 11, 1948, Spellman to Stritch, KC, *Enrico Galeazzi Papers, No. Amer. Coll, financial management 1946-1948 & Undated*, Box 13, File 7.

exchange for the blocked lire, they could ask for construction bids for the College. Spellman, still pushing to downsize the seminary, added, "If the bids are beyond the potentialities of $3,000,000 then it seems to me that we should meet and decide on new plans to build as large and as good an institution as we can get with the money available."[259] Spellman ended by referring to the last paragraph in Connellan's letter:

> Of course, there are many holders of Blocked Lire in the Country but presently we do not know of any sizable concentration and, considering the length of the contract as well as changes, both political and economic, which may take place at that time, it is our view that if a satisfactory price base can be agreed upon, it is highly desirable to deal with one group rather than many.[260]

Responses from the Episcopal Board members arrived in New York. Spellman answered each one, and again repeated his insistence that a smaller building might be the answer on the Janiculum if they could not secure sufficient funds, despite the earlier and repeated decisions of the Board to retain the original larger plans.[261]

As the January 4th meeting drew near, O'Connor did what he always did prior to big meetings concerning the College: he wrote and cabled repeatedly, asking the members of his Roman team to pray and to offer Masses for success of the College plan. This time, he added his good humor to the request:

---

[259] New York December 20, 1948, Spellman to NAC Trustees, KC, *Enrico Galeazzi Papers, No. Amer. Coll, Financial Management 1946-1948 & Undated*, Box 13, File 7.

[260] New York December 15, 1948, Thomas J. Connellan to Spellman, KC, *Enrico Galeazzi Papers, No. Amer Coll, Financial Management 1946-1948 & Undated*, Box 13, File 7.

[261] New York December 31, 1948, Spellman to Stritch, NYC, Box S/C-73, Folder 13: *To Card. Spellman, N. Amer. Coll.*

Despite my good intentions, there has not been much opportunity for a rest. I have had a complete physical examination, which gives me a clean bill of health. Nevertheless, the spot below Archbishop Kennedy in the Campo Santo [the College mausoleum] is inviting, and the possibility that I will be there must not be excluded, as Monsignor McKeough would say.[262]

The meeting was held at Spellman's residence on January 4th, with Cardinals Mooney, Spellman and Stritch,[263] Archbishops Cushing, Keough, Ritter, and Bishop O'Connor present, along with Monsignors Fitzgerald and Maguire, and Messrs. James Bohen and Thomas Connellan of the National City Bank.

Spellman opened with his caveat that the new College construction must be restricted to the purchasing power of $3 million. He reported that O'Connor had initiated negotiations with the Italian Minister of Foreign Commerce who:

> will entertain the petition of the College Board to release Blocked Italian Lire for construction of the College in extra-territorial Rome on the basis of a sale of such Lire at the official rate of 575 to the dollar and a donation of the differential between the official rate and the negotiated rate.[264]

[262] Scranton January 1, 1949, O'Connor to Burns, CUA, *O'Connor Papers*, Box 36: *MJ O'Connor Rel. Org/Priests Corr,* Folder: *Burns, Msgr. Richard K (1947-54)*. Cable January 1, 1949, O'Connor to Burns, CUA, *O'Connor Papers*, in above ref: "Special Board Meeting January 4. Asking prayers faculty students. Happy New Year All. Bishop O'Connor"

[263] Scranton January 7, 1949, O'Connor to Burns, CUA, *O'Connor Papers*, Box 36: *MJ O'Connor Rel. Org/Priests Corr,* Folder: *Burns, Msgr. Richard K (1947-54)*: Dougherty was unable to attend the meeting because he had already left on January 1st for Florida.

[264] New York January 4, 1949, "Minutes of a Special Meeting of the Board of the American College of the Roman Catholic Church of the United States, held at the Residence of His Eminence, Francis Cardinal Spellman", NYC, Box S/C-73, Folder 14: *To Card. Spellman, N. Amer. Coll.*

He continued, "There are elements of risk that must be considered", and he listed four: The attitude of the Italian government, "now most friendly, might change. With a hostile ministry it could be difficult to complete our transaction if it were to be made on an installment basis with new permissions required for each transfer of funds"; The future of the Motion Picture Industry in Italy "is not too secure. Only recently the question of withdrawing from the country [Italy] was discussed. It was decided to retain the *status quo* but further restrictions might force the reconsideration of this decision." Any negotiations must, therefore, be exclusively "for the sale of Lire actually on hand". The danger of inflation was real, and so, to protect the Church, Spellman suggested that "we should determine the rate on a percentage basis, X percentage over the official rate at the time dollars are paid over." If there were uncontrolled inflation, the Church would still be unprotected; The danger of deflation, "If the official rate for Lire were lowered a correction of costs and prices would lag behind, and this would be temporarily disadvantageous to us." Despite these risks, Spellman ended his report, "However, it seems that that is a risk we must assume."

He then reported that Cardinal Stritch had obtained from Warner Brothers a commitment for 150,000 lire at an exchange rate of 830 lire per dollar, but that it was valid only until February 1, 1949, contingent upon the granting of a license from the Italian government. Likewise, Stritch was negotiating with 20th Century Fox for the sale of 1,500,000 lire at a rate of 805 lire per dollar, as compared with the official exchange of 575 lire per dollar, to be paid in installments over an 18 month period. However, it was unsure whether 20th Century Fox actually had that much lire on hand. A third "preliminary and unofficial offer" had been made by the Motion Picture Association of America:

> This group controls 1,500,000,000 Lire in blocked accounts and is willing to sell these at 835 Lire for the dollar, payment to be made in dollars on the transfer of Lire or possibly an arrangement could be made to finance part of the transaction on notes maturing within one year.

The Board accepted the Warner Brothers proposal, because the other two were too risky. Archbishop Ritter motioned that this be accepted, and Spellman seconded the motion, that Stritch be authorized to sign the contract with Warner Brothers, and that Mr. Connellan review the wording of the contract and submit his comments.

Finally, a motion was made by Ritter, seconded by Keough and carried unanimously, "that Cardinals Stritch and Spellman be empowered and authorized by the Board to continue negotiations for blocked lire and to execute on behalf of the Corporation a contract or contracts that in their judgment are to the best advantage to the American College." They were also instructed to inform the Italian Ambassador to the United States of the accepted offers and ask him to expedite the license from the Italian government for use of the blocked lire.

O'Connor hoped the negotiations would be favorable and result in a contract, which he could bring back to Rome at the end of the month, so he could approach the Italian ministry once more to secure the required license for the blocked lire deal. If all worked well, he could bring the government's license and the construction bids for the new seminary back to the States in March for another special Board meeting. The Rector asked Burns that Masses be offered in thanksgiving for the successful meeting, and for the future success of the blocked lire negotiations for the College.[265] He reported everything to Galeazzi, ending his letter: "My trip to America has been successful in many ways, and I see that progress cannot be achieved without regular contact."[266]

---

[265] Scranton January 7, 1949, O'Connor to Burns, CUA, *O'Connor Papers*, Box 36: *MJ O'Connor Rel. Org/Priests Corr, Folder: Burns, Msgr. Richard K (1947-54)*: "I received your cable of thanks and I am grateful for the prayers. I wish that you or Father Lacy would give a check for $100 for 100 Masses in honor of the Holy Spirit to Monsignor Angelini who gave the conference to our domestic help last year. You can reach him through the Catholic Action Office. The intention of these Masses is for the Faculty and students of the College, and the American Hierarchy, particularly the Board of Trustees."

[266] Scranton January 7, 1949, O'Connor to Galeazzi, KC, *Enrico Galeazzi Papers, No. Amer. Coll, Corresp, Most Rev. Martin J. O'Connor, 1949*, Box

Spellman and his team, and O'Connor and his team, continued their work. Spellman met with the Italian Ambassador to the United States, Alberto Tarchiani, and obtained his assurances that Italy "would do everything possible to favor us with the issuance of a license."[267] He also received new proposals from 20th Century Fox and the Association of Motion Picture Producers. He immediately wrote O'Connor, instructing him to come to New York to meet with Maguire, and then to go to Washington, D.C. to meet with the Ambassador to explain the details of the blocked lire transaction.[268] The Rector wrote Burns that he would leave for Washington, D.C. on January 13th, and that:

> it seems that the Italian Ambassador is well impressed by our proposal and that we have very favorable offers from the firms concerned. In other words, we will have a third miracle on this side of the ocean, after which I will have to return and present it to the Minister of Finance.[269]

As the New Year began, reports about the Janiculum excavations were good, but those about the Umiltà, disappointing. With strikes and work stoppages, the return of the students into the City was again postponed. Promises by the contractors were repeated that the students would soon be able to settle into the Umiltà. "But, I'd take no bets on it," Lacy reported:

30, File 10.

[267] New York January 11, 1949, Spellman to Stritch, NYC, Box S/C-73, Folder 14: *To Card. Spellman, N. Amer. Coll.*

[268] New York January 11, 1949, Spellman to O'Connor, NYC, Box S/C-73, Folder 14: *To Card. Spellman, N. Amer. Coll.*

[269] Scranton January 12, 1949, O'Connor to Burns, CUA, *O'Connor Papers*, Box 36: *MJ O'Connor Rel. Org/Priests Corr*, Folder: *Burns, Msgr. Richard K. (1947-54)*. O'Connor wrote Burns a second letter on January 12th: "I will probably not be in Rome for the Purification and presentation of the candle to PPXII: please take care of the function as you see fit." Same CUA reference.

However, it certainly is going to be a beautiful building and perhaps worth the delay. The hole on the Janiculum [foundation excavations] is vast and deep but the Count seems satisfied and I have heard that the soundings made to date give every indication that our house will not be built on sand.[270]

---

[270] Rome January 14, 1949, Lacy to O'Connor, CUA, *O'Connor Papers*, Box 25: *MJ O'Connor Misc & Unfiled Corr*, Folder 11.

*Arnaldo Mengarini, Contractor; Bishop Martin J. O'Connor (center),
and Count Enrico Galeazzi, Architect, inspect a plastic model
of the new seminary.*

(courtesy Pontifical North American College Archives)

Above, Demolition of old buildings on the Janiculum property, with the dome of St. Peter's in the distance, and the Urban College at above right. Below, Excavation work as of December 14, 1948.

Excavation work on the new College construction site,
as of December 14, 1948.

15 - STATO DEI LAVORI AL 14 DICEMBRE 1948: LO SCAVO PER IL II°SCANTINATO PROCEDE NEL BRAC
CIO VERSO LA PINETA -

Excavation work as of December 14, 1948.

Excavation work as of February 28, 1949.

Seminarians return to the Umiltà, 1949.

*January 1950: Avenue of Pines. View of the excavated property
for the new College, with Saint Peter's Dome at right.*

March 1950: excavations and retaining walls.

Excavations and construction of retaining walls.

August 1950: new College construction, looking north to St. Peter's.

August 1950: new College construction, looking northwest to St. Peter's.

August 1950: new College construction: to the right is the City
and the Bambino Gesu Hospital.

September 1950.

September 1950.

February 1951.

Refectory, January 1952.

February 1952.

Francis Cardinal Spellman and Count Galeazzi
at the new College construction site, June 1952.

At the center: Count Galeazzi, Cardinal Spellman, and Bishop O'Connor.

April 1953, from the sports field.

Pontifical North American College postcard:
central cortile and chapel exterior.

Pontifical North American College postcard central cortile and chapel exterior.

Upper Crypt.

Bishop O'Connor admires some of the new sculptures for the chapel.

Count Galeazzi in front of the new College, 1953.

Samuel Cardinal Stritch, Edward Cardinal Mooney,
and Francis Cardinal Spellman.

Chapter 5

Building a Seminary

"I beg you to believe in the optimism that I show you, and to face with perfect tranquility the problems before you. Your work is greatly appreciated, and has been given to your care by Divine Providence, because of your intelligence and rare ability and competence."
—Count Galeazzi to Bishop O'Connor, 1950

To counter Spellman's repeated insistence that the College building project was too large, Galeazzi began offering the Rector information about other large Italian construction projects that he might use to convince the Episcopal Board that the College construction project was not an isolated phenomenon. There were a number of substantial construction projects under way in Rome, "consequent to private initiatives and interests", and not due to the government:

> You know the railway station [Stazione Termini] which is surely the largest enterprise of the city, which is in full development, and it is hoped that for the end of the year it will be completed in all its essential parts . . . . Restoration work of the many buildings which have suffered from the war, especially in the outskirts of the city, has been largely completed.[271]

---

[271] Rome January 16, 1949, Galeazzi to O'Connor, KC, *Enrico Galeazzi Papers, No. Amer. Coll, Corresp Most Rev. Martin J. O'Connor, 1949*, Box 30, File 10.

The Vatican was also involved in a few projects of its own. Two groups of buildings, each with a housing capacity for more than 200 families, were recently begun near the Vatican. Two other sizeable buildings were nearing completion in preparation for the Holy Year, located at the beginning of the Via della Conciliazione, near Castel Sant'Angelo.

Galeazzi enclosed a clipping from the Milanese newspaper *L'Italia*, with photos of the various Roman projects, including the restoration work at the College Umiltà property, which his office had supplied the editors. He sent this information to O'Connor just in case he might find it useful in his conversations with donors and bishops that the Janiculum project should be viewed in light of the steady trend in Roman construction. "I hope that in this general frame the plan of the new College will appear quite feasible, and in agreement with the general progress of these activities." O'Connor used Galeazzi's information. He transcribed the clippings from *L'Italia* about the Umiltà construction, and copied photos of the Janiculum foundation excavations in his circular letters to the Episcopal Board to bolster his campaign to move forward with the unaltered plan for the Janiculum construction, in a city where other massive construction projects were successfully moving ahead.[272]

In order to shore up their position, and to demonstrate the progress to date, Galeazzi and O'Connor secured a private audience with the Pope for February 23rd. In preparation for the meeting, the Count and the Rector prepared a memorandum for the Holy Father. It outlined the decisions of the Episcopal Board meetings of November 15 and 17, 1948, and the special meeting of January 4, 1949, clearly stating that "The Rector was present at all these meetings." The memorandum then outlined the resolutions adopted by the Episcopal Board concerning bids, contracts and the negotiations with the Italian government and American film companies to purchase blocked lire. O'Connor continued that he had already met with Cesare Merzagora, Minister of Foreign Commerce, and with Alcide De Gasperi. He

---

[272] Rome February 18, 1949, O'Connor to Episcopal Board Members, KC, *Enrico Galeazzi Papers, No. Amer. Coll Corresp with Rector, Martin J. O'Connor, Financial Management, 1949-1952*, Box 13, File 8.

concluded his memorandum to the Pope with the news that the excavation work for the new seminary was practically concluded.[273]

O'Connor then returned to the United States for the upcoming March Episcopal Board meeting.[274] He delivered reports on his work and a package from Galeazzi to Spellman, and then was debriefed by Spellman and Maguire, especially concerning the Pope's reaction to the blocked lire negotiations with the De Gasperi government. O'Connor told them that the Holy Father hoped the negotiations could be concluded as soon as possible as another sign of Italian/Vatican cooperation with the United States, to continue the American political and financial support of the reconstruction of post-war Italy and the defeat of the Communist Party. To save time, instead of mailing the reports or sending O'Connor to Chicago to meet with the archbishop, Spellman phoned Stritch, to discuss O'Connor's news, and they approved the Rector's plans to move ahead.[275]

A meeting was held with representatives of the film companies, of bankers, of Spellman, and of the College in Maguire's New York office on March 2, 1949, and, according to the Rector, it seemed all

---

[273] Rome, February 22, 1949, "Memorandum for His Holiness", KC, *Enrico Galeazzi Papers, No. Amer. Coll, Financial Management, 1949-1952*, Box 13, File 8.

[274] New York March 1, 1949, O'Connor to Galeazzi, KC, *Enrico Galeazzi Papers, No. Amer. Coll. Corresp with Rector Martin J. O'Connor, Jan-March 1949*, Box 50, File 6: O'Connor described his long flight to the States, giving an idea how interminable and dangerous cross-Atlantic air travel was in 1949: "We went over the Alps to Zurich. From Paris we went to the Azores, and after arriving in New York we were unable to land except at Washington as the airport was closed yesterday because of inclement weather." He told the Count that, while in Paris, awaiting a flight to New York, the Rector took the train to Lisieux, and offered Mass at the Shrine of the Little Flower for the intentions of the College and the successful outcome of the negotiations.

[275] New York, March 1, 1949, O'Connor to Galeazzi, KC, above reference. Long distance was still very expensive in 1949. For Spellman to incur such an expense was a sign how important it was to conclude this matter quickly. This is the second letter the Rector wrote the Count on March 1st. He ends this letter: "My visits have been satisfactory, and again I am convinced that time and anxiety have been saved by personal contact. I'll continue to write you from time to time to keep you informed, but there is no need to answer all these letters as I know you are already heavily burdened."

would accept the proposed agreement. The next step was to secure the signatures of the legal representatives of the movie companies on a master application for presentation to the Italian Minister of Foreign Commerce in Rome. Likewise, Spellman and Stritch would both sign in the name of the Episcopal Board. O'Connor was given the assignment to bring the document to Chicago and return to New York with the completed application by the early part of the following week.

Since the Holy Father had urged that all be concluded as soon as possible, O'Connor decided to send the application to Burns via air mail. Once the document arrived at the College, Burns and Silvestri were to take it to the Minister of Foreign Commerce and secure the needed license, a process, all hoped, that would take no more than three weeks to conclude. The Rector ended by informing Galeazzi that, following the meeting, he visited Cardinal Dougherty, and returned to New York the same day. "He takes a deep interest in the progress we are making and enjoys listening to the accounts of the work."[276] On March 9th, Galeazzi reported that the unofficial approval by the Minister of Foreign Commerce "appears to be effectively confirmed. I am convinced it will conclude well."[277]

On March 11th, Galeazzi wrote O'Connor that he had a meeting the day before with two gentlemen, Mr. Zellerbach and Mr. Freudenthal, who were interested in Cardinal Spellman and the negotiations about blocked lire. Galeazzi informed them that things were moving along, and that the Italian government had given verbal authorization for the license, and were waiting for the document from America, signed by the movie companies and Cardinals. The gentlemen had seen an article in the March 10th number of Rome's *Daily American*,

---

[276] March 3, 1949, O'Connor to Galeazzi, KC, *Enrico Galeazzi Papers, No. Amer. Coll Corresp with Rector Martin J. O'Connor*, Box 50, File 6: Air mail, while more expensive than surface mail in 1949, would assure that the document would arrive in Rome much more quickly than if O'Connor personally carried it and returned by ship. While he could have returned by air, there was a limit to Spellman's willingness to spend money: air mailing the letter would be cheaper than air mailing O'Connor with it.

[277] Rome March 9, 1949, Galeazzi to O'Connor, KC, above ref: "Thank you for calling on my daughter in New York City."

and told Galeazzi that there were many deals in the planning stages for use of the blocked lire owned by Hollywood corporations, and it would be wise for Cardinal Spellman to make haste, "to avoid these funds being earmarked and used for other projects."[278]

O'Connor wrote Galeazzi the same day, telling the Count that an article from Hollywood appeared in the *New York Times* ["Italy May Release Frozen Film Funds; U.S. Film Men make Vatican Lire Deal"] on March 9th; another article appeared the next day ["Seminary in Rome closing Lire Deal"], from the offices of the Motion Picture Association of America; and one more article in the March 11th number of the *New York Times*, ["Italy May Abolish Taxes on U.S. Films"]. One of the articles mentioned a change of directors for the Ministry of Foreign Finance, but Silvestri told O'Connor such a change would have no effect on the negotiations, since the Ministry had given a verbal approval for the blocked lire license. The master application still had not been signed by the American principals, but Maguire expected it within days, and O'Connor told the Count he hoped Burns and Silvestri would have it by March 23rd.[279] Burns had been approached by reporters in Rome, seeking confirmation of the news stories, "the origin of which was in the States", but "I pleaded ignorance of the whole matter."[280]

Another article appeared in the March 16th number of *Variety*, which hinted at more far-reaching results of the deal:

> Fears that the Communist press would capitalize on the report last week of a frozen lire deal between the Vatican and the U.S. film industry led to the quick and bitter denials of the arrangement from Rome and New York. Church authorities were afraid the Communists would misuse the report to support

[278] Rome March 11, 1949, Galeazzi to O'Connor, KC, above ref.
[279] Scranton March 11, 1949, O'Connor to Galeazzi, KC, *Enrico Galeazzi Papers, No. Amer. Coll. Corrisp. With Rector Martin J. O'Connor*, Box 50, File 6.
[280] Rome March 14, 1949, Burns to O'Connor, CUA, *O'Connor Papers*, Box 36: *MJ O'Connor Rel. Org/Priests Corr*, Folder: *Burns, Msgr. Richard K (1947-54)*.

the type of charges recently made against Cardinal Mindszenty of Hungary and other religious leaders accused of black market operations.[281]

Variety continued that the uproar was caused by the erroneous reporting by the *New York Times* that the blocked lire deal was worth $3,000,000 and involved the Vatican. In reality, it was only $975,000, and did not involve the Vatican but the North American College. "Actually, this type of deal is not at all unusual", the *Variety* article continued. American film companies had very little "frozen coin" in Rome, because arrangements had been made with Jewish and Catholic charitable organizations since the end of the war, with the approval of the Italian Government.[282]

There now began to appear letters in which the Rector mentions his various health issues. Never a robust man, O'Connor had also been pushing himself in his work for the College, with extended travels, very long hours, improper diet, and exceptional stress. While maladies that today could be treated with little difficulty, in 1949 and the early 1950's, they posed serious threats. In a letter to Monsignor Burns about College matters, he urged the Vice Rector to be sure to write him at least weekly with reports about the seminary, the graduate house of studies, the construction projects, and in answer to his numerous written instructions. He continued, "Since March 5, the day I returned to Scranton, I have had neuritis in my left arm which has made me a bed patient at Marywood, but not in the

---

[281] One of the numerous false charges brought against Cardinal Mindszenty at his trial in February 1949 by the Communist government in Hungary was that of currency speculation on the black market and conspiring to steal the Crown of St. Stephen, turning it over to the Americans for safekeeping, all with an eye to undermining the government and re-establishing the Hapsburg monarchy.

[282] *Variety*, March 16, 1949: pp. 5 and 53: During the previous three years large deals also had been made between film companies and the Joint Distribution Committee, aiding "thousands of European refugees to get to Palestine", supplying them with food and clothing in the camps throughout Europe and to charter ships from Italian ports to bring them to Palestine.

hospital. The doctor says it will clear up in a few days."[283] But his illness did not stop him from continuing his work for the College. He continued dictating letters to Sister John Chrysostom, IHM his American secretary at Marywood College in Scranton, who must have been exhausted by the end of the construction project, since O'Connor maintained an immense correspondence throughout his years as Rector.

In a letter to Galeazzi, O'Connor reported on his health problems, and that there was no news about the signatures on the master application for blocked lire. He reported his illness, and then concluded:

> As soon as I have any worth-while information, I will get in touch with you promptly. If you have an opportunity to take up the question of the manner of signing contracts and by whom, I think it would be a good idea. If the Trustees are satisfied from the point of view of finances, I think we should have as little time as possible elapse before the actual construction begins.[284]

Galeazzi recognized the importance of this statement, and underlined all of this in red pencil.

Soon after, Burns shared great news with the Rector: the students finally moved from Castel Gandolfo into the Umiltà property on March 2nd,

> in the middle of one of the coldest weeks we have had this winter. In fact at the Villa on Monday the snow fell for about three hours and was still on the ground Tuesday morning. However, we were able to take

---

[283] Scranton March 9, 1949, O'Connor to Burns, CUA, *O'Connor Papers*, Box 36, *MJ O'Connor Rel. Org/Priests Corr*, Folder: *Burns, Msgr. Richard K (1947-54)*.

[284] Scranton March 9, 1949, O'Connor to Galeazzi, KC, *Enrico Galeazzi Papers, No. Amer. Coll. Corresp with Rector Martin J. O'Connor, Jan-March 1949*, Box 50, File 6.

care of the boys at dinner on Tuesday right on time, and from the very beginning all essential services have been maintained. So far we have not been able to use the down-stairs chapel, but the up-stairs chapel is finished, even to the baldacchino.[285]

Knowing O'Connor's interest to publicize the College to boost donations and student enrollment, Burns added:

We had the photographer here at the College the day we moved in and he was able to get several excellent pictures, copies of which have already been sent to Frank Flynn. Father Sullivan has also taken a couple of pictures which he will use in a story about the reopening of the College.

The construction work continued. On March 5th, Galeazzi sent an updated cost sheet for the Umiltà work. O'Connor wrote immediately after receiving it, that work had to commence immediately:

If the transaction concerning the blocked funds is satisfactory, as soon as you receive the news that the license has been granted and the funds transferred to our account I think you should be prepared to buy quantities of construction material, such as steel and stone, at once. My reason is that we will have accumulated too many lire and that these should be expended safely and yet rapidly. This is not quite the same idea as the stockpile, but rather like your own when you were able to purchase steel after authorization from me while I was in America. Stockpiling of other materials seems to be risky and subject to all kinds of hazards. However, I feel that

---

[285] Rome March 14, 1949, Burns to O'Connor, CUA, *O'Connor Papers*, Box 36, *MJ O'Connor Rel. Org/Priests Corr*, Folder: *Burns, Msgr. Richard K (1947-54)*.

you could place these orders if you were authorized to do so. All this depends, however, on the preparation and the signing of the contracts, and the complete agreement of the Board.[286]

O'Connor used high-tech office methods of the day by sending a photostatic copy of Galeazzi's updated cost sheet to the Board members on the Ides of March.[287] In his report, the Rector pointed out that there were unexpected cost overruns: the original estimated cost for renovations at the Umiltà totaled $550,000 [$5,317,090.34], including the architect's fees. The final figure would be $564,700 [$5,459,201.66], at the present 600 lire per $1 exchange rate, which did not include the architect's 5% fee, although the legal expenses had been paid. He continued:

The principal causes of the increase in cost over the original estimate were the condition of the Palazzo Tomba [at the Umiltà property], labor strikes, no electrical power two days each week, and, as stated in a previous report, an influenza epidemic.

In this report, particular attention is called to the necessity of renovating the means of water supply from the Trevi Fountain. The probable cost of which will be about 1,000,000 Lire.[288]

---

[286] Scranton March 14, 1949, O'Connor to Galeazzi, KC, *Enrico Galeazzi Papers, No. Amer. Coll. Corresp with Rector Martin J. O'Connor, Jan-March 1949*, Box 50, File 6.

[287] Scranton March 15, 1949, O'Connor to Galeazzi, KC, *Enrico Galeazzi Papers, No. Amer. Coll, Corresp with Rector Martin J. O'Connor, Jan-March 1949*, Box 50, File 6: The next day was also his 25th anniversary of priestly ordination, "However, as no one knows about it here, we will pass it over quietly."

[288] Scranton March 15, 1949, O'Connor to Board of Trustees, KC, *Enrico Galeazzi Papers, No. Amer. Coll, Corresp with Rector Martin J. O'Connor, Jan-Mar 1949*, Box 50, File 9.

As work progressed, there were more unforeseen costs.

Maguire's letter and the signed American document authorizing the lire deal arrived in Rome on March 18th. Burns brought it to Silvestri that afternoon, and it was in the hands of the Italian Ministry the next day. Burns cabled O'Connor in the morning, and wrote him a few hours later, "Please accept my most sincere congratulations on the successful outcome of your negotiations: what you have accomplished on this trip should bring us a great step closer to the realization of the new College on the Janiculum."[289]

Burns' letter was delayed in the mails, and O'Connor responded on March 25th:

> Little by little, the pieces of our program seem to fit into place. I can only attribute it to prayers. Please take another $100 from the emergency fund and have 5 Masses in all said by Monsignor Fitzgerald, Father Lacy, and yourself in honor of St. Therese in thanksgiving for the accomplishment of this mission. If you are not too heavily burdened with intentions, I would be grateful if these Masses could be said soon.[290]

In another letter to Burns, O'Connor wrote that he had shown Burns' cable to Spellman and Maguire, and all were delighted the license would be granted soon. O'Connor told his Vice Rector that Spellman was writing the Board members "so he can notify me that I will have the authority to sign the contracts instead of the

---

[289] Rome March 18, 1949, Burns to O'Connor, CUA, *O'Connor Papers*, Box 36: *MJ O'Connor Rel. Org/Priests Corr*, Folder: *Burns, Msgr. Richard K (1947-54)*. New York March 22, 1949, O'Connor to Burns, CUA, *O'Connor Papers*, Box 36, above ref: O'Connor was on the road on College business, having gone to Washington, D.C., then to Detroit, where he received Burns' cable, then on to Chicago.

[290] Scranton March 25, 1949, O'Connor to Burns, CUA, *O'Connor Papers*, Box 36, above ref.

Treasurer [Spellman] as it was originally decided by the Board."[291] The construction bids for the Janiculum work were to be catalogued, examined and summarized for Spellman by the New York archdiocesan lawyer and architect, "in order to give the assurance that the total amount of the bids is within the purchasing power of $3,000,000."

Burns and Silvestri "had a brief but profitable visit with the Minister" on the morning of March 23rd. He approved the blocked lire contract and promised to sign the license within a few days.[292] In a second handwritten letter the same day, Burns broke the news to the Rector that "Carl Castiglione, a student from Detroit Archdiocese, has had a very light attack of scarlet fever." The student was immediately isolated, a male nurse hired, and the doctor reported him recovering:

> There is no reason to be disturbed; and you may be
> sure that no one in Rome knows the story except us.
> I hope, I hope, I hope. We have told no one including
> the *personale* and the students, although all knew
> from the precautions that Castiglione has had some
> contagious disease.[293]

The license for the blocked lire was finally granted to the College on March 28th, and Burns cabled the good news to the Rector. But it was a limited license, and the amount of lire released would not pay for the entire construction project on the Janiculum. The Rector

---

[291] New York March 22, 1949, O'Connor to Burns, CUA, *O'Connor Papers*, Box 36, above ref: "A number of Bishops is expected in Rome after Easter: I'm sure you, Lacy and Fitzgerald will look after them."

[292] Rome March 23, 1949 Burns to O'Connor, CUA, *O'Connor Papers*, Box 36, above ref: Burns gave a report on the continuing work at the Umiltà property. They were beginning work on the "Red Room", the formal reception room. "We are fortunate in that we can use about a dozen chairs and two couches that were formerly in this room. The workmen are gradually finishing up in that part of the College which we occupy, and by the time you return we should be pretty much in sole possession of our part of the College."

[293] Rome March 23, 1949, Burns to O'Connor, CUA, *O'Connor Papers*, Box 36, above ref.

wrote Galeazzi that Maguire was kind enough to telephone him the good news after Burns notified Spellman. In order not to lose time by waiting for O'Connor to sail back to Rome, he wrote Galeazzi:

> I think it would be worthwhile, if the bids are in by the end of this month, for you to invite Msgr. Burns, in my absence, to be present at the opening and cataloging of these bids so that you and your staff could have the whole matter summarized to await my return.[294]

Spellman thanked Burns for the news of the license, wrongly taking full credit for the accomplishment: "For me it is the end of a long battle of many years since I first proposed the use of blocked lire for our college and all of us together should and will offer a fervent prayer of thanksgiving."[295] He later noted that, while the license would not solve all the College's immediate financial woes, it left open the possibility for future licenses from the Italian government.[296]

Since the Italian government had given only a limited license authorizing the sale of an amount of lire much smaller than needed to cover construction costs for the new seminary, Spellman's plan to reduce the size of the seminary and sell the Umiltà still had a chance, or at least so he thought. O'Connor and Galeazzi knew they should tread warily, especially with the presentation of bids for the construction work. It was decided that only "partial information" about the bids be given to Spellman, hoping that he would rely on Galeazzi's judgment in the end, which, of course, was O'Connor's

---

[294] Scranton March 28, 1949, O'Connor to Galeazzi, KC, *Enrico Galeazzi Papers, No. Amer. Coll. Corresp. Most Rev. Martin J. O'Connor, 1949*, Box 30, File 10.

[295] New York March 28, 1949, Spellman to Burns, NYC, Box S/C-73, Folder 14: *To Card. Spellman, N. Amer. Coll.*

[296] New York, n.d., draft Memorandum to Board Members, NYC, Box S/C-73, above ref: In red pencil is the note: "sent to all members of the board." Spellman also requested the Board to approve that O'Connor would sign all construction contracts.

judgment.[297] Galeazzi answered his friend the same day: "Agreeing fully your opinion about delaying partial information bids to treasurer. Good Journey."[298]

Unwittingly, the New York archdiocesan architect supported the plan of O'Connor and Galeazzi, by acknowledging that he was ignorant of Rome, of the costs of building materials and labor, or even the price of basic commodities. Therefore, while the bids and projected costs were being sent to him for analysis, he had little to say. "I do not believe," he wrote in a memorandum to Monsignor Maguire on the same day that O'Connor and Galeazzi were exchanging cables, "that the Bishop [O'Connor] will want us to appraise the reasonableness of bids on costs, so that quantity, surveys, unit prices and other phases of the cost would serve little purpose. I have no way of determining costs in Rome."[299] *Per forza*, the decisions concerning the construction project in Rome would have to be made by those on the ground in Rome: O'Connor and Galeazzi.

By early June, O'Connor sent a summary of bids to Spellman and to the Episcopal Board members, explaining that the Italian method for bidding on construction work was different than in the United States. O'Connor, Galeazzi, and Silvestri recommended the acceptance of three bids: Ravello and Mengarini of Rome, submitted a bid for 440,036,780 lire for general construction; Dell'Orto and Chierigatti of Rome and Milan, submitted a bid 26,735,660 lire for heating; DeGirolami of Rome submitted a bid of approximately 50,000,000 lire for "general items". O'Connor did not include estimates for the electrical work, because Galeazzi and Silvestri advised against recommending anyone at that time, because of the great disparities among those companies bidding, and the great

---

[297] Cable Vatican March 31, 1949, Galeazzi to O'Connor, KC, *Enrico Galeazzi Papers, No. Amer. Coll, Most Rev. Martin J. O'Connor Corresp, 1949*, Box 30, File 10.

[298] Cable Vatican March 31, 1949, Galeazzi to O'Connor, KC, *Enrico Galeazzi Papers*, above ref.

[299] New York March 31, 1949, Thomas A. Kelly to Maguire, KC, *Enrico Galeazzi Papers*, above ref.

possibility of large price drops in material within six months. The explanation of the Italian methods for bidding followed:

> The amounts indicated above do not represent the cost of each individual contract but comprise the results of the various bids after an examination of the principal items involved in the contract, such as steel, cement, labor, etc. Fifty items were catalogued. This is the business practice here to enable the owner to select the most preferable bidder, which does not mean that the total cost of the contract will not exceed the figure indicated. As a matter of fact, the actual heavy construction may be 800,000,000 lire. However, the estimate of the total cost remains as outlined by the architect.[300]

In other words, all this was an educated guess, at best. In the end, Galeazzi stood by his estimated costs from October 1948: The new seminary construction would cost $3,230,000, plus fees amounting to $323,000 or 10 % of the total cost as contingencies, and for safety's sake, an additional $100,000 for the "unforeseen" costs, which the Rector explained "is purposefully high but is included to guard against a possible spiral of labor costs in the next two years as well as a provision for contingencies." In short, this post-war construction project would be a game of Russian Roulette, played by the Americans and the Italian construction industry, with headaches.[301]

---

[300] Rome June 4, 1949, O'Connor to Spellman, KC, *Enrico Galeazzi Papers, No. Amer. Coll, Financial Management 1949-52*, Box 13, File 8: Based on an exchange rate of 600 lire per $1 [$9.67 in 2012 dollars].

[301] The Knights of Columbus Archives, housing the Enrico Galeazzi Papers, contain innumerable hand written pages of figures, cost sheets, balance sheets, comparative studies for commodities and services, and reports to O'Connor, Silvestri, Spellman and Maguire, and the College Episcopal Board members.

He then gave the figures for the financial resources along with costs for construction of the new seminary and for the restoration of the Umiltà and Villa Santa Caterina properties:

Financial Resources as of May 25, 1949:[302]

1938-1946	Diocesan quotas received:	approx. $ 598,000. [$ 5,781,127.31]
1947	Pledges:	$3,059,000.[$29,572,689.71]
1948	Alumni Chapel Fund:	$ 200,000.[$ 1,933,487.39]
1949	Blocked Lire Funds Benefit:	$ 332,000.[$ 3,209,589.08]
	Total:	$4,189,000.[$40,496,487.08]

New Seminary:

Construction, Fees, Furnishings, Extras:	$3,553,000. [$34,348,403.57]

Via dell'Umiltà:

Construction, Fees, Furnishings, Extras:	$ 657,861. [$ 6,359,829.76]

Villa Santa Caterina:

Construction:	$ 151,281.[$ 1,462,499.53]
Total Costs:	$4,362,142.[$42,170,732.86]

O'Connor ended his report with the news that there would probably be an operating deficit for the College for the 1949-1950 academic year of between $17,000 [$164,346.43] and $20,000 [$193,348.74]; but that seemed unimportant compared to the other figures.

Spellman and Maguire responded on July 7th, but less vehemently than might have been anticipated. Their primary questions, which were expected, concerned the lack of firm construction bids and the seemingly large line item listed as "unforeseen" in O'Connor's report.

---

[302] Rome June 4, 1949, O'Connor to Spellman, KC, *Enrico Galeazzi Papers, No. Amer. Coll, Financial Management 1949-52*, Box 13, File 8: Based on an exchange rate of 600 lire per $1 U.S. dollar.

The Rector responded with Galeazzi's words that "the total cost of building and furnishing should not exceed the figure" of $3,230,000 [$31,225,821.43] and includes the item listed as "unforeseen" of 10% of the total cost, as a margin of safety.[303] He also insisted that the 10% "is not indispensable", serving only as a financial cushion to any possible increases in labor and materials during the subsequent two years. Since "to-day the general trend is downward", O'Connor insisted that the 10% should not be considered a real cost, and more than balanced the foreseen 1949-1950, operating deficit of $173,142 [$1,673,839.37] of the College. The Rector ended his response in his usual optimistic fashion, stating, "while we cannot now know accurately possible future increased costs, we can consider the probability of increases in revenue", especially the "benefits from blocked lire, which could be repeated in the future."

During the July 25, 1949 meeting, the College Board[304] reviewed O'Connor's report and Spellman's comments, and concluded "It appears that it is impossible to obtain firm bids and that, therefore, it is necessary to rely on the estimates as made by the architects."[305] Since the cost was computed on an exchange rate of 600 lire to the dollar:

> The Lire cost is therefore 2,131,800,000 Lire. We have already purchased 975 million Lire, so the Lire balance required is 1,156,000,000, or $1,926,666. On the assumption that all pledges for the New College will be paid and that $200,000 will be raised by the Alumni, we shall have raised $3,259,000. We have paid for Blocked Lire $1,167,500, so we

---

[303] Rome July 16, 1949, O'Connor to Maguire, KC, *Enrico Galeazzi, No. Amer. Coll, Financial Management, 1949-1952*, Box 13, File 8.

[304] The Board members present were Cardinals Mooney, Spellman and Stritch, Archbishops Cushing, Keough and Ritter, with Monsignor Maguire serving as acting secretary.

[305] "Minutes of Special Meeting of Board of Trustees of the American College of the Roman Catholic Church of the United States, Held in New York City, July 25, 1949", KC, *Enrico Galeazzi Papers, No. Amer. Coll, Financial Management, 1949-1952*, Box 13, File 8.

have a balance of $2,091,500, or $174,834 more than required. With this margin, and taking into consideration the safety features incorporated in the estimated cost of the new College, it was decided to proceed.

The bishops approved O'Connor's plans. Ritter moved and Mooney seconded the motion, and it passed unanimously that the Board,

> confirms the exercise of the power granted to the Treasurer [Spellman] to give the Rector word to proceed with construction and to delegate to the Rector authority to sign the contracts, contingent, however upon examination by their Eminences Cardinal Mooney and Cardinal Stritch concerning exchange [of lire] arrangement and their decision that these arrangements are in accord with the understanding of the Board.

In one motion, Spellman's control of the construction project ended, and was placed in the hands of Cardinals Mooney and Stritch. The question of the College's operating deficits was seen "as incidental to the reopening of the College, and that as the student body increases they will diminish and perhaps disappear. No action was taken." In other words, so far as the Episcopal Board was concerned, O'Connor could build his College, as originally planned, and was free from Spellman—with Mooney and Stritch now taking the lead, and they were O'Connor's supporters. "Everything seems to be satisfactory. Step by step!" the Rector wrote Galeazzi."[306]

Mooney and Stritch traveled to Rome to visit the worksites and to speak with Galeazzi and Silvestri about their numbers. They cabled Spellman the results of the meeting, countering some of

---

[306] Rome August 15, 1949, O'Connor to Galeazzi, KC, *Enrico Galeazzi Papers, No. Amer. Coll, Most Rev. Martin J. O'Connor Corresp 1949*, Box 30, File 10.

his objections and his continued insistence to reduce the size of the new College: "Calculations cited in minutes meeting July 25 not borne out by our examination STOP. Study reveals correctness figures given in Rector's letter June 4 and conclusions noted in Maguire letter July 7 STOP." They continued that by reducing the reserve 10%, and by deferring the complete finishing of sections of the chapel and auditorium, while still providing a usable building, "Galeazzi strongly advises proceeding with building and we are in accord STOP. All things considered we advise authorizing rector to proceed STOP. Please cable your agreement or disagreement."[307]

O'Connor related to Galeazzi that "Cardinal Stritch just told me he had a reply from Cardinal Spellman: 'Agree with Your Eminences.'" He invited the Count to join O'Connor for lunch later in the week at the Villa Santa Caterina with Cardinals Stritch and Mooney, "in order to get things going."[308]

With the support of Cardinals Mooney and Stritch, O'Connor, Galeazzi, Burns, and Silvestri now swung into full action to complete the work at Castel Gandolfo and the Umiltà, in order to turn their full attention and the full resources of the bishops to the Janiculum project. This is reflected in a slew of detailed memoranda by O'Connor to Galeazzi,[309] revealing the scope of the practical work

---

[307] Cable August 18, 1949, Mooney & Stritch to Spellman, CUA, *O'Connor Papers*, Box 44 NAC, Folder: *Report to Board (1949)*.

[308] Rome August 20, 1949, O'Connor to Galeazzi, KC, *Enrico Galeazzi Papers*, above ref.

[309] Rome September 14, 1949, O'Connor to Galeazzi, KC, *Enrico Galeazzi Papers, No. Amer. Coll, Notices, Reports of work, 1949-1952*, Box 13, File 10: There are three memoranda outlining work: The memo about the Via dell'Umiltà contains 25 points, including preparation of ceremony for Cardinal Pizzardo to take possession of the College as its cardinal protector; new lighting for the refectory and chapel; design for the College coat of arms; restoration of the marble statue of St. Cecilia and the moving of the statue of the Blessed Mother from the Casa San Giovanni [both in today's Casa Santa Maria]; tree removal and a light for the Cortiletto; door stops; small trucks for supplies; necessity of advancing work on workers' quarters; water supply: "has a new pipeline been laid to Trevi?"; final building approvals. The memo about the Villa Santa Caterina contains 12 points, including "cost of tiling swimming pool. Preparation of a three or five year plan for the development of the gardens. Erection of walls and repair of roads"; door

entered into during the summer months, not to mention the usual College correspondence, the practical preparations to accommodate new and returning seminarians, and priests in graduate studies, as well as attending to American pilgrims and visiting prelates and alumni at the College.

In 1949, once the seminary returned to the Via dell'Umiltà, O'Connor opened the College Audience Office to assist American pilgrims to the Vatican, in anticipation of the 1950 Holy Year, which would be extended by the Holy Father through 1951. The operating cost for the office during its first year totaled $4,932.40 [$47,683.67], funds for which came from a grant of $5,000 [$48,337.18] by the National Catholic Welfare Conference, with one anonymous donation of $500 from an American bishop. Soon, however, the operational costs for the office were turned over to the College, but

---

stops, either marble or mechanical; chapel lighting; suggestions for building maintenance; "is it possible to divert planes from flying directly over the Villa by an appeal to the proper authorities? In past planes went wide of Villa"; purchase statue of S. Catherine of Siena for entrance gate niche; Appian Way entrance gate unusable "because the car cannot pass over the drain"; leather pads for chair legs as silencers; final building approvals. The memo about the Janiculum project contains 10 points, including "Date for signing the contract: probably the week of September 18th, 1949"; "Date for beginning the actual construction: immediately after signing"; photos of signing "for historical purposes"; "it is suggested that there be no ceremony for either the signing or the beginning of construction, especially in Italy. Probably it will be wise to have no publicity in the U.S., because there is a general belief that we have begun the work"; Discussion of laws governing extra-territorial land: "On my return to the College to-day I found a letter from Mr. Silvestri with regard to the question of duties [to be paid] and the difference of opinion between the authorities of the Vatican City and the Italian State on that subject in so far as it concerns the Janiculum property"; "Decisions concerning the absence of the rector that cannot wait can be taken up with Monsignor Burns and Mr. Silvestri regarding the signing of the contracts"; arrange appointment with Fr. Engleberg regarding the community of German nuns to do domestic service of the College, "so that the architect will have the benefit of their counsel in planning details in the laundry, kitchen, infirmary, etc"; "What is cost of general construction alone?"; budget line items "furnishings" and "furniture" must be clarified, since there is only one heading now for $250,000; "include in architectural plans a trunk room to accommodate trunks and baggage for 320 persons".

without the American bishops allocating funds for it, thereby adding to the College's growing operational deficit.

At first, O'Connor's office for American visitors to the Vatican was staffed by the faculty priests. But the number of visitors grew so rapidly that a full-time priest, Father Claiborne Lafferty [NAC 1935], was named assistant to the Rector by the end of 1949 for the Holy Year, and a secretary was hired. As the number of visitors continued to increase, a part-time stenographer, file clerk and receptionist were hired, but these soon became full-time positions. During the summer months, the number of American pilgrims was so large that the full-time paid staff numbered seven assistants, along with the Rector, the faculty priests and two seminarians who volunteered full-time every day. Not only did these services occupy most of the staff and seminarians' time, the office also kept the Rector's driver, Mr. Primo Spaghetti, on the road three to four hours daily, delivering audience tickets and performing "other services for those recommended by American Bishops."[310] And all these services were provided free of charge. O'Connor reported:

> The office was open all day long. Sometimes as many as sixty people were in the office before breakfast and often the phone rang as late as 10:30 or 11:00 at night. Someone was on duty all day long, from eight in the morning until eight in the evening. During the busy season the secretary stayed practically every day until 9:30 or 10:00 P.M. The office was also open all day on Sunday.

This was madness. And it only became more hectic as the Holy Year warmed up. It was thought that 20,000 people might seek papal audiences through the College during the Holy Year. But, from the opening of the Holy Door at Saint Peter's through October 1, 1950, the number of American visitors applying for papal audience tickets

---

[310] "Report of the Assistant to the Rector for Holy Year Activities, Rev. Claiborne Lafferty For Period Dec. 24, 1949-Oct. 1, 1950", CUA, *O'Connor Papers*, Box 42: *NAC subfiles*, Folder: *Papal Audiences (1949-50)*.

through the College office was more than 52,000! 34,000 of whom came, not with pilgrimage groups but individually, simply arriving at the College doorstep during the Holy Year, seeking audience tickets. The Vatican would not accept individual or private applications for audiences until the people requesting tickets were actually in Rome, so that ruled out any early processing of private requests by mail. The pilgrimage groups registered with the American Holy Year Committee in Washington, D.C. prior to departure from the United States, which gave O'Connor's staff some idea of the number of requests for any given week. But to accommodate the tens of thousands of Americans who simply walked in off the street, and who stayed in Rome for only a few days, that "required a great deal of attention and many trips to the Vatican in order to see that these people had the opportunity of receiving the Pope's blessing." He added, "As a matter of fact almost as much work is required to arrange an audience for one person as it is for a group."

The usual practice was that a priest or bishop in America would send a letter to O'Connor's office requesting a papal audience. By the end of September 1950, 5,940 letters were received requesting papal audiences. Each letter was answered, either by an acknowledgment card or by personal letter. Many more letters were received from priests asking O'Connor for information about offering Mass at Roman shrines, or asking that O'Connor make reservations for them to celebrate Mass at a particular place or altar, on a specific day and time. Likewise, his office filled requests to secure relics of saints, rosaries, medals, papal blessings and pictures of the Pope. When one of the numerous beatifications or canonizations took place, the office work increased, because "every pilgrim in the city wished to attend". That doubled the work, because a special request for tickets had to be made for each person.

Besides requests for tickets to papal audiences, Masses, and ceremonies, there were the innumerable requests for information "ranging from when will they see the Pope to where they can get the best bargains in linen." Information about tours in the City, opening hours of museums, arranging visits to Saint Peter's Basilica, the Vatican Gardens or to the then recently opened *Scavi* beneath the Basilica, even street addresses for priests and laymen living or studying in Rome, were all requested through the College office. All these services were provided by the Rector and his staff as they continued to run a seminary and oversee the Janiculum construction project, as well as steering the blocked lire negotiations with the Italian government and title negotiations with the Propaganda.

O'Connor saw all these services offered by the College as important because "it is felt that the Bishops would like to have those they recommend be given every service practicably possible", which helped secure the support of those bishops for the College in the form of financial assistance for the construction projects and the assignment of seminarians to the College.

The Rector left Rome for the States in late September, to the chagrin of Spellman, who, after wiring O'Connor in early October, and having been informed of the Rector's absence from the College, expressed his displeasure to Monsignor Burns. After informing O'Connor that Spellman was looking for him, Burns relayed the Rector's response to the Archbishop of New York, telling him that:

> if the Rector had known your wishes before he had left Rome and before he had made all arrangements necessary for his return to America, it would have been possible for him to regulate himself accordingly. However, in the present case he had already left Rome, and everything had been done for his return to America.[311]

Burns continued, "The Bishop asked me to write Your Eminence that he would like very much to make a visit to America at this time for personal reasons, and that he is quite willing to bare [sic] the expenses of the trip himself."

Spellman was still annoyed at the Rector, especially since the Board had supported O'Connor's plans over his own, and since his oversight of the Janiculum construction project had been given by

---

[311]   Rome October 20, 1949, Burns to Spellman, CUA, *O'Connor Papers*, Box 36: *MJ O'Connor, Rel. Org/Priests Corr*, Folder: *Burns, Msgr. Richard K (1947-54)*.

the Board to O'Connor's friends, Cardinals Mooney and Stritch.[312] O'Connor and Galeazzi wrote each other about how to respond to Spellman. In the meantime, the Archbishop of New York underscored the unsatisfactory financial status of the College in his report to the Board in late October, in preparation for their November meeting. As of October 15, 1949, the total of $625,383.86 [$6,045,859.05] had been received for the Umiltà project. Spellman told the bishops that funds were insufficient to pay for the full restoration of the Umiltà, and bishops who had not yet paid their quotas were encouraged to do so. Then, knowing the Rector enjoyed the support of many of the bishops, of Galeazzi and of the Pope, he offered a back handed compliment to O'Connor: "The work on the Via dell'Umiltà is now practically complete and gives to those of us who have been privileged to see it full evidence of the foresighted practical planning of the Rector and his architectural staff."[313]

O'Connor wrote Galeazzi that upon arriving in New York he paid a visit to the Cardinal, but was told he "was out". Galeazzi knew all about the tiff with Spellman, since the Rector had cabled him the details from Paris on his way home. So, O'Connor reported in more detail his observations about the importance of his frequent trips to the States, the outward reason for the Cardinal's annoyance with the Rector:

> The last six months of work with the Bishops has borne fruit, and the reports on the College and the work accomplished in Rome are good as far as I can see. I am well satisfied that I put all the efforts into receiving the Bishops in Rome, because I think they appreciated everything we did . . . I was very much disturbed, but I think it would have been a grave mistake to remain away from the [bishops'] meeting this year in Washington. The interest of the Bishops

[312] Cardinals Mooney and Stritch were members of the College class of 1909.
[313] New York October 28, 1949, Spellman to College Board of Trustees, KC, *Enrico Galeazzi Papers, No. Amer. Coll, Financial Management 1949-1952*, Box 13, File 8.

has been awakened and a spirit of good will created, and I think we should profit by it.[314]

Galeazzi responded to his friend on November 5th:

I have your telegram from Paris, and have followed the events by means of the updates courteously sent me by Monsignor Burns. It is useless that I express to you how much this saddens me, because I know well the sentiments of your heart and your lively interest in the 'welfare' of the College. On the other hand, there is nothing I can do, other than being always ready to lose no occasion whenever you wish, that I say a word of clarification and to express my well wishes.[315]

The Episcopal Board meeting was postponed for two days until November 14th, and met at the Stattler Hotel in Washington, D.C. The Rector had received an invitation marked "Urgent please forward" to attend the meeting. He reported that the rehabilitation work at the Villa in Castel Gandolfo was complete. All building projects had slowed because of the cold winter weather "which caused suspension of all outside work and of inside plastering", then there were two months of strikes and slowdowns. Because of this, the seminarians had remained at Castel Gandolfo commuting daily to the universities until March 1st, when they moved into the partially restored Umiltà property. By the time of the bishops' meeting, the Umiltà "is now at the disposal of the college administration, and the formal transfer by the contractors is expected to take place on the

---

[314] Scranton November 1, 1949, O'Connor to Galeazzi, KC, *Enrico Galeazzi Papers, No. Amer. Coll Corresp with Rector Martin J. O'Connor, Oct-Dec 1949*, Box 50, File 9.

[315] Rome November 5, 1949, Galeazzi to O'Connor, KC, *Enrico Galeazzi Papers, No. Amer. Coll Corresp with Rector Martin J. O'Connor, Oct-Dec 1949*, Box 50, File 9.

return of the Rector."[316] In accordance with the Board's July 25, 1949 permission, the Rector signed the contract for general construction of the new seminary on September 26, 1949, and work began on October 3rd.

O'Connor later told his Vice Rector that, even though there was no mention of Spellman's cablegram about O'Connor's returning home, a resolution was passed that the Rector should return annually to the States for the fall Board meeting, but that he needn't attend the April meetings. "The resolution regarding the presence of the Rector is not retroactive and accordingly, I must be responsible for the expense of this trip."[317] The only other point that interested the Board members concerned the College investments totaling $451,810.25 [$4,367,847.12], which was a welcome surprise to the bishops, about which Spellman had not referred prior to this meeting.[318] After attending the meeting of the entire American Hierarchy, O'Connor observed in a second letter to Burns:

> All the bishops are interested and I am particularly impressed by the fact that many of the younger and middle-aged Bishops know a great deal about the internal history of the College and speak very frankly concerning it.[319]

The Rector reported that in September 1948 there were 48 seminarians enrolled, four having left "honorably", having no priestly vocation. At the time of this report, the number had risen to

---

[316] "Report of the Rector of the North American College in Rome to the Episcopal Administrative Committee for the Hierarchy of the United States, November 14, 1949", CUA, *O'Connor Papers*, Box 44: *NAC*, File: *Rector's Report (Nov, 1949)*.

[317] Scranton November 22, 1949, O'Connor to Burns, CUA, *O'Connor Papers*, above ref.

[318] Minutes of the North American College Board Meeting, November 14, 1949, NYC, Box S/C-73, Folder 14: *To Card. Spellman, N. Amer. Coll*: Bonds: $267,637.50; Preferred Stock: $129,438.00; Common Stock: $54,734.75.

[319] Scranton November 22, 1949, O'Connor to Burns, CUA, *O'Connor Papers*, Box 36: *MJ O'Connor Rel Org/Priests Corr.*, Folder: *Burns, Msgr. Richard K (1947-54)*.

85 students. Their general health was good, "colds, low continuous fever, dysentery, and radical tooth decay were the commonest ailments. There was one case of scarlet fever and one case of partial temporary paralysis." The decision to make vaccinations compulsory was taken in January 1949, as well as an annual physical examination at the English Hospital for each student. Likewise, there were 21 student priests at the graduate house of studies, the Casa San Giovanni atop the Janiculum.

The Rector reported on the number of visitors to the College, as well. Up to November 1, 1949, 84 American bishops visited the College and nearly all inspected the College properties.[320] The number of lay and priest visitors was also large, with 1,500 persons in July alone having applied for papal audience tickets through the College.[321]

During the Holy Year, Spellman began insisting that the College and the Audience Office become money-making operations. For instance, he suggested that the College might serve as a priests' hostel during the summer months of the Holy Year, while the seminarians were at the Villa Santa Caterina. O'Connor objected that additional domestic staff would need to be hired, since the College closed down during the summer.[322] Likewise, even without providing meals, other difficulties would present themselves such as "the impossibility of control over those who are given accommodations, especially with regard to hours and company." To say nothing of possible damage to property, so recently restored and re-opened.[323]

---

[320] Rome December 4, 1949, Burns to O'Connor, CUA, *O'Connor Papers*, Box 36: *MJ O'Connor Rel Org/Priests Corr.*, Folder: *Burns, Msgr. Richard K (1947-54)*: Burns reported that Bishops McCarty and Greco came to supper at the College. "Both of them were very much impressed with the work that has been accomplished."

[321] "Rector's Report, North American College, November 1949", p. 9, VII: *Visitors*, CUA, *O'Connor Papers*, Box 44: *NAC*, File: *Rector's Report (1949-Nov)*.

[322] New York June 8, 2012, Edward Cardinal Egan to DiGiovanni: "Bishop O'Connor said often, and he was right! 'We must never let visitors and outsiders damage the proper rhythm of a seminary.'"

[323] Rome January 9, 1950, O'Connor to Spellman, NYC, Box S/C-73, Folder 15: *To Card. Spell, No. Amer. Coll.* New York January 28, 1950, Spellman

Later in the year, Spellman took aim once again at O'Connor concerning fundraising for the College. From his first year as Rector, following his visit to the seminary in Detroit, O'Connor had wanted to design and print informational brochures about the College. This, he hoped, might be sent to the bishops providing them information about the seminary program and the construction projects, to spur them on to support the program financially and to send seminarians. During the Holy Year, O'Connor approached the Cardinal Treasurer for permission to print brochures for the Visitors' Office. Spellman, taking credit for the brochure idea, which was O'Connor's, shot back:

> I wish to say that you have misunderstood my suggestion concerning the desirability of a brochure presenting data concerning the new American College . . . . The chief use of the booklet should be to help you as Rector of the American College and your associates to interest visitors to Rome in our College. This should not be difficult since you are privileged to come in contact with the most distinguished Catholics in the United States.[324]

As the Holy Year continued, Spellman repeated his jabs at the Rector, especially concerning construction costs and operational deficits, with barbed, snipping comments about O'Connor's ideas, such as raising student tuition to help cover operational expenses. In 1951, again referring to O'Connor's work at the Audience Office, Spellman thanked him for his courtesy to some of his friends, the Schedler Family, during their visit to Rome. Then, he attacked:

---

to O'Connor, NYC, above ref: Spellman answered O'Connor, writing that he had written Archbishop Cicognani, "so that he might be informed of your views in regard to the use of the American College property during the Holy Year, views in which the Trustees and his Excellency, the Apostolic Delegate, concur", even though he, himself, did not.

[324] New York July 8, 1950, Spellman to O'Connor, KC, *Enrico Galeazzi Papers, No. Amer. Coll Corresp, Francis Cardinal Spellman, 1950-51, 1953-1954*, Box 30, File 17.

I am also pleased to see that they made a contribution to the New College Building Fund which is along the lines that I have been stressing to you for several years, because I believe that you have great opportunities in the simplest and most natural manner to enlist interest and obtain assistance from American visitors who go to Rome. Certainly that was the method followed by your distinguished predecessors, Archbishop Kennedy and Monsignor O'Hern, who, without help from the Hierarchy, made it possible to purchase the land on which the new college is being erected. Assuredly something will have to be done to supplement the most generous contributions of the Bishops who are giving fifteen times their annual quota to the Building Fund of the North American College, if the tuition is not to be raised to a point where Bishops simply cannot afford to send men to study in Rome. I repeat I am delighted to see that you and your efficient staff are making progress in supplementing the efforts of the Bishops in this regard.[325]

O'Connor answered a month later, writing that,

no important contributions were received during the whole year of 1950. Some gifts came from bishops to pay for diners for students they hosted; others for books or vestments we need here. A detailed account is kept by the Economo, and he will send you a copy.

In this instance I can see that Your Eminence is considering a comparison with some Rectorships

---

[325] New York March 20, 1951, Spellman to O'Connor, KC, *Enrico Galeazzi, No. Amer. Coll. Corresp, Francis Cardinal Spellman, 1950-1951, 1953-1954*, Box 30, File 17.

of the past and the excellent work accomplished at various times. Nevertheless, I think that the present demands of the college itself on the Faculty are much more pressing than they were in years gone by. Speaking for myself, however, I must confess that, much to my regret, I am not especially talented for any unusual success in soliciting donations and thereby assuring a stable course of income for the College.[326]

Following the initial excavation work and studies of the soil of the Janiculum property, Galeazzi and his team decided to change their original Z-shaped design.[327] Because of the unique and varied substrata of the land, a reconfigured P-shaped building was settled upon, requiring the driving of 1,644 piles into the sandy clay [totaling 10 miles of piles, end-to-end],[328] as well as the construction of more extensive retaining walls and a more complicated drainage system than originally anticipated.[329] This included new basement levels and cellars, which delayed the laying of the foundation, since the further excavations and driving of piles pushed the work schedule back into the winter months, and increased labor and material costs.

During the spring and summer months, the pouring of the concrete foundations for the basement was completed, except for those of the chapel, which designs were being reconsidered, resulting from Thomas Kelly's suggestions. Galeazzi hoped to begin that work by mid-October. Work on the reinforced concrete skeleton, at the other side of the building, facing the *viale dei pini* and the Basilica of

---

[326] Rome April 30, 1951, O'Connor to Spellman, NYC, Box S/C-73, Folder 16: *To Card. Spellman, N. Amer. Coll.*

[327] Vatican March 13, 1950, Galeazzi to O'Connor. This formed part of O'Connor's March 1950 Rector's Report, CUA, *O'Connor Papers*, Box 44: *NAC*, File: *Rector's Report (1950, March)*, pp 2-3.

[328] Tournier, Francis, *The North American College, Historical Summary and Guide to the New Site on the Janiculum Hill*, private printing, p. 9.

[329] Vatican September 30, 1950, Galeazzi to O'Connor, found in O'Connor's November 1950 Rector's Report, p. 1, CUA, *O'Connor Papers*, Box 44: *NAC*, File: *Rector's Report (1950, November)*.

Saint Peter had progressed to the floor above the *rappresentanza*, at the formal entrance.

Galeazzi hoped the pouring of the reinforced concrete skeleton for the second floor of the largest portion of the building might be completed by mid-November. In fact, despite the initial slowdown in work, because of the changed plans and excavation work, Galeazzi hoped the entire work in reinforced concrete to be completed by April 1951.[330] He was also optimistic about the completion of the sewer and drainage systems, which had to be modified because of the new basement excavations and unanticipated ground water and seepage.

Contracts with the DeMicheli and the Fusi & Macchi Companies were recently signed to provide the hydraulic, sanitation, and the heating systems. Galeazzi requested cost updates from those who submitted bids for the electrical contracts, and was about to send out a request for proposals for the Travertine and other stone for both the exterior and interior of the building. Plaster scale models of various architectural design work had also been requested and were nearly complete. Galeazzi reported that the number of workmen on the site had risen to 110 men.

The Rector returned to the States, again preparing for an upcoming bishops' meeting in November. He wrote his Roman team nearly every day, sometimes twice daily, and received as many reports from Rome. Galeazzi supplied him with a written chronology of the Janiculum construction to be used at the meeting. He reported that the work progressed well, but because of bad weather, the work was about three months in arrears, and the opening date should be pushed back to the autumn of 1952, although that would leave some "finishing work" and the furnishing of the building undone.[331]

Spellman was not speaking with O'Connor at the time, except for the bare minimum of communication about the College during the annual meetings. Both Galeazzi and Burns reported to the

---

[330]   Galeazzi, ibid, p. 2.
[331]   Vatican November 9, 1950, Galeazzi to O'Connor, KC, *Enrico Galeazzi Papers, No. Amer. Coll. Corresp, Rector Martin J. O'Connor, Oct-Dec 1950*, Box 50, File 12.

Rector about the hospitality recently offered to Spellman, Cicognani and numerous other American bishops at the College. During the Washington meetings, Cicognani and other bishops personally commended the Rector for his staff's work and hospitality during their Roman visit at the time of the definition of the Dogma of the Assumption. "Of course, I met with the Cardinal Treasurer [Spellman] both on Tuesday evening and at a meeting of the Legion of Decency," the Rector reported to Burns, "but he did not mention his visit to Rome and neither did I."[332]

Galeazzi had written his friend earlier, knowing the Cardinal's cold demeanor towards the Rector, as if to steel O'Connor for upcoming difficulties:

> I beg you to believe in the optimism that I show you, and to face with perfect tranquility the problems before you. Your work is greatly appreciated, and has been given to your care by Divine Providence, because of your intelligence and rare ability and competence.[333]

As they prepared for the bishops' meeting, Spellman informed the Rector of his intention to begin a second round of discussions with the Italian government about another blocked lire deal. O'Connor dutifully informed his Roman team, which began arranging the necessary meetings.[334]

---

[332] N.p. November 18, 1950, O'Connor to Burns, CUA, *O'Connor Papers*, Box 36: *MJ O'Connor Rel. Org/Priests' Corresp*, Folder: *Burns, Msgr. Richard K (1947-54)*.

[333] Vatican November 9, 1950, Galeazzi to O'Connor, KC, *Enrico Galeazzi Papers, No. Amer. Coll, Corresp, Rector Martin J. O'Connor, Oct-Dec 1950*, Box 50, File 12.

[334] Vatican November 24, 1950, Galeazzi to O'Connor, KC, *Enrico Galeazzi Papers, No. Amer. Coll. Corresp., Rector Martin J. O'Connor, Oct-Dec 1950*, Box 50, File 12: Galeazzi thanked O'Connor for his two letters of November 18th, and continued: "I have asked for a meeting with Undersecretary of State Andreotti, and I think it will take place in the next few days" [Galeazzi received the appointment date prior to mailing this letter, because he penciled in "it has been fixed for tomorrow at 1 p.m."]. Washington, D.C. March

An agreement with Warner Brothers Pictures International Corporation had already been worked out by Spellman, news of which he reported to Galeazzi, but not to the Rector. The deal was for the sale of 1,000,000,000 lire to the College at an exchange rate of 775 lire per dollar, approximately $1,292,000 [$12,334,847.30], but was valid only until December 28, 1950, and the College had the burden of securing the Italian government's approval.[335] The bishops gave the task to O'Connor during their annual meeting.[336]

Galeazzi informed Spellman that the Italian government would not grant the license for the deal with Warner Brothers, which, he suggested, "might also induce them somehow to better the conditions offered for the transaction." He continued:

> May I add that if Your Eminence will inform the movie company of the negative answer . . . they will probably understand that their blocked lire here are really much more blocked than they think, . . . I believe that the Italian Government would be willing to grant this permission at our request more than at that of anybody else, and, as a matter of fact, it

10, 1950, Alberto Tarchiani to Spellman, NYC, Box S/C-74, Folder 7: *To Card. Spellman, N. Amer. Coll*: Tarchiani, the Italian Ambassador to the United States, wrote in Italian diplomatic style thanking Spellman for his March 4th letter, assuring the Cardinal that "I have not delayed in bringing the matter [of blocked lire] to the knowledge of the Ministry for Foreign Affairs and to warmly recommend that the Ministry of Finance be invited to consider the possibility of having the question settled along the lines you have indicated."

[335] New York November 17, 1950, John J. Glynn to Spellman, KC, *Enrico Galeazzi Papers, No. Amer. Coll, Corresp. Rector Martin J. O'Connor, Oct-Dec 1950*, Box 50, File 12. Spellman sent copies of everything to Galeazzi for his input. Galeazzi sent copies of everything from the New York chancery concerning the College to O'Connor, to keep him informed.

[336] N.p. December 9, 1950, O'Connor to Galeazzi, KC, *Enrico Galeazzi Papers, No. Amer. Coll, Financial Management, 1949-1952)*, Box 13, File 8. This same letter, but addressed to Silvestri, is in NAC Archives, *Coll. Amer, Corresp Rett e Card. Spellman—M.C. Geough* [sic]: O'Connor had addressed the American bishops, "probably 150 of them" on November 15th, the day following the College Board Meeting.

should have already been granted to us, had it not
been for the present delicate situation between the
Government and the movie companies.

Mr. Andreotti remembers quite well that there is a
moral understanding between the Italian Government
and the North American College for this second
permission, and the movie companies should
appreciate that an eventual licence [sic] would be
more easily released at our request than at theirs.[337]

Count Galeazzi told the Cardinal that the College should wait
before submitting another blocked lire petition, until a "new regime
for the granting of licences [sic]", which would give Andreotti more
time to "hasten the matter". He suggested obtaining a "prorogation
in the terms of the agreement with the movie company for another
month or so", and then proceed with a new application to the
government. Likewise, "we are quite willing to start any other action
that would be considered advisable." Spellman followed his friend's
advice.[338]

Right on cue, as the New Year arrived, Spellman wrote a letter
to Alcide De Gasperi, asking that his government grant the license
permitting the blocked lire deal with Warner Brothers. In typical
Spellman subtlety, he ended his request by "hinting" at the financial
benefits to Rome if the College were granted the license, writing,
"When the new College is operating at capacity, three-hundred
thousand dollars will be spent annually in Rome for the students'
maintenance."[339] Spellman sent his completed letter for De Gasperi
to Galeazzi, asking that he discuss the letter with Mario Zama of

[337] Vatican November 29, 1950, Galeazzi to Spellman, KC, *Enrico Galeazzi Papers, No. Amer. Coll, Corresp, Francis Card. Spellman, 1950-1951, 1953-1954*, Box 30, File 17.

[338] N.p. December 7, 1950, O'Connor to Burns, CUA, *O'Connor Papers*, Box 36: *Rel. Org/Priests*, Folder: B*urns, Msgr. Richard K (1947-54)*.

[339] New York [draft], Spellman to Alcide De Gasperi, KC, *Enrico Galeazzi Papers, No. Amer. Coll, Corresp, Francis Cardinal Spellman, 1950-1951, 1953-1954*, Box 30, File 17.

Warner Brothers in Rome, and then determine the strategy for presenting the letter, if at all, and explain both the film company's position and that of the College to De Gasperi.[340]

Silvestri contacted Zama, and Galeazzi spoke on the phone with Andreotti, who counseled waiting until March before presenting any request.[341] The Count told Spellman he would discuss the matter with O'Connor. However, since the exchange rate in the city was nearly equal to that offered by Warner Brothers, Galeazzi suggested that it might be more advantageous to await a better offer from another corporation, unless Warner Brothers could improve their offer. There the matter ended, for the time being.[342]

O'Connor was again ill, and about to enter the hospital.[343] The constant traveling; the mounting stress running the College and directing the construction in Rome while in the States; the antagonism of Spellman; and simple exhaustion all sent his blood pressure plummeting, in a man never considered to enjoy a robust constitution. Both O'Connor and Galeazzi complained of low blood pressure, unrelenting stress, and interminable work hours, as seen in their correspondence. These shared characteristics and experiences contributed to the forging of their friendship as they worked together for years to re-open the College and to build its new home on the Janiculum.[344] It is at this time that O'Connor first makes mention of his thoughts to resign his position as Rector, mentioning a conversation with an unnamed priest friend in the

[340] New York January 4, 1951, Spellman to Galeazzi, KC, *Enrico Galeazzi Papers*, above ref: "I am not sure that this request should be made now or postponed until after the proposed meeting. I defer to your good judgment."

[341] Vatican January 19, 1951, Galeazzi to Spellman, KC, *Enrico Galeazzi Papers, No. Amer. Coll, Corresp Most Rev. Martin J. O'Connor, 1951-1953*, Box 30, File 19.

[342] Cable New York February 3, 1951, Spellman to Galeazzi, KC, *Enrico Galeazzi Papers, No. Amer. Coll, Corresp, Francis Cardinal Spellman, 1950-1951, 1953-1954*, Box 30, File 17.

[343] Rome December 2, 1950, Burns to O'Connor, CUA, *O'Connor Papers*, Box 36: *Rel. Org/ Priests*, Folder: *Burns, Msgr. Richard K (1947-54)*.

[344] N.p. n.d., O'Connor to Galeazzi, KC, *Enrico Galeazzi Papers, N.Amer. Coll, Corresp Most Rev. Martin J. O'Connor, 1950-1951*, Box 30, File 11.

west, who encouraged the Rector to try to keep going despite the pressures.[345]

Despite his poor health, O'Connor continued his travels around the country visiting bishops, repeatedly making his pleas for financial support for the construction of the new seminary, and asking bishops to send new seminarians to Rome.[346] The Rector also continued to carry on the usual, daily College work, writing scores of letters to his Roman team, as well as to bishops, alumni, the New York chancery, and various Board members, concerning College business.[347]

His visits with bishops, as well as the positive feedback from those who had visited the College and spoken with O'Connor's Roman team, made him optimistic that he had growing support among them for his work at the College, as he wrote to Silvestri: "The reaction is very favorable to the work in Rome, and I feel the visits of the Trustees to your office and your personal meeting with many of the Bishops has been productive of much good for the whole project."[348]

Galeazzi urged O'Connor to write to Spellman, despite the lack of any communication between the two during the past months. The Count wrote the original draft in Italian, which O'Connor had translated word for word, and sent it to the Cardinal on February

---

[345] Scranton December 2, 1950, O'Connor to Galeazzi, KC, *Enrico Galeazzi Papers*, above ref.

[346] Scranton January 4, 1951, O'Connor to Galeazzi, KC, *Galeazzi Papers*, above ref: Cardinal Dougherty gave O'Connor a check for $48,000 as the final payment on the quota he accepted in 1938. n.p. January 4, 1952, O'Connor to Burns, CUA, *O'Connor Papers*, Box 36: *MJ O'Connor to Rel. Org/Priests Corr*, Folder: *Burns, Msgr. Richard K (1947-54)*. He spent December 31st with Msgr. Fitzgerald in New Rochelle, Jan 1st with Msgr. Burke in Hackensack, January 2nd with Bishop Boland in Paterson, and January 3rd with Cardinal Dougherty and Archbishop O'Hara in Philadelphia.

[347] CUA, *O'Connor Papers*, Box 36: *Rel. Org/Priests Corr*, Folder: *Burns, Msgr. Richard K (1947-54)*: just the number of his letters to Burns is staggering, responding to reports and questions about construction, the daily life of the College and graduate house, the hiring of nuns to run the College kitchen and laundry, the legal matters with Propaganda and the Italian government, and, of course, finances.

[348] Scranton January 4, 1951, O'Connor to Silvestri, NAC, *Coll. Americano, Corrisp Rett. Card. Spellman—M.C. Geough* [sic].

26th.[349] The Rector wrote that he read the Cardinal's February cable to Galeazzi, agreeing to postpone approaching the Italian government for the time being. O'Connor reported that the Italian government decided to approach the film companies directly, concerning their future in Italy. The Italians had arranged meetings with representatives of the American film corporations in New York City during the first weeks of March to discuss the whole question of blocked lire. The Rector reminded the Cardinal that Andreotti "has let us know that it would be pleasing to the government if the petition of the College could be somewhat delayed in order not to interfere with these negotiations."

Representatives from Warner Brothers had recently met with Silvestri and Galeazzi, he continued, asking about the progress of the College's petition to the Italian government about the Warner Brothers deal. Silvestri and Galeazzi explained to Mr. Mario Zama, General Manager of Warner Brothers in Italy, and to Mr. Joseph Hummel, Vice President of the same division, that the College was not pushing the government for a license, especially in view of the high dollar exchange on the free market. Repeating the points he had made to Spellman earlier, Galeazzi gave his "private opinion" that the College might consider opening new negotiations with Warner Brothers if better terms were offered and if the offer were based on a fluid rate of exchange, "that is, it would be based on the free market rate on the day of closing the operation, with the addition of a certain number of points, insuchwise [sic], however, that the variations in exchange would not disturb the substantial value of the transaction."

Further, Galeazzi and Silvestri made it clear that:

> the operation the College intended to persue [sic] with the authorization of the Italian Government (hope for which we feel is founded in the general

---

[349] Rome February 26, 1951, O'Connor to Spellman, KC, *Enrico Galeazzi Papers, No. Amer. Coll, Corresp. Most Rev. Martin J. O'Connor, 1951-1953*, Box 30, File 19. Both Galeazzi's hand written draft and a copy of O'Connor's translation are here.

assurances of Mr. Andreotti) bears no relation to the agreement that may be reached in New York in the first fortnight in March between the representatives of the Italian Government and the film companies regarding the regulations of the latters' [sic] funds which are blocked in Italy.

O'Connor continued:

It will be necessary to insist on this point during negotiations in order to let the Warner people know the true position, namely, that the provision made by the Italian Government is a particular concession to the American College because of the nature of its work and not, instead, the result of any agreement which the film companies may conclude in the near future.

O'Connor stated that he did not attend the meetings, so as not to give the impression of a commitment by the College, and "in order to emphasize the fact that they [the meetings of Silvestri, Galeazzi and the Warner representatives] were of a private character only." Hummel was scheduled to return to New York, and hoped to meet with Monsignor Maguire. O'Connor and Galeazzi suggested that Maguire insist that the negotiations be based on a fluid rate of exchange, and that a more reasonable time to conclude negotiations be granted the College by Warner Brothers, "for example at least until the end of March 1951. He concluded:

It seems important to me to inform you of these Roman conversations, and of their private nature, not only that you may know of the evident desire of Warner's to sell their blocked lire, but also in order, if you wish, to forewarn Monsignor McGuire [sic] of the coming visit of Mr. Hummel and of the circumstances surrounding it.

By March 1951, the entire basement excavations, the driving of support piles for the remaining foundations, and the laying of sewer lines were complete. The construction of the retaining walls, interrupted because of the redesigning of the building that included basement work in certain areas, was to resume. Bids had been requested for supplying the Travertine, for the new furniture and fixtures in wood and iron, and for the passenger and freight elevators.

The weather had turned particularly nasty in November and continued through early March, with "unprecedented" continuous and driving rains, stopping all open air work, which comprised most of the construction at this stage of the project. The previous three months were lost, and hindered the completion of the pouring of foundations and the erection of the reinforced concrete skeleton. A lack of accurate and detailed technical plans of each section of the recently redesigned building also hindered the work.

Another unanticipated difficulty was the recent notable cost increase for building materials. Galeazzi suggested that the purchase and storage of large quantities of the building materials required on the Janiculum might prove helpful. He reported that he had already purchased as much ironwork, cast iron and lead piping, drainage, and sewage hardware for the water and sanitation systems, the tubing, wiring and casings for the electrical works, and the iron rebar rods for the reinforced concrete work, and other building materials as he could lay his hands on. He reported that this unexpected increase would raise the construction total to about $3,379,858 [$29,909,793.38].[350]

In the middle of these months of incessant work, it was the Rector's turn to help his friend, who was feeling poorly. In a handwritten note, thanking the Count for the gift of a papal medal, the Rector wrote:

---

[350] Vatican March 5, 1951, Galeazzi to O'Connor, included in the Rector's Report, April 2, 1951, CUA, *O'Connor Papers*, Box 44:*NAC*, Folder: *Rector's Reports (April 1951)*, p. 2.

Last year you encouraged me at a time when I needed it badly. This year it is my turn to use your words but in a different sense—'*La supplico*'—please take some rest, at least at Easter Time. You cannot stand so much work and worry too long—and we would like you present for the dedication and when we take over the Bambino Gesu Hospital in 1965!! I will hold you to your promise about a visit to Circeo when the weather is warmer. Happy Easter![351]

The trip was made, O'Connor traveling south to Circeo to meet the Count, who was resting at his summer home in the ancient seaside town, as O'Connor wrote in another note:

I am most grateful to you for pleasant days and good company at Circeo. I needed it very much indeed. I thank you always for the example of charity and kindness. Sometimes I am inclined to be bitter and resentful for reasons already explained and your guidance and sense of forgiveness has been an inspiration. I am glad I had the opportunity to talk, however, because I was under a great strain when I first arrived. The whole visit did me much good.[352]

In March and April, following the Episcopal Board meeting, Spellman and Maguire returned to the problem of the operational deficit of the seminary. As O'Connor told the Board in his November 1950 report, he was well aware of the problem, and that the operational deficit was made up by drawing on the Building

---

[351] Rome March 16, 1951, O'Connor to Galeazzi, KC, *Enrico Galeazzi Papers, No. Amer. Coll, Corresp Martin J. O'Connor, 1950-1951*, Box 30, File 11.

[352] "Sunday" O'Connor to Galeazzi, KC, *Enrico Galeazzi Papers*, above ref. This letter, and that below from Villa San Giralomo, while undated, are all filed by Galeazzi together with other letters dated during the spring and summer months, 1951.

Fund."³⁵³ In strenuous terms, Spellman wrote the Rector, "I wish to notify you that we cannot further permit you to draw on the Building Fund for any operational deficit."³⁵⁴

While the operational deficit was a problem, it certainly did not merit the time and anxiety lavished upon it by the New York chancery. In his April 2, 1951 report to the Board, O'Connor reported that, for the period of September 31, 1950-January 31, 1951, the Rector and Galeazzi had recorded the works completed under budget. He called them "financial surpluses" on the construction project at the Umiltà of $20,289.89 [$179,553.82]; a surplus on the construction project of the Villa Santa Caterina of $18,165.16 [$160,751.19]; a surplus on the construction so far completed of the new seminary of $119,563.43 [$1,058,067.38]. The College appeared to have a combined surplus for the daily operation of the Umiltà and the Villa of $61,142.68 [$541,077.44]; and an anticipated "break even" for the Casa San Giovanni, due principally to the increase of annual tuition, room and board charges, from $750 [$6,637.07] to $800 [$7,079.54].³⁵⁵

The well-understood reality was that a certain fluidity existed between the three College bank accounts: one for the Castel Gandolfo property, one for the Umiltà property, and one for the Janiculum property projects. College operational expenses were paid from burses established by dioceses, investment income, and annual charges to dioceses for tuition, room and board for seminarians and student priests, and from the G.I. Bill, at least for a while. And, it had been a commonly accepted and Board-approved practice that the Rector could borrow funds from one account for use in the other,

³⁵³ Rector's Report, November 1950, CUA, *O'Connor Papers*, Box 44: *NAC*, Folder: *Report Board of Trustees (1950)*. The estimated deficit for ordinary expenses for 1950-1951 academic year was $6,851.00 [$65,445.81].

³⁵⁴ New York April 18, 1951, Spellman to O'Connor, NYC, S/C-73, Folder 16: *To Card. Spellman, N. Amer. Coll.*

³⁵⁵ "Rector's Report, North American College, April 2, 1951", *Financial Report*, pp. 6-12, CUA, *O'Connor Papers*, Box 44: *NAC*, Folder: *Rector's Report (April 1951)*.

eventually paying back the borrowed sum to the original account.[356] Everyone knew this was a type of institutional shell game;[357] the bishops themselves having approved the practice specifically during their November 1949 meeting.[358] Even earlier, when O'Connor had raised the question of the operating deficit during a special Board meeting on July 25, 1949, the bishops tabled any discussion.[359]

Until the bishops made provisions so the College could actually pay its way, by raising student fees to a realistic level, for example, there simply was nothing else the Rector could do. For the bishops, the completion of the new seminary was of prime importance; operational deficits and other matters could be attended to after the opening of the new College on the Janiculum, no matter what Spellman thought.

[356] New York May 2, 1951, Maguire to Spellman, "Memorandum for His Eminence Re: North American College", NYC, Box S/C-73, Folder 16: *To Card. Spellman, N. Amer. Coll*: For example, the repair and restoration costs for the Villa Santa Caterina totaled $150,000. "Most was paid from accumulated income from Burse investment; the balance was charged to the Building Fund."

[357] "Rector's Report, North American College, April 2, 1951", above ref, p. 11: Receipts for the Umiltà seminary as of Sept. 1, 1950 were: "On Hand", Guaranty Trust Co, NYC: $15,106.62; "On Hand"—Banca di Roma: $826.99; Burse Income—"from Treasurer of NAC": $17,664.90; Unused Burse Income—"from Treasurer of NAC": $5,790.74; Board & Tuition to Jan 31, 1951: $64,629.43; transfer from Credito Italiano: $7,405.00; Total Receipts: $111,423.68. Total Expenditures for the Operation of the College at the Umiltà and Castel Gandolfo: $50,281.00, leaving positive balance on hand of: $61,142.68, comprised of "On Hand" funds as of January 31, 1951: Guaranty Trust Co: $28,226.26; Istituto Opere Religione [Vatican Bank]: $32,156.42; Banca di Roma: $760.00 [$1 equals $9.55 in 2012 dollars].

[358] New York June 5, 1951, Maguire to Spellman, "Memorandum to His Eminence: Re: Attached Correspondence North American College", NYC, Box S/C-73, Folder 16:*To Card. Spellman, N. Amer. Coll*: This is attached to O'Connor's April 30, 1951 letter to Spellman, in which the Rector reminded Spellman of that approval.

[359] *Minutes of Special Meeting of Board of Trustees of the American College of the Roman Catholic Church of the United States Held in New York City, July 25, 1949*, KC, *Enrico Galeazzi Papers, No. Amer. Coll, financial Management, 1949-1952*, Box 13, File 8.

The actual College operational deficit for September 1, 1950-September 1, 1951 totaled $23,016 [$203,678.32]. The Rector had informed the Board repeatedly that the College was operating in the red:

> Nevertheless, as I have explained on several occasions, an operation deficit could not have been avoided. Of course we are trying to reduce this deficit year by year, and, as a matter of fact, this year it promised to be less than ever. At the same time I was of the opinion that the resolution numbered four of the Board expressed in the minutes of its meeting of November 14th, 1949, described the general thought of the members on the deficit."[360]

As the Rector continued to inform the Cardinal Treasurer of the actual financial situation of the College, the reality was that part of the deficit was due to the "added extras" Spellman urged upon the College Board and Rector, such as a salary increase for the faculty, the hiring of additional secretarial staff for the Audience Office at Via dell'Umiltà, and the operational expenses for that office, which were covered by the College—but without any additional funds being allocated to cover the expenses. In other words, more expenses and services were added, but no funding was provided.[361]

The Archbishop of New York developed a singular notion that the Rector of the College should help raise money to offset the operational expenses of the College, at least by means of the Audience Office. He repeated this to O'Connor in various letters, as seen earlier. That he must have spoken of this to others is evident from memoranda from Maguire. It might be interpreted that Spellman was trying to replace O'Connor with a Rector of his own choosing,

---

[360] Rome April 30, 1951, O'Connor to Spellman, NYC, Box S/C-73, Folder 16: *To Card. Spellman, N. Amer. Coll.*

[361] New York April 5, 1951, Spellman to O'Connor, Box S/C-73, above ref: there are two separate letters of the same date: one treats of salary raises; the second, of financing the Audience Office.

or simply to discredit his administrative abilities before the other bishops, so that Spellman's plans to reduce the size of the seminary construction project and his continued insistence to sell the Umiltà could be adopted.[362]

By May, the pressure returned concerning the blocked lire negotiations with the Italian government. Galeazzi wrote Spellman a letter marked "PERSONAL" on May 9th, telling the Cardinal that Joseph Kennedy came to Rome "by air" to spend May 8th—just one day—with Galeazzi to discuss the blocked lire negotiations and other matters. Kennedy was scheduled to see Spellman the following Monday "and tell you directly of his experiences in Rome."[363] During his one day in Rome, Kennedy "had an informal and confidential lunch with Monsignor Montini, Bishop O'Connor, Father [Vincent] McCormick and Prince Carlo Pacelli attending." Galeazzi reported that he had contacted the Italian government frequently, but no response had yet come about the blocked lire license, writing:

> In the meantime, Mr. Kennedy mentioned the fact that, following recent arrangements with our Government, the movie companies apparently will have a certain amount of their blocked lire available, while, besides, they are in very hard need of money, and therefore he thinks that the companies should be ready to meet any condition for the remaining share of blocked lire. The real problem is to get the Italian Government approval.

---

[362] N.p. May 2, 1951, O'Connor to Galeazzi, KC, *Enrico Galeazzi Papers, No. Amer. Coll, Corresp Martin J. O'Connor, 1950-1951*, Box 30, File 11: O'Connor sent Galeazzi a copy of his April 30, 1951 letter to Spellman, adding "I do hope the difficulty will be surmounted. I wrote an official letter for Cardinal Mooney in case of a meeting and a private one to stress the importance of this affair."

[363] Vatican May 9, 1951, Galeazzi to Spellman, KC, *Enrico Galeazzi Papers, No. Amer. Coll, Corresp Francis Card. Spellman, 1950-1951, 1953-1954*, Box 30, File 17.

In early July, Galeazzi approached the Italian government once again, this time writing Andreotti. He repeated his request for a meeting, and informed him that O'Connor was leaving for a brief vacation, but would delay his departure if Andreotti would grant an appointment to discuss the blocked lire.[364] Andreotti finally replied on July 14th in a letter marked *"personale"*:

> I ought to add in the most confidential manner that on the part of the Americans (in a group that was almost entirely Jewish and Protestant), during a number of these painful negotiations, was underscored with accents of biting irony about the 'ecclesiastical means' by which the lire had been remarkably unblocked in the past. Naturally, statements clarifying the legal reasons that justified the various past transactions were not lacking on my part.[365]

He ended by offering his help in "any of your future works", if needed. But, nothing could be done, at least not for the moment.

O'Connor and his staff prepared for the first ordinations to the subdiaconate and to the priesthood since the College had closed in 1940, to take place in the Umiltà chapel on the morning of July 16th, the Feast of Our Lady of Mount Carmel. The Rector wrote both Galeazzi and Silvestri inviting them to be present at the ceremony. To Galeazzi he wrote that July 16th would be:

> a symbol of all the efforts of the College: the preparation of young men for the priesthood for the Catholic Church in the United States. Possibly these young men do not recognize how much your work has been a part of their preparation, but we who are

---

[364] Vatican July 3, 1951, Galeazzi to Andreotti, KC, *Enrico Galeazzi Papers, No. Amer. Coll, Corresp Most Rev. Martin J. O'Connor, 1951-1953*, Box 30, File 19.

[365] Rome July 14, 1951, Giulio Andreotti to Galeazzi, KC, *Enrico Galeazzi Papers, No. Amer. Coll, Corresp, Giulio Andreotti 1951*, Box 30, File 18.

constantly working with you know how much you have dedicated your time and your strength, . . .[366]

To the Silvestri he wrote:

I write to invite you to assist at this ceremony which fills our hearts with great joy. Your presence will be a great pleasure to us, because of your splendid work completed for the rebirth of the College . . .[367]

Following the ordinations, O'Connor took the train to Lucerne for a vacation. He left with the weight of unanswered questions about the future of the College, and was in no rush to return to Rome. He wrote Galeazzi:

For the first time since 1940 I am having a long quiet vacation; resting, walking, reading and praying. It is only now that I am feeling better but I am going to stay here some weeks or as long as the money lasts! I am alone but the Hotel is filled, few Americans but many Belgians, Dutch and Swiss.

I hope and pray that the contractor difficulty [Mengarini, one of the partners of the construction company, suddenly died, and his widow had raised legal problems that stopped work on the Janiculum], the blocked lire problem and the Propaganda affair will have more satisfactory settlement soon.[368]

---

[366] Rome July 10, 1951, O'Connor to Galeazzi, KC, *Enrico Galeazzi Papers, No. Amer. Coll, Corresp, Martin J. O'Connor, July-Dec 1951*, Box 50, File 14.

[367] Rome July 10, 1951, O'Connor to Silvestri, NAC, *Coll. Amer., Corrisp Rettori, Card. Spellman—M.C. Geough* [sic].

[368] Lucerne July 25, 1951, O'Connor to Galeazzi, KC, *Enrico Galeazzi Papers, No. Amer. Coll, Corresp Martin J. O'Connor, 1950-1952*, Box 30, File 11.

He wanted to keep Galeazzi informed of his health and to ask about the status of some of the questions. The operational deficit was one of the burdens lightened for him by Cardinal Mooney:

> I wrote Cardinal Mooney asking him to settle the difficult problem [College deficit] in some way he thought fit and if necessary ask the approval of the individual members of the Board. Evidently he preferred to avoid this as appears from the inclosure [sic]. Please keep it for the time being, and give it to me when I return. I am glad he settled it easily without the formality of voting. I also sent to him as the new Chairman of the Board, new material and a new Economo whom I hope will be here in September. The first draft of the New Constitution [for the College] is about ready also.

O'Connor's reference was to the cable Mooney had sent to the College on July 24th,[369] which Lacy forwarded to the Rector on July 27th,[370] and which O'Connor sent along with his letter to Galeazzi: "Telephone conversation with Treasurer [Spellman] give assurance that 1949 practice regarding deficit holds for this year. Letter to follow. Regards, + Mooney."[371]

The good news about Spellman's defeat concerning the College deficit, at least for the present fiscal year, was followed by more good news and some bad news from Galeazzi: despite the sudden death of one of the partners of the construction company, the Janiculum work

---

[369] Cable Detroit July 24, 1951, Mooney to O'Connor, CUA, *O'Connor Papers*, Box 46: *MJ O'Connor, Personal*. Folder: *O'Connor, Martin J. Rector—Personal*.

[370] Cable Rome July 27, 1951, Lacey to O'Connor, KC, *Enrico Galeazzi Papers, No. Amer. Coll, Corresp Martin J. O'Connor, 1950-1952*, Box 30, File 11.

[371] Cable Detroit July 24, 1951, Mooney to O'Connor, CUA, *O'Connor Papers*, Box 46: *MJ O'Connor, Personal*. Folder: *O'Connor, Martin J. Rector—Personal*.

continued; but Andreotti and the Italian government were in crisis, so nothing could now be done about the blocked lire.[372]

O'Connor was a weakened man, and his health problems and stress continued. He wrote this to Galeazzi, enclosing copies of letters from Cardinals Mooney and Stritch about the College deficit:

> you will see that Cardinal S [Stritch in reference to the College property title] has done a complete *volte-face*. But it looks like difficulty after difficulty, again.

> My conversations with you have been and will always be confidential. I am grateful that during this time of extreme worry I have had your understanding. We should not blind ourselves to the fact that the situation [tension between Spellman and O'Connor] is known and is being observed. For much has occurred for it not to be known. When the August 'feria' are past we should give careful thought to the report for the Fall, it seems to me, in order to have a minimum of problems in Washington.[373]

On his way back to Rome, O'Connor stopped at the Villa San Girolamo in Fiesole, outside Florence. He wrote the Count that he intended to remain at the nursing and retirement home in the care of the Irish nuns, and then proceed to Rome, "When I do, I think I will go directly to the English Hospital and await the arrival of the Boston pilgrims." He continued:

> Here I have been spending about fifteen hours a day in bed. As I suspected my blood pressure was 60-90;

---

[372] Vatican July 27, 1951, Galeazzi to O'Connor, KC, *Enrico Galeazzi Papers, No. Amer. Coll, Corresp, Most Rev. Martin J. O'Connor, 1951-1953*, Box 30, File 19.

[373] Lucerne August 7, 1951, O'Connor to Galeazzi, KC, *Galeazzi Papers, No. Amer. Coll, Corresp, Martin J. O'Connor, 1950-1951*, Box 30, File 11.

90 a maximum, makes me feel as if the end of the world were just around the corner. It is a sure antidote for too much success.

By the time I return to Rome I hope the pressure will be up to my normal, which is 120.

I have thought over many of the things we talked about [at Circeo], too much I suppose for my own peace of mind. I do hope everything works out satisfactorily. However I cannot permit myself to attempt the impossible simply through fear of resigning. To think of making up a deficit according to the suggestions [of Spellman that the Rector do fundraising work] would kill me physically and is totally unnecessary. However we will wait and see and prepare as thoroughly as possible for November [bishops' meeting].

Please do not think it necessary to answer this note. I will see you soon in Rome and by that time, I hope, my pressure will permit me a brighter outlook on life. As a fellow sufferer, you will understand.[374]

---

[374] San Girolamo, Fiesole 1951, O'Connor to Galeazzi, KC, *Enrico Galeazzi Papers*, above ref.

Chapter 6

Unblocking the Lire, Completing the Construction

> *"This additional percentage is rather minimal in relation to a construction project begun in 1947 and that will come to an end, with most of it paid for, in 1954; in other words, more than seven years; a long period in which the rise in costs reflected above, in light of the unique market conditions created following upon various international events, whose repercussions have affected both the construction work and the administration of the College."*
> —Francesco Silvestri, College Attorney, 1953

Once the vacations of *ferragosto* were over, the Roman world began to move once again. On September 1, 1951, De Gasperi wrote Spellman about the blocked lire negotiations. De Gasperi presumed Galeazzi had kept Spellman informed that any deal should not use the term *blocked lire*, especially while the Italian government continued its own negotiations with the American film companies. The government would consider assisting the College because of the "unique nature of the request", which would not be a new concession by the government, but which could be considered the "logical and conclusive next step to the release of funds in 1949 at the beginning of construction work on the College . . . and rather as a completion of that earlier decision." The one caution was that this could not in any way negatively impact the Italo-American film industry relationships and discussions.[375]

---

[375] Sheen, Erica, "Un-American: Dmytryk, Rossellini, and *Christ in Concrete*", in Krutnik, Frank [ed], *Un-American Hollywood*, New Brunswick, 2007, p. 39 ff. The Italian government's negotiations with the film companies had

Possibly recalling the international publicity launched by the *New York Times* at the time of the initial government license in 1949, De Gasperi cautioned Spellman that this should not be publicized, and that this would be a one-time and limited provision, which His Eminence should bear in mind. Always keen to shore up American financial and political support for his government, and knowing that Spellman was a key figure in maintaining American governmental foreign aid and Catholic charitable assistance to Italy,[376]De Gasperi clearly stated that the young Americans who would study in Rome at the new College atop the Janiculum, ". . . could not but become, by merely living within the Capital, sincere and true friends of Italy."[377]

Andreotti followed, writing Galeazzi on the same day, including along with his note detailed financial information about three of the American film companies that might prove helpful to the College construction, adding "this should show that it might be most advantageous to look to Metro Goldwyn Mayer [Loew's International Corporation] instead of to Warner Brothers, as Spellman noted."[378]

This made perfect sense, because Spellman had a long relationship with Louis B. Mayer. In 1944, Mayer, head of Metro-Goldwyn-Mayer, struck up a working relationship with Spellman. The friendship continued for years, and was the subject of one of many articles about Spellman, so often based on rumor or worse, by Drew Pearson

---

much to do with attempting to align their productions with the social and political program of De Gasperi and his government. Spellman, likewise, found himself embroiled in an American legal controversy about his condemnation of Roberto Rossellini's *The Miracle* and its New York City showing in January 1951, which ultimately went to the state supreme court, and Spellman's defeat.

[376] *Mission Bulletin*, May, 1957, Vol. IX, No. 5, p. 318: Working with the United States Government, the American Catholic Relief Services and the National Catholic Welfare Conference were the largest distributors of U.S. surplus food overseas after the War.

[377] Rome September 1, 1951, Alcide De Gasperi to Spellman, KC, *Enrico Galeazzi, No. Amer. Coll, Corresp Francis Cardinal Spellman, 1950-1951, 1953-1954*, Box 30, File 17.

[378] Rome September 1, 1951, Andreotti to Galeazzi, KC, *Enrico Galeazzi Papers, No. Amer. Coll, Corresp Giulio Andreotti, 1951*, Box 30, File 18.

in 1944. The barb was published in his *Merry-go-Round*, syndicated in numerous American newspapers around the country, as a literary caricature of persons of influence. Pearson was particularly interested in the Catholic-Jewish relationship, and its influence as exercised in electing Franklin D. Roosevelt. In his 1944 piece, Pearson stated that Mayer hoped to produce a movie version of the European Passion Plays, and requested Spellman's permission that a priest of the Archdiocese of New York play the part of the Savior. According to Pearson, Spellman agreed, so long as Mayer promised not to offer the priest a film career.[379]

Nasty innuendo aside, the Spellman-Mayer relationship was more than professional, and, in an age when anti-Semitism and anti-Catholic sentiments were quite alive and well in Protestant America, it raised some eyebrows that so powerful a Jewish movie mogul and so influential a Catholic prelate should join forces.[380] Mayer kept an oil painting of the Cardinal in his library, and dined with Spellman each time he was in New York City.[381] Spellman was even named an honorary pallbearer at Mayer's funeral in 1957, along with President Harry Truman and dozens of other American "celebrities". And now the friendship came in handy for the College.[382]

By September 3rd, the deal was done, and Andreotti notified Galeazzi that Spellman had sent the favorable response of the Italian

---

[379] Drew Pearson, *Merry-go-Round*, May 25, 1944, a copy of which can be found in NYC, S/C-35: *National Legion of Decency*, Folder 3. Another appeared in the July 28, 1949 number of various American newspapers, entitled, *On the Catholic-Jewish Political Bond*.

[380] Twentieth Century Fox produced the 1947 sensation, *Gentleman's Agreement* starring Gregory Peck about anti-Semitism in upper class Protestant America.

[381] Gabler, Neal, *An Empire of Their Own*, New York, 1989, p. 285.

[382] N.p. October 25, 1950, Louis B. Mayer to Spellman, NYC, SC-32, Folder 4: *To Card. Spellman, Louis B. Mayer*: "There is so much for which I am thankful and grateful to you, but one of the outstanding lessons which have come to me is the inspiration I receive from our friendship. It grows greater every time I see you." Mayer went on to thank Spellman for his gift of cufflinks bearing the Cardinals' initials.

government to New York.[383] The agreement involved the purchase of 1 billion lire, blocked in the account of Loew's International Corporation (MGM). Of that, 900 million lire was transferred to the College account in the Roman office of Credito Italiano on October 15th; the remaining 100 million lire would be paid during 1952.[384]

Galeazzi was still concerned about O'Connor's health, and accompanied the Rector to the Rome airport when he left for New York on October 12th. O'Connor expressed his thanks after his arrival in New York: "I deeply appreciated this delicate act of kindness very much."[385] He reported that he had met with Spellman the next day, presented a package from Galeazzi, and discussed the College. Spellman was intent that the students move into the new seminary by October 1952. But O'Connor had to break the news that, even though the construction was moving ahead, the earliest transfer of the students might not be until February 1953, with a possible May inauguration date. He continued to Galeazzi:

> I do not think His Eminence was too pleased with deferring the transfer of the students, but when he has more time to think it over and I have more chance to explain, I do not anticipate serious objections. I also mentioned having expressed to the Holy Father the hope that he would be present at the inauguration . . .

O'Connor had a number of private audiences with Pius XII during the previous few years to discuss the College construction and the seminary program, among other topics of importance.[386] The

---

[383] Rome September 3, 1951, Andreotti to Galeazzi, KC, *Enrico Galeazzi Papers, No. Amer. Coll, Corresp Giulio Andreotti, 1951*, Box 30, File 18.

[384] Rome October 18, 1951, Burns to Maguire, NAC, *Coll. Amer, Corresp Rettori, Card. Spellman—M.C. Geough* [sic].

[385] Scranton October 20, 1951, O'Connor to Galeazzi, KC, *Enrico Galeazzi Papers, No. Amer. Coll, Corresp Martin J. O'Connor, 1950-1951*, Box 30, File 11: This is marked "Personal, No Copy."

[386] Stamford, May 31, 2012, Interview of Mr. Thomas McKee by the author. Mr. McKee was a student at the new College from 1954 until November

most recent was on October 11th, at which he invited the Holy Father to preside at the inauguration of the new building in the spring of 1953.[387] The Rector continued to Galeazzi:

> At the airport, I had little time or privacy to tell you that the Holy Father was tenderly kind to me on my departure. He was much interested in the photographs, and I am afraid is sometimes gently amused by my enthusiasm when he has the worries of the world.

The relationship between O'Connor and the Pope is attested to in a very interesting original document found in the O'Connor Papers at the American Catholic History Research Center and University Archives in Washington, D.C. It is entitled, *Report of Mother Pascalina*, dated June 30, 1960, handwritten and signed by Madre Pascalina, the housekeeper for Pope Pius XII, and a woman of great influence. The document is formally notarized, and witnessed by Father William Bachman [NAC 1935], then the College spiritual director, and by Father Robert McNamara [NAC 1936], College alumnus and then Professor of Church History at Saint Bernard Seminary in Rochester, New York. It is worth quoting in full:

> One day His Holiness, returning from an Audience which he had granted, asked me: 'Mother, have you heard that His Excellency, Bishop O'Connor, is scheduled to return to America? They want to make him Bishop of a small diocese in the United States. Cardinal Spellman is in favor of this. However, I have indicated that Bishop O'Connor is to remain here in Rome. I know Bishop O'Connor quite well; he is

---

1956. He told me that during these years when the United States had no formal diplomatic relations with the Holy See, O'Connor served as the sole unofficial American contact in Rome who had access to the Pope, who worked to express the policies and concerns of the American government and to uphold the interests of the Church in the United States to the Holy Father.

[387] Rome October 27, 1951, O'Connor to Episcopal Board Members, CUA, *O'Connor Papers*, Box 44: *NAC*, File: *Rector's Report (Nov 1951)*.

very well informed and is extremely well disposed to assist Us in every way possible. The Bishop is a very understanding person and I do wish him well. But if he goes, we have no idea what his successor will be like.'

To which I replied: 'No, I haven't heard anything.'

Later, while at table, His Holiness remarked: 'Mother, I wonder if you could find out how Bishop O'Connor feels about the proposed change; because I would not like to interfere if the Bishop prefers to return to America.' I thereupon assured His Holiness that I would inquire right away.

Upon inquiry, I discovered that His Excellency had placed himself at the complete disposition of his superiors. He was quite willing to remain or to leave, according to their decision in his regard.

His Holiness was pleased to learn this and said: 'That is fine, because we would not like to impose any burden on Bishop O'Connor after so many years of loyal service.' And later that evening, in the presence of Count Galeazzi, Carlo Pacelli and myself, His Holiness repeated the same thoughts, which He had earlier expressed to me. The Holy Father made it clear that it was His will that Bishop O'Connor remain. However, He said that He had already given an order to this effect. His Holiness singled out Bishop O'Connor in view of his fine record over the years and said that there wasn't the slightest fault to be found in all that time.[388]

---

[388] *Report of Mother Pascalina*, June 30, 1960, CUA, *O'Connor Papers*, Box 24: *MJ O'Connor Misc & Unfiled Corr*, Folder: *Correspondence to 1972*.

It can be reasonably assumed that, during these years, the interests of the College and its Rector were made known to the Pope and Madre Pascalina by Count Galeazzi. He was considered the most influential layman in the Vatican because of his long and close personal friendship with Pius XII, his decades of work in the Vatican during the war, and as the representative of the Knights of Columbus in Rome.[389]

O'Connor appreciated his own friendship with Galeazzi. As he prepared for the November 1951 bishops' meeting, he expressed his gratitude to the Count:

> All in all, I am feeling very much better than on my previous visits before the meeting. Probably there are two causes: one spiritual, and the other very physical in the form of a rest in Switzerland last summer. I feel better prepared for this meeting than for others in the past, and I hope and pray that the delicate situations will be adjustable. Needless to say, I will always be profoundly grateful for your sympathetic support

---

[389] Note pad, "11 a.m., Friday 24", O'Connor to Burns, CUA, Box 42: *NAC subfile*, Folder: *Galeazzi, Count, NAC-talks with*: There are 7 pages of O'Connor's handwritten notes in pencil on yellow legal pad paper listing things to do. There are a number of these notes throughout the various archives, reminders to himself. Among items on this "to do" list, is an entry concerning a meeting of O'Connor:
"Cornerstone; Mother Pasqualina [sic]—Tuesday—10:30." The cornerstone of the Janiculum seminary chapel was a gift from the Pope, taken from the foundations of Saint Peter's Basilica then recently uncovered during the discovery of the ancient Roman cemetery, today known as the *Scavi Vaticani*, in which was re-discovered the tomb of St. Peter. That Count Galeazzi had a hand in obtaining this singular gift of the Pope to the College is quite possible, because he was the chief architectural consultant for the excavations, as well as a personal friend of the Pope, Madre Pasqualina, Prince Carlo Pacelli and O'Connor. The inscription reads: *Lapis Auspicialis E Vaticanae Basilicae Hypogeis Erutus*: "This cornerstone was excavated from the deepest foundations of the Vatican Basilica."

last spring, without which I am afraid I would have experienced serious consequences.[390]

The College Board was scheduled to meet on November 14th, and O'Connor planned to address them, as well as all the members of the hierarchy gathered for their annual meeting the next day. Soon after arriving home, O'Connor visited both Cardinals Stritch and Mooney, writing to Galeazzi, "It makes me very happy to be able to tell you how much pleased they are with your work for the College."[391]

The Rector had the support of both Cardinals, and they intended to make proposals about the College to the Board themselves, rather than have the Rector make them.[392] Two weeks before the meeting, the Rector sent a memorandum summary of the more important points to the Board members, detailing the construction, finances, legal and seminary matters, "as I am anxious to have direct authorization for a number of decisions which will have to be made."[393] He had prepared the report with Galeazzi, Silvestri, Burns, and Lacy, and it was an end-run around Spellman, worked out by the Rector with Stritch and Mooney to push College matters forward.

The Rector's report for the November 14, 1951 meeting was clear and very detailed, and it included those reports by Galeazzi, Silvestri, Burns, Lacy and Lafferty as separate chapters. Spellman had insisted that O'Connor's reports offer more detail.[394] The Rector gave the Cardinal Treasurer exactly what he asked for in this 52-page report.

---

[390] Scranton, October 20, 1951, O'Connor to Galeazzi, KC, *Enrico Galeazzi Papers, No. Amer. Coll, Correspond Martin J. O'Connor, 1950-1951*, Box 30, File 11.

[391] Scranton November 2, 1951, O'Connor to Galeazzi, KC, *Enrico Galeazzi Papers*, above ref.

[392] O'Connor was also working with Cardinal Stritch to secure a community of Swiss religious Sisters to head up the domestic service at the Janiculum.

[393] Scranton November 10, 1951, O'Connor to Galeazzi, KC, *Enrico Galeazzi Papers*, above ref.

[394] New York April 5, 1951, Spellman to O'Connor, NYC, Box S/C-73, Folder 16: *To Card. Spellman, No. Amer. Coll.*

O'Connor knew well what he was doing, counseled by both Galeazzi and Silvestri as he prepared this report. Spellman demanded a more detailed Rector's report. Here it was. He wanted costs cut, and so the Rector cut them, and informed the Board of the very real reasons for higher construction costs in Italy, of which the Rector was entirely powerless to change. If the Board wanted the new seminary, then the Board would have to figure out how they would pay to build and operate one. It was not the Rector's responsibility, since he had been charged with the restoration of all the College properties and re-opening of the seminary and graduate house of studies after the war; the opening and operation of the Audience Office to the Vatican; the construction of a new seminary on the Janiculum; the securing of episcopal support for the new construction; the recruitment of new students for the seminary; and the daily running of the seminary and graduate house. Any one of those was sufficiently burdensome, especially in post-war Italy; that he should be responsible for raising funds for all this as well, was impossible. If the Board or Spellman did not like his work, then the Rector was prepared to resign his office. Kealy had faced similar challenges, although he had enjoyed Spellman's friendship and favor, and still he resigned.

O'Connor knew well, as did Galeazzi, that neither the Board nor Spellman would want another Rector resigning, not from a project that had become so high-profile in the Vatican, Italy, and the United States. O'Connor had the upper hand—and the support of many bishops, along with that of at least the Cardinal Archbishops of Detroit, Philadelphia, and Chicago, of Count Galeazzi, of Madre Pascalina, and of the Pope, himself.[395]

The Rector presented his annual report during the November 14th meeting of the Episcopal Board.[396] While the construction costs were still within the 1947 estimated budget, the line item "unforeseen

---

[395] Washington, D.C. December 11, 1952, Msgr. Joseph Christopher to Msgr. Florence D. Cohalan, NYC, Box S/C-12, Folder 2: *About Cardinal Spellman*: "The Pope, Galeazzi & Spellie (in that order) are running the Church. I knew S.[pellman] disliked Bp. O'Connor who has done a magnificent job, but unfortunately was not chosen by Spellie!"

[396] *Report of the Rector of the North American College in Rome to the Members of the Episcopal Administrative Committee for the College in Preparation*

expenses" had been spent because of various types of cost increases since January 1, 1951. Contributing to these additional costs was the repeated insistence by the contracting company for a revision of their contract based upon the increased prices of material and labor since the contract signing. To round out the report on construction and financing, O'Connor made mention that "in the estimate there is only a provision made for the essentials in the construction of the church." The Alumni Fund had "more than $100,000 less in it than the predicted cost of the Chapel or $350,000. I had instructed the architect accordingly to restrict the costs to essentials and consequently to exclude all decorations." The chapel fund was Spellman's responsibility, as were the alumni contributions.

The financial report, written by Monsignor Joseph Lacy, opened with a note by the Rector, repeating his annual warning about the seminary operational costs:

> "I am still of the opinion that our ordinary income will not be sufficient to maintain the college even if the pension rate is increased considerably. At present, the Rector of the Scots College, with more than thirty years experience in Rome, charges 190 pounds a year and has a deficit which is absorbed yearly by the Archdiocese of Glasgow. It is expected that the tuition is to be increased there."

Lacy's report bore this out: even with increased charges for tuition, room and board, other sources of income would be necessary. Funds for the operation of the seminary were derived from direct student room and board payments from individual dioceses, the G.I. Bill, and the income on used and unused burses, created for just this purpose. "Originally, a burse of $5,000 [$44,247.12] was supposed to yield the sum sufficient for the support of a student for twelve months. Today, seven times that amount is necessary to defray only the figures tentatively set by the Board." Lacy reported that the

---

for Their Meeting on November 14, 1951, CUA, *O'Connor Papers,* Box 44: *NAC,* Folder: *Rector's Report (Nov 1951).*

operating deficit had been covered by drawing on the interest income from the College Building Fund account at the Credito Italiano: the deficit for 1950-1951 totaled $6,996.26 [$61,912.86].[397]

Expenses for the upcoming academic year would be only slightly reduced. Various factors were responsible for this, such as the fluctuating currency exchange rates; costs for food and utilities, which had recently increased; the salary increase for the faculty, including that for the superior of the graduate house of studies; and, now, the full expense for the Audience Office would be borne by the College alone. Lacy continued reminding the Board that they had mandated the salary increases and that the cost for the Audience Office be covered by the College budget, yet had not provided funding for them, so the College would begin the year with an operational deficit.

To the repeated insistence by Spellman and Maguire that the potential for fundraising through the Audience Office could be lucrative, Lacy included a page entitled "Gifts". During the year, the College had received a grand total of $4,746.10 [$42,000.25] in the form of 43 gifts, which "range in number from offerings of $1.00 usually sent to the College with a note of thanks for arranging the audience, to a single gift of $2,500.00 [$22,123.56] by a friend of the institution who insisted that he remain anonymous." This detail of numerous small gifts could only have galled Spellman and Maguire, who repeatedly insisted that the Rector was lax in mining the fundraising potential of the Audience Office and College. Lacy informed the Board that these gifts were not listed in the general report on College income, because the amounts varied from year to year, and were never large. Likewise, when a gift was given it usually was accompanied by a "suggestion as to its use", something for the chapel, library, or "for some form of entertainment or refreshment for the students." These funds were used during the 1950-1951 academic year to pay for "altar linens, altar furnishings and vestments . . . .", which should have been included by the Board in the annual College operational budget, but were not, and for a

[397] *Report of the Rector, November 14, 1951*, CUA, *O'Connor Papers*, Box 44: NAC, Folder: *Rector's Report (Nov 1951)*, p. 6.

"special entertainment for the students, and necessary disbursements in gratuities and charity."[398]

As a means of addressing the problem of an annual operational deficit, the Rector suggested the creation of "a special fund of approximately $20,000 [$176,988.46], which would remain constant from year to year." That would take the place of the College Building Fund, which was serving the purpose to cover temporary deficits, and then was paid back.[399]

Besides the progress in the construction, both O'Connor and Galeazzi knew that the bishops would be interested in the cost, especially the Cardinal Treasurer. Their October report stressed this, despite all the delays and increased costs of building materials, the Rector and architect felt sure that, as of August 31, 1952, the complete cost for construction of the building "would remain within the estimated limits of 2.027.914.800 lire. However, they cautioned that this was dependent upon the exchange rate remaining at least 600 lire per $1.[400] Likewise, this did not include the final costs for the artistic decorations for the chapel interior, including the high altar and the side altar, the bronze *Via Crucis*, the various frescoes, carved marble holy water stoups, "and in general, for all the furnishings of the Chapel and the Crypts."[401]

---

[398] *Report of the Rector*, ibid., p. 21.

[399] *Report of the Rector*, ibid., p. 24.

[400] Ibid, p. 2: They claimed this included the increase of 1.035.000.000 lire for the bonus for the construction company of Ravello and Mengarini at the conclusion of the project. Silvestri reported that the process for transferring the title of the Umiltà property from Propaganda Fide still dragged on.

[401] Cable Vatican November 6, 1952, Galeazzi to O'Connor, KC, *Enrico Galeazzi Papers, No. Amer. Coll, Corresp Most Rev Martin J. O'Connor, 1950-1953*, Box 30, File 9: Galeazzi provided the Rector more detail about costs for the November bishops' meeting: the costs for all artistic decorations in the chapel and annexes, including costs for the altars and furnishings, mosaics, paintings, bronze Stations of the Cross, stained glass windows, and other items, were not included in the general estimate for the chapel costs. These might cost an additional $75,000. Scranton November 17, 1952, O'Connor to Galeazzi, KC, above ref, Box 30, File 12: "Informally I can assure you that the Episcopal Committee was disposed to proceed with the work of decorating the Chapel at your estimate of $75,000 [$663,706.73 in 2012 dollars]. However, before

As the year progressed, other such expenses were incurred for the completion of the College that were not included in the original construction budget.[402] They were noted by O'Connor, Galeazzi, and Spellman, and reported to the Board.[403] The bishops showed little concern, presuming that these would be paid somehow and at some time. The ambiguity of the situation would result in angry finger pointing by June 1953, when all these extras were added up, apparently bursting the construction budget wide open.[404]

There had been a six month work stoppage, from March through the end of September, 1951, due to the untimely and sudden death of Arnaldo Mengarini, one of the partners of the general contracting company of Ravello & Mengarini, responsible for constructing the new College; an unusually severe winter; difficulty in obtaining building material; and the problem of retaining skilled workers in

---

we go ahead, it will be better for me to have the minutes of the meeting as an instruction for both of us."

[402] Cable Vatican November 12, 1952, Galeazzi to O'Connor, KC, in above ref: The rough estimate for the total reconditioning of the Casa San Giovanni for use as a convent for the sisters after the graduate priests moved to the Umiltà, was $60,000 [$530,965.38 in 2012 dollars], without furnishings.

[403] New York January 22, 1953, Spellman to Board Members, NYC, Box S/C-73, Folder 2: *To Card. Spellman, N. Amer. Coll*: Spellman approved O'Connor's recommendation to pay Silvestri a $3,000 [$26,548.27] bonus, "as special compensation for his important, exacting and time consuming efforts in connection with the litigation with the Propaganda and transaction in blocked lire." Spellman also hinted at another enormous, yet unbudgeted expense: the price to obtain the civil transfer of the property title for the Palazzo Orsini from the Propaganda.

[404] New York July 1, 1953, Maguire to O'Connor, CUA, *O'Connor Papers*, Box 25: *MJ O'Connor Misc & Unfiled Corr*, Folder 5: Maguire sent Spellman's new list for inscriptions on enormous marble slabs, which are today found on the *Terra* and *Piano Nobile* floors of the College, in the chapel and throughout the seminary: three bear the names of the American bishops in attendance at the October 14th dedication ceremonies; another lists the members of the Episcopal Board; another, excerpts from the Pope's address on dedication day of the College; another bears the Pope's 1948 letter to the American bishops, and many more with commemorative messages and names of donors. This is a small fortune's worth of massive marble plaques, representing one of many substantial costs ordered by Spellman but never included in the construction budget. And there were many more such expenses.

reinforced concrete, since most were members of the Communist Party, who caused "considerable trouble" among the workers on the Janiculum site, because it was Vatican territory.

Despite these setbacks the work had progressed, including the completion of the reinforced skeleton superstructure of the entire building and the facing in Travertine and white brick of some lower portions of the building begun. The construction of interior walls and work on the plumbing and heating systems had also begun, and the terraces had been waterproofed. O'Connor wrote that it was hoped that the

> building will be finished in October, 1952, with the exception of fixtures, furnishings, decorations, and gardens. It will not be hygienically a safe building into which to put students at that time, and besides which workmen will still be present in large numbers.[405]

The Rector informed the Board that, "It is proposed to move the students from the Via dell'Umiltà to the new building during the 1952-1953 academic year, possibly in February." Likewise, one plan was that the 21 student priests would occupy one of the wings in the new seminary by October 1952, remaining one year until the Umiltà property could be prepared for their permanent residence. Spellman insisted on these early dates, which the Rector opposed because he knew they were unrealistic, which was the reason for their inclusion by O'Connor in this report to the Board members now.

The Rector ended his report asking that the Board permit him to pursue negotiations with a community of German religious Sisters and one of Swiss religious Sisters, with the purpose of hiring one of the communities to oversee the domestic services provided by the College for the students and faculty. Cardinal Stritch had assisted O'Connor in his initial negotiations with the Sisters, as had Galeazzi.

---

[405] *Report of the Rector of the North American College in Rome to the Members of the Episcopal Administrative Committee for the College in Preparation for Their Meeting on November 14, 1951,* CUA, *O'Connor Papers,* Box 44: *NAC,* Folder: *Rector's Report (Nov 1951).*

O'Connor preferred the Swiss congregation, whose members had experience working in two seminaries.[406]

One reason for hiring religious Sisters was the reduction of paid laypersons. While this would help reduce payroll costs, there was another benefit. Not only were the Italian labor laws complicated, but the labor unions, and the type of people applying for these jobs had changed since before the war. "Service is no longer a career, especially in metropolitan centers, and a criminal and faithless element has invaded domestic service to a very dangerous degree."[407] The College provided room and board for many of their lay employees, as well as religious services for their spiritual welfare. A priest from Catholic Action in Italy provided two spiritual conferences, monthly; Sunday Mass and daily Rosary were provided the employees; and, once the new College opened, they would have their own chapel.[408] O'Connor cabled Galeazzi: "Report accepted. Future optimistic. Arriving Rome December six. Grateful Regards."[409]

O'Connor spent the winter continuing his work to secure the property title from the Propaganda; overseeing the construction project on the Janiculum; securing new students for the 1952-53 academic year; hiring religious Sisters; and running the daily life of the seminary [with 154 students during the 1951-52 academic

---

[406] Scranton November 2, 1951, O'Connor to Galeazzi, KC, *Enrico Galeazzi Papers, No. Amer. Coll, Corresp Martin J. O'Connor, 1950-1951*, Box 30, File 11.

[407] *Report of the Rector*, November 14, 1951, CUA, *O'Connor Papers*, Box 44: *NAC*, Folder: *Rector's Report (Nov 1951)*, p. 51.

[408] *Report of the Rector*, ibid., p. 7.

[409] Cable Washington, D.C. November 17, 1951, O'Connor to Galeazzi, KC, *Enrico Galeazzi Papers, No. Amer. Coll, Corresp Martin J. O'Connor, 1950-1951*, Box 30, File 11. O'Connor sent a second cable to Galeazzi the same day: "Hope you can accept invitation Ordination and dinner December Eighth." In above KC reference. Rome January 8, 1952, O'Connor to Abp Filippo Bernardini, CUA, *O'Connor Papers*, Box 1: *MJ O'Connor Gen. Corr*, Folder B: *(1947-52)*: O'Connor wrote the Nuncio to Bern that the December 8, 1951 ordination "was the first full post-war class for ordination to the priesthood and it gave me much consolation after the difficulties attendant on the reconstruction of the College."

year, from 67 American dioceses], graduate house of studies, and Audience Office.[410]

On December 6, 1951, one student, James Markham [NAC 1951] was ordained a deacon. On December 8th, 21 deacons were "raised to the priesthood in the chapel of the College" by the Rector. Two men were too young to be ordained on December 8th, and they were ordained priests on February 12, 1952. Ceremonies for minor orders were also celebrated for the second and third year theologians.

In his April 1952 report to the Episcopal Board, O'Connor told them that the American Express Company predicted the upcoming tourist season to be the greatest "in history." Quoting from the company's monthly *News Bulletin* for March 1952, the Rector told the bishops that steamer bookings to Europe and the Mediterranean were already difficult to obtain, even though six new ocean liners had been added to the already existing fleet. "With virtually all tourist flights already booked from 78 to 100% full through July, Europe's greatest season is definitely assured." That meant record numbers of American visitors might be expected at the College. "At the end of this year we will give a summary of the work of the audience office and make definite recommendations, for a permanent arrangement."[411]

---

[410] Rome December 18, 1951, O'Connor to Rev. Raymond A. McGowan [NAC 1912], CUA, *O'Connor Papers*, Box 25: *MJ O'Connor Misc & Unfiled Corr*, Folder 10: The Rector also was busy preparing a new library collection at the College, and asked various priests and bishops for donations and recommendations for important approved theological works. Rome June 11, 1952, O'Connor to Spellman, KC, *Enrico Galeazzi Papers, No. Amer. Coll, Corresp Most Rev Martin J. O'Connor, 1952*, Box 30, File 12: Cardinal Spellman sent some books, delivered to the College by Count Galeazzi.

[411] *Report of the Rector*, April 22, 1952, p. 15, CUA, *O'Connor Papers*, Box 44: *NAC*, Folder: *Rector's Report (April 1952)*. The volume of correspondence by O'Connor during these years is staggering, even for the 1950's when letter writing was more frequently used than was the telephone, which was expensive and cumbersome, especially international service after the war. In the archives I visited, there is an immense number of O'Connor's letters and reports: responses to seminary applications, letters to bishops for fundraising, support of the College, or seminarian enrollment; letters to visitors to Rome concerning papal audience tickets; construction and financial statements and reports; letters to Italian tradesmen, American corporations and business

During the next six months, work at the new College site slowed, the result of further labor problems in Rome, financial problems suffered by the contractor Ravello & Mengarini following Mengarini's death, and the continuing escalation of costs for building material in Italy. Likewise, Mengarini's widow, the Contessa Pia Buonaccorsi, brought legal action against the College, demanding a change in the contract following the death of her husband. Despite this, it was still hoped that the basic structure would be completed sometime in late 1952,[412] leaving only the final outfitting and furnishing of the interior. Work on the grounds would take a few months longer to complete.[413]

---

officials eager to sell the College American products or to use the College name for advertising; letters to seminarians and their families; letters to faculty members and alumni; even responses to Christmas cards or Easter greetings, all personalized, commenting on how pretty the card might be, or how charming the poetic saying enclosed. His responses, either short notes or lengthy letters, are never perfunctory; most are lengthy and all are individualized. The only exceptions can be found to simple notifications that applications for audience tickets had been received, and that was only because the number of requests skyrocketed as the years passed.

[412] Chicago February 27, 1951, Kealy to O'Connor, CUA, *O'Connor Papers*, Box 37: *MJ O'Connor Rel. Org/Priests Corr. Folder: Kealy, Msgr. J. Gerald (1946-56)*: The former Rector asked if the 1952 alumni meeting might be held at the new College, which reportedly would be opened and inaugurated in the Spring, 1952. Rome March 8, 1951, O'Connor to Kealy, CUA, above ref: Acknowledges some misunderstanding, since he had been telling people the basic structure of the College would not be completed until later in 1952. "Only recently I discussed with Count Galeazzi the question of a possible date for the inauguration and we both seem to think that the Spring of 1953 would be the best date, practically speaking." O'Connor suggested an alumni meeting at the College in 1959, in conjunction with the College centennial observances.

[413] Vatican March 20, 1952, Galeazzi Report to Episcopal Committee, in *Report of the Rector of the North American College in Rome to the Members of the Episcopal Administrative Committee for the College in Preparation for Their Meeting on April 22, 1952*, CUA, *O'Connor Papers*, Box 44: *NAC*, Folder: *Rector's Report (April 1952)*, pp. 2-3. Galeazzi reminded the bishops, "the interior artistic decorations of the Chapel, the vestments, and in general the 'furnishings', are not included in the original estimated cost."

By the beginning of July 1952, one of O'Connor's problems had been solved: the revision of construction prices demanded by the construction company, Ravello and Mengarini.[414] They requested a 6% increase of the total cost of the project, which totaled $100,000 [$884,942.31] above the fee originally agreed upon.[415] Both Galeazzi and Silvestri agreed this should be paid, not as a legal requirement under the terms of the original contract, but "under the aspect of equity". Both agreed there should be no revision of prices, but merely the paying of this sum to the contractor after the completion of the work, as a type of bonus. "Such a practice is not uncommon in Italy."[416] While this was not thought to exceed the estimated construction budget, the final decision would be left to the Board. Because Galeazzi recommended this, the Executive Committee of the Board, Cardinals Mooney, Stritch and Spellman, approved the plan.[417]

---

[414] Vatican July 10, 1952, Galeazzi to O'Connor, KC, *Enrico Galeazzi Papers, No. Amer. Coll., Corresp Most Rev Martin J. O'Connor, May-Aug 1952*, Box 50, File 16.

[415] Ibid, October 1, 1952, Report of the College Lawyer, Francesco Silvestri, p 6-14: The Italian courts decided against any modification of the original contract between Ravello & Mengarini and the College, following the sudden death of Mengarini, as his widow, Contessa Pia Buonaccorsi had insisted. The court observed that clause #12 in the contract explicitly prohibited revising the cost of building materials. The court ruled that the contracts were still in effect, having been signed in good faith by the College and by the construction company, despite the unexpected deaths of both partners. Nevertheless, because the market price for building materials had risen so exorbitantly, both Galeazzi and Silvestri suggested a type of "bonus" be offered the widow and her son, following the completion of the project, even though, strictly speaking, there was no legal obligation. One reason for this was to encourage the Contessa to return the workmen to the site after months of inactivity while awaiting the court's decision, and to assure that the men would complete their work quickly and well.

[416] Rome July 11, 1952, Burns to Cardinals Mooney, Stritch & Spellman, NAC, *NAC Construction 1925-1954*, #224, Folder: *NAC Construction 1952, Increased Costs.*

[417] Cable Detroit July 17, 1952, Mooney to Burns, NAC, above ref. New York August 4, 1952, Spellman to Burns, NAC, in above ref: For some reason, Spellman had the urge to clarify Mooney's cable: "Just to complete the record I wish to acknowledge your letter of July 11th and to say that immediately

The 1952-53 academic year opened with 157 seminarians, representing 73 American dioceses, living at the Umiltà property, and 21 student priests, representing 15 dioceses, at the Casa San Giovanni on the Janiculum. The pension rate approved by the Board was $800 *per annum* for both the seminarians and student priests, even though both the seminary and graduate house offered nearly twelve months of services, including the summer weeks at the Villa Santa Caterina. The Rector prepared the bishops for an inevitable tuition increase, both for the seminarians and student priests. He also shared with them the estimated costs for the renovation of the Umiltà property to accommodate the graduate student priests, after the new seminary was opened on the Janiculum. Because the building had only recently been renovated, with new plumbing and heating systems already installed, the cost would be minimal, $50,000 [$434,122.64], and the conversion of the building to provide 60 two-room suites for single occupancy (complete with a sink providing hot and cold running water in each room) could be completed by the summer of 1953.[418]

O'Connor used this opportunity to offer a two-page synopsis of the graduate program as an advertisement, assuring the American bishops that they could assign their priests to the new program at the Via dell'Umiltà with confidence. The College of Our Lady of Humility, as it was to be called, was located at the heart of the Eternal City, in an hygienic, modernized, well-run, and disciplined institution. There the student priests could pursue their higher academic degrees at some of the world's best universities, while strengthening their priestly vocations at the shrines and tombs of the Apostles and martyrs. The bishops could rest assured that their serious financial investment in the education of their student priests would be worth the cost and effort.

---

after its receipt I discussed its contents and the report accompanying it with Cardinal Mooney and Cardinal Stritch, and Cardinal Mooney agreed to telegraph you expressing our agreement with your proposal."

[418] *Report of the Rector of the North American College in Rome to the Members of the Episcopal Administrative Committee for the College in Preparation for Their Meeting on November 12, 1952,* p. viii-xi, CUA, *O'Connor Papers,* Box 44: *NAC,* Folder: *Rector's Reports, (Nov 1952).*

Silvestri reported to the Rector by mid-October 1952 that the Credito Italiano had renewed the College contract bringing the interest rate from 4 ½% to 5%. "This new rate is really exceptional and constitutes a big advantage for the North American College", he wrote.[419] Even Spellman reported on the positive status of the fundraising efforts for the seminary construction in his November letter to the Episcopal Board: $3,153,370.00 [$27,378,986.28] had been pledged for the new College. "It is anticipated that this amount, when fully paid, together with contributions received from the American College alumni, will be adequate to defray construction and furnishing costs."[420] The Rector reported these numbers to the bishops, who were as elated as he was:

> When I think that in 1946, there was only $300,000 [$3,539,769.23] on hand, the fact that we have received up to the present, in cash, $2,419,787.38 [$21,009,689.79] on the pledges and $256,000 [$2,222,707.92] in cash from the Alumni, the situation is encouraging.[421]

Along with his report, the Board approved O'Connor's suggestion that Columbus Day, October 12, 1953, be chosen for the inauguration of the new College, leading the Rector to cable Galeazzi, "Future optimistic.[422]

By March 1953, the Rector reported the construction of the walls of the new seminary was relatively complete, except for the finishing touches to the exterior, work being done floor by floor. Most

---

[419] Rome October 13, 1952, Silvestri to O'Connor, NAC, *Corresp Rettori e Card. Spellman—M.C. Geough* [sic].

[420] New York November 3, 1952, Spellman to Episcopal Board Members, KC, *Enrico Galeazzi Papers, No. Amer. Coll. Financial Management, 1949-1952,* Box 13, File 8.

[421] Scranton December 1, 1952, O'Connor to Galeazzi, KC, *Enrico Galeazzi Papers, No. Amer. Coll, Corresp Most Rev Martin J. O'Connor,* Box 30, File 12.

[422] Cable Washington, D.C. November 17, 1952, O'Connor to Galeazzi, KC, above ref, Box 30, File 11.

of the Travertine facing was finished, both inside and outside the building. Work on the four student residence floors continued, with those exterior walls completed, as well as much of the interior work. The interior plastering, the heating, water and electrical systems and installation of fixtures were nearing completion, with only the final installation of the marble work in the student bathrooms and showers at the end of the hallways, and the painting and covering of the walls in the student rooms with a newly developed plastic wallpaper left to complete. The interior walls on the *piano nobile*, or main ceremonial floor around the entire interior courtyard, were nearing completion as well, linking the chapel, library, refectory, and auditorium.

Work on the chapel was also going well. The reinforced concrete foundations and walls had set successfully; the upper portion of the cupola had not yet been poured. The exterior northern and eastern walls were closed up, and the Travertine facing would soon begin. In the two crypts, the final work on the walls had also begun, with the installation of radiant heating panels in the walls, which meant that the mosaic work on the floors and decoration of the walls could begin, as well.[423]

Notwithstanding the deaths of both Mr. Ravello and Mr. Mengarini, the increased material costs, labor difficulties, slowdowns, and strikes, the Rector and architect assured the bishops that the construction of the seminary would be completed, excluding complete furnishing and final interior decoration, by September 1953. Galeazzi reported that the number of workmen on site and in various workshops for the College project numbered 280 men; it would soon rise, he told the bishops, to around 310 men, in order to complete the work by the desired September 1953 date. The students might occupy the building by October.

On January 23, 1953, the tenth anniversary of his episcopal consecration, O'Connor wrote to Galeazzi, reflecting on their friendship and work in Rome:

---

[423]   Ibid, October 3, 1952, Report of the Architect, Count Enrico Galeazzi.

On this anniversary in particular my thoughts turn gratefully to you, whose patience and understanding have largely enabled me to persevere.

There have been occasions when I have been extremely discouraged and I assure you that your prudence and moral support helped me immeasurably.

Your generous and thoughtful gift of the series of exquisite silver medals issued during this Pontificate will always be a precious personal reminder of your interest in this anniversary. Strangely enough, I have always wanted some of these medals and now I have many of the most desirable ones.

It is true that my years in Rome have, through the College, associated me with this Pontificate. Such an association comes to very few persons and it has had a profound influence on my thought and life. Your gift is most appropriate for me and I value it not only because it comes from you but because it represents an association that has been priceless.

Again, my thanks and, if, from time to time I try your patience, forgive me! We are on the home stretch.[424]

But he found the "home stretch" to be somewhat bumpy, beginning with Cardinal Spellman. Soon after his success at the bishops' meeting, O'Connor invited the Pope to preside over the inauguration of the College on October 12th, but the Pontiff's schedule permitted October 14th, instead. Spellman was displeased that the decision to change the inauguration date was made without his knowledge or input—although both Cardinals Mooney and Stritch knew. Their growing influence on the Board during these final years of work on

---

[424] Rome January 27, 1943, O'Connor to Galeazzi, KC, *Enrico Galeazzi Papers*, above ref, Box 30, File 13.

the College he had worked on so diligently nettled the Archbishop of New York. He immediately notified Mr. William V. McCarthy of the Catholic Travel League that he would not attend the College inauguration, because his presence at the annual Al Smith dinner in New York City was essential[425], and informed Galeazzi in a brief note on February 7th.[426] The rumor arrived in Rome more quickly than did the mail. O'Connor learned of it from Monsignor Giovanni Montini's office, when he was given a date to meet with the Vatican acting Secretary of State about the College.[427]

Galeazzi sent off a letter marked *"Personale"* to Spellman on February 12th, urging him to attend, telling him that his presence at the inauguration would:

> be a sign of the completion of this work, which is in a great part due to your prudent initiative and ardent interest. The importance of this event, which is so relevant for American Catholics, will be notably lessened without you.[428]

[425] Alfred E. Smith (1873-1944) was the three-term Governor of New York and the first Roman Catholic presidential candidate. Beginning in 1945, the Alfred E. Smith Memorial Foundation hosts a white tie dinner at the Waldorf-Astoria Hotel to benefit Catholic Charities annually on the third Thursday in October. Since its beginning, the annual dinner attracts some of the most influential and powerful Americans, Catholic and non-Catholic alike.

[426] New York February 7, 1953, Spellman to Galeazzi, KC, *Enrico Galeazzi Papers, No. Amer. Coll, Corresp, Francis Cardinal Spellman, 1950-1952, 1953-1954*, Box 30, File 17.

[427] Rome "Sunday" [February 9, 1953], O'Connor to Galeazzi, KC, *Enrico Galeazzi Papers, No. Amer. Coll, Corresp Most Rev. Martin J. O'Connor, 1953-1954*, Box 30, File 13: In two notes attached to this letter, O'Connor had written in pencil: "Mr. McCarthy received a jolt", and, referring to Montini, "This is the effect of which I spoke and will be a helpful force. Excuse pencil." Montini was the future Pope Paul VI.

[428] Vatican February 12, 1953, Galeazzi to Spellman, KC, *Enrico Galeazzi Papers, No. Amer. Coll, Corresp, Francis Cardinal Spellman, 1950-1952, 1953-1954*, Box 30, File 17.

Spellman responded that, "Solely because of your urgent appeal am I arranging at considerable difficulty to transpose the date of the annual Al Smith Dinner." He continued:

> It is true, as you say, that for many motives I have had a deep interest in this project, but since Cardinal Mooney and Cardinal Stritch both plan to be present at the exercises and my participation will be purely incidental, it did not seem to me to be justifiable to take a long trip to Rome and back just for the purpose of participating in one brief ceremony, especially because of the necessity of my being present at the Al Smith Dinner. However, as I have stated, I shall now make arrangements to participate. I would prefer that you keep this information confidential for the present.[429]

Throughout March, April and May, the Cardinal Treasurer wrote a number of letters to O'Connor and Galeazzi asking for information concerning the new seminary chapel. Galeazzi sent him a cost list for the chapel decorations and furnishings. Spellman was especially interested in the high altar, which Galeazzi told him would cost $10,000 [$86,174.16] to build in carved marble and cast bronze.[430] During the April meeting of the Episcopal Board, Spellman renewed his decision to provide the cost of the chapel High Altar:

> for the sum of $15,000, which I have contributed to the Chapel fund. It is my desire that on the front of the altar there be this inscription: 'TO THE MOTHERS OF THE SONS OF ALMA MATER'. I do not wish my name or my mother's name to appear

---

[429] New York, February 21, 1953, Spellman to Galeazzi, KC, *Enrico Galeazzi Papers*, above ref.

[430] Vatican, April 18, 1953, Galeazzi to Spellman, NYC, S/C-74, Folder 5: *To Card. Spellman, N. Amer. Coll.*

in connection with this dedication even though I am giving the altar in memory of my own mother.[431]

The Cardinal also told the Count that he had found donors to cover the cost for half of the 45 crypt altars. He himself took ten of the altars, "one for each of my predecessors in the office of Archbishop and for other friends of the College",[432] and that he would be "subscribing one to bear your name as a memorial of my affection for you and one also in memory of Bishop Louis F. Kelleher" [NAC 1915].[433] Following the May alumni meeting, Spellman wrote Galeazzi, "I have succeeded in arousing enough enthusiasm so that the whole forty-five altars were taken with offerings of $2,500 [$21,543.54] each."[434]

In March, Galeazzi provided the Rector with his last report on the construction of the new seminary before the October dedication, to be included in the April Rector's report.[435] Most of the construction work was completed or near completion, with only some of the interior finishing work remaining. The plumbing, electrical and heating systems, were nearing completion as well. The chapel exterior walls were finished, and some of the interior Travertine was in place. Nearly all of the interior artwork for both the chapel and crypt had been commissioned. The heating system in the two crypt floors had been finished, and the plaster work was nearly completed, as well as the decorative mosaic floors and the cutting of the marble for the 45 altars. The auditorium and the courtyards had all been finished, leaving only various decorative works to be completed and installed. The exterior retaining walls along the sports field and behind the tennis courts were finished, and the drainage

---

[431] New York April 29, 1953, Spellman to O'Connor, NYC, Box S/C-74, Folder 5, *To Card. Spellman, N. Amer. Coll.*

[432] New York April 24, 1953, Spellman to Fr. Andrew McEntee [NAC 1935], NYC, above ref.

[433] New York, April 29, 1953, Spellman to Galeazzi, NYC, above ref.

[434] New York, May 12, 1953, Spellman to Galeazzi, NYC above ref.

[435] Vatican March 15, 1953, Galeazzi to O'Connor, included also in the Rector's Report of November 14, 1953, CUA, *O'Connor Papers*, Box 44: *NAC*, File: *Episcopal Committee (1953)*.

systems begun. The last Italian families who had refused to leave the remaining decrepit cottages nearest the boundary wall with the Urban College next door, finally were moved to new housing on the Via Aurelia.

By late April, O'Connor informed Spellman that Stritch, Mooney, Galeazzi and he had been negotiating for the third purchase of blocked lire, this time from the Metro-Goldwyn-Mayer Studios.[436] O'Connor met with Monsignor Fiorenzo Angelini, who assured the Rector that his friend, Giulio Andreotti, the Undersecretary of the Presidential Council, was favorable to the operation.[437] In fact, on Tuesday, April 28th, Andreotti was to visit the new College along with Galeazzi, Silvestri, Angelini and O'Connor. Andreotti, however, insisted on two essential elements: that the petition to the government be made immediately, because Italian elections were near, and that this should be done in total secrecy.[438]

O'Connor had told Angelini that 1 billion lire were available, and informed Spellman, "The MGM people here are disposed to sell that amount." O'Connor had already informed Mooney of these conversations, asking that he communicate the information to Spellman, and approve O'Connor's return home for the negotiations. Now, after the fact, he asked Spellman to reply with his opinions and permission.

Spellman did, on April 29th, informing the Rector that Mooney had already contacted him on April 23rd, and that, indeed, he had relayed O'Connor's request to come to New York:

> I could see no reason for your coming, but wishing to cooperate with Cardinal Mooney I assented to the proposal.

---

[436]   Rome April 25, 1953, O'Connor to Spellman, NYC, Box S/C-74, Folder 2: *To Card. Spellman, N. Amer. Coll.*

[437]   Angelini was friends with Andreotti and served as chaplain to the *Azzione Cattolica* during the years 1945-1959; he was the Papal Master of Ceremonies during the years 1947-1954, and a friend of Galeazzi.

[438]   Rome April 25, 1953, O'Connor to Spellman, NYC, Box S/C-74, Folder 2: *To Card Spellman, N. Amer. Coll.*

We ourselves have been in communication with different moving picture corporations to get competitive prices for blocked lire but we do not know anything about the price which has been offered to you. Therefore I suggest that you give me this information.

We also are interested in keeping the transaction secret but since you speak of a billion lire we have had inquiries from this end concerning the same sum it would seem as if there have been some inquiries from Rome about this matter. Moreover, as you know, we are not in a position to purchase a billion lire. We should be disposed to purchase a sufficient amount of lire to finish the commitments we have undertaken. Beyond that we are not in a position to commit ourselves.[439]

O'Connor cabled Spellman on May 4th that he had received the Cardinal's April 29th letter, assuring him that no steps had been taken, and that he was simply gathering information. Likewise, to calm Spellman, the Rector continued, "Happy to know trip unnecessary. STOP. Urgency however advises presentation request here before May 9. Respectfully suggest consideration largest feasible figure grateful earliest reply."[440] Maguire was instructed to respond to the

---

[439] New York April 29, 1953, Spellman to O'Connor, KC, *Enrico Galeazzi Papers, No. Amer. Coll, Corresp, Francis Cardinal Spellman, 1950-1951, 1952-1953,* Box 30, File 17. New York April 29, 1953, Spellman to Mooney, NYC, Box S/C-74, Folder 2: *To Card. Spellman, N. Amer. Coll*: "I assented to your proposal that Bishop O'Connor come home, even though I see no reason for so doing. After receiving his letter I still see no reason but I imagine that Your Eminence has already given permission and that he may be on his way even though his last sentence says 'awaiting your reply'."

[440] Cable Rome May 4, 1953, O'Connor to Spellman, NYC, Box S/C-74, Folder 2; *To Card. Spellman, N. Amer. Coll.*

Rector the next day by telephone, and that "License up to 600 million lira [sic]. Exact amt. depends upon rate and funds here."[441]

The third blocked lire transaction was completed on June 29th, for 600 million lire, purchased for $816,326.53 [$7,034,625.08] at a rate of 735 lire per $1 dollar. In order to make the payment, a loan of $100,000 [$861,741.57] was taken at 3% interest. The extent of the transaction was determined by the analysis prepared by the College Business Manager, Monsignor Robert Sennott, which he sent to Maguire on March 7, 1953, "with a substantial allowance for contingencies."

Spellman sent the information to the Episcopal Board members. These were the numbers including some construction costs:

Lire required to complete NAC projects:	1,256,668,032 Lire [$14,735,780.90]
Lire on hand in Rome:	1,098,655,816 Lire [$12,646,557.39]
Lire deficit:	158,012,216 Lire [$ 1,853,778.47]
Added Projects:	----------
Price Revisions:	200,000,000 Lire [$ 2,344,884.99]
Chapel Decoration:	45,000,000 Lire [$ 572,601.28]
Casa San Giovanni Renovation:	36,000,000 Lire [$422,081.12]
Umiltà Restoration:	30,000,000 Lire [$ 415,359.44]
Total:	311,000,000 Lire [$ 3,646,287.12]
Lire Required:	469,012,216 Lire [$ 5,616,124.94]
Lire Purchased:	600,000,000 Lire [$ 7,034,396.46]
Surplus Lire:	130,987,784 Lire [$ 1,483,462.27]
Or Approximate Contingency Fund:	$200,000. USA [$ 1,723,483.14][442]

Even while this blocked lire transaction was being negotiated, O'Connor repeated his concerns about the construction costs and growing operational deficit, which were becoming more worrisome

---

[441] Cable, same as above: Spellman's handwritten instructions to Maguire are found on the bottom of the above cable.

[442] New York June 29, 1953, Spellman to Board of Trustees, NYC, Box S/C-74, Folder 3: *To Card. Spellman, N. Amer. Coll.*

as the October inauguration date drew nearer. He wrote Cardinal Mooney on June 11th, informing him that Monsignor Robert Sennot had rushed home to attend to his dying brother in Boston. The Rector continued:

> For some reason I have been anxious for a further check on our expenditures in relation to our whole program. It will be recalled that our annual reports have shown that the [construction] cost of the seminary would be within the estimate. In the last report this was changed to read 'within estimated resources.'

Sennot was completing an up-to-date report when he was called home, and, following discussions with Galeazzi and Silvestri, the Rector felt that "a general outline of the situation should be presented to you and the Board at once."[443]

He then listed the projects that constituted his entire work in Rome during the previous six years, and which costs all added up to an enormous amount of money, including the preliminary rehabilitation of the Casa San Giovanni on the Janiculum property; the complete renovation and refurnishing of the Castel Gandolfo and Umiltà properties and the College Mausoleum; the architect's fees and administrative costs for those projects; "incidental expenses" to the re-opening of both properties, along with the operational deficits of both institutions; the opening and operation of the Audience Office during the Holy Year and subsequent years; the construction and furnishing of the new seminary, with those administrative, legal, and architectural fees; the conversion of the Umiltà buildings for graduate studies; the conversion of the Casa San Giovanni into a convent; and the eventual payment of taxes to the Italian government for the transfer of the Palazzo Orsini, "ordered by Cardinal Spellman, January 1953."

---

[443] Rome June 11, 1953, O'Connor to Mooney, CUA, *O'Connor Papers*, Box 42: *NAC subfile*, Folder: *Increased Cost for NAC*.

Likewise, the Rector continued, the bishops in their November 1952 meeting had approved the estimated costs for chapel decoration of $75,000 [$651,183.96] and the conversion of the Casa San Giovanni into a convent for $65,000 [$564,359.43], as well as the conversion of the Umiltà for graduate studies. In January, Cardinal Spellman had approved the price adjustments in connection with the new seminary construction, which would not be known for another six months, and which "were, however, inevitable and occurred all through Italy as a result of the Korean War." The Rector continued with his bad news, that there would be additional unbudgeted costs for the transferring of the Umiltà facility and the students to the new College, as well as operational deficits that would likely occur during the first years of operation on the Janiculum. "No one can foretell exactly what they will be, but it is certain that they will occur."

Since the two programs of graduate students at the Umiltà and seminarians in the new facility on the Janiculum would begin in October:

> I feel the situation should be referred to you and the Episcopal Committee for any instructions you deem necessary. Even though I have received authorization it would not be possible for me to go into debt without special permission.

O'Connor cabled Mooney the same day, alerting him to the posting of his letter,[444] and then, after discussing the problem with Silvestri, sent a second cable, "Reference to Letter June Eleven Total Figure might be approximately three hundred thousand dollars but not certain this conclusion after conference with lawyer today."[445]

On June 15th, O'Connor wrote Sennott, asking about his brother's condition, and included a copy of his letter to Mooney. He told his *Economo* that he had met with Galeazzi and Silvestri "several

---

[444]   Cable Rome June 11, 1953, O'Connor to Mooney, CUA, *O'Connor Papers*, Box 42, *NAC subfile*, Folder: *Increased Cost NAC*.

[445]   Cable Rome June 11, 1953, O'Connor to Mooney, CUA, above ref.

times", and that "their different methods of book-keeping have been responsible for a part of the difficulty."[446]

By June 18th, the Rector's letter arrived in Detroit, and the Cardinal President of the Episcopal Board cabled O'Connor, "Received letter had telephone discussion with Sennott STOP Latest Silvestri figures needed before checking with Treasurer's [Spellman's] books. Explanatory statement from architect essential before placing matter before Board. Letter Follows. Regards +Mooney."[447]

Cardinal Mooney was on retreat, yet penned an eight page handwritten letter the same day, answering O'Connor's letters of June 10th, 11th and 12th. The man who submitted O'Connor's name to become the Rector of the College, and supported that nomination, addressed his beleaguered colleague:

> Caro Mio, I received the bad news [Letter of June 11th] about the prospective deficit just as I was leaving for retreat here at the Seminary. I only got in touch with Sennott last night.
>
> I fully share your own disappointment for I counted on having a surplus that would cover operating deficits until the enrollment is up to capacity at which time we could set a board and tuition charge that would cover expenses.[448]

Mooney thought the best course of action would be for Sennott to sit with Maguire to compare the Roman team's figures with those of the Cardinal Treasurer's office, and to explain the apparent discrepancies in Silvestri's reports. Mooney said he would call Spellman to arrange that meeting. Then they could approach the Board to decide their next course of action:

---

[446] Rome June 15, 1953, O'Connor to Sennott, CUA, above ref.

[447] Cable Detroit June 18,1953, Mooney to O'Connor, CUA, above ref.

[448] Plymouth, MI [St. John's Seminary] June 18, 1953, Mooney to O'Connor, CUA, above ref.

When the deficit is verified in a definite figure, I don't
see what else we can do than to ask the Bishops of
the country for a supplementary assessment to cover
it—and, I hope, provide a cushion for prospective
operating deficits during the years of transition. This
is going to be hard . . .

because, as Mooney knew well, the American bishops had voted
recently to support the building of the National Shrine of the
Immaculate Conception in Washington, D.C., promising money they
did not have, just as they had done in the past few years concerning
the re-opening and construction of the College. He then reflected on
the divisions of loyalty among the bishops, writing:

It is hard, too, because from the very beginning, as
you will remember, there was a tendency, utterly
unreasonable of course, to set the two causes—the
College and the Shrine—in opposition as to their
claims on the interest of the Bishops.

The increase in construction costs, the most recent a 35% increase,
was due to the Korean War, and so beyond anyone's control. But,
"The worst of it is that the architect and contractors (and possibly
Silvestri's accountant) were so slow either in discovering it or
making it known. Thus it hits us suddenly as well as hard just when
we thought the end was in sight."

Mooney insisted that both Galeazzi and Silvestri prepare a
report containing the actual numbers "that reveals the extent of this
increased cost and justifies the factors that go to make it up." And the
report was to be signed by them. Both knowing quite well the source
of the heaviest criticisms, Mooney then continued to O'Connor: "I
would not want to call a meeting of the Committee without having
this report in hand, with an extra copy (for the Treasurer) and a copy
of an English translation for every member of the Committee."

O'Connor had questioned whether he should continue with the
chapel decoration, and the refurbishing of the Casa San Giovanni
and the Umiltà, even though the bishops had approved those projects

during their November 1952 meeting. Mooney told him the only necessary work was the refurbishing of the Casa San Giovanni as the new convent for the Sisters. The chapel decoration might be limited to the sanctuary, and the Umiltà work could simply be postponed, since the present state of the building "will serve the new inmates", as he termed the student priests.

As for the dedication ceremonies, Mooney told the Rector to proceed, and to include the costs in the deficit, that would have to be paid, anyway. He continued:

> But the newly arisen situation is an added reason for keeping the affair simple and expenses as low as possible. In any case simplicity will make as good impression on the American Bishops in attendance. They will be struck by good singing, good ceremonies, and the demeanor of the students. All the rest matters little.

O'Connor had asked about calling an emergency meeting of the Board in Rome, before the October 14th dedication. But Mooney cautioned against such a move; better to wait and see which bishops actually came to the dedication. "I think it will be better to arrange it informally when we are there rather than alert them in advance."

The President of the Episcopal Board then tried to calm his friend, the Rector:

> "Please do not let this financial difficulty get you down. We just have to face it and do what we can. The fact that it comes up in a report of Galeazzi and Silvestri will help in the quarter from which most rumbling will come [Spellman]. But, I want to have Sennott well armed with statistics before arranging the New York Meeting. He needs only totals, but totals that are definite. I may call Cardinal Spellman about the matter before he hears from other sources that Sennott is in the States."

So, here was the plan of action, and the tactics fashioned by Mooney to face this last minute hurdle to the completion of construction and the opening of the new College; and this would continue all summer. Mooney was determined to solve the problem, so that the College project would open as planned, and the candidate he had supported for the job of College Rector could survive the tempest and retain the respect and support of the American bishops, so necessary to his successful administration of the College after the dedication ceremonies and the new seminary opened.

Mooney spent the summer months in constant contact by telephone, cable and postal services to arrive at the bottom of this challenge: he was a task master with Maguire and Sennott, supportive and clear with O'Connor, and tactful in his handling of Spellman, all while running his own Archdiocese of Detroit, and suffering from ill health, himself, going over numbers, and seeking the reasons for the mix-up, as his lengthy correspondence with each man reveals. So frequent were the communications and requests for information, that the mails proved insufficient in the timely delivery of facts and figures needed to meet the demands of the process, resulting in a storm of cables and telephone calls to and from Mooney, Sennot [in Boston], O'Connor, Maguire, and Spellman, in order to exchange and clarify information.[449]

O'Connor worked feverishly on his end with his team members to meet Mooney's demands, while, at the same time, completing the construction on the Janiculum; planning for the dedication ceremonies; running the seminary at the Villa Santa Caterina; preparing for the arrival of new students; the transfer of the seminary and graduate houses to their new homes by September; and running the Audience Office.

Mooney's first demand was for exact numbers, total receipts and expenditures, and an exact tally of the total cash on hand. Reports

---

[449] The Archives of the Catholic University of America has the entire collection of scores of letters, cables and reports, collected and amassed by O'Connor, possibly intent on setting the record straight about his work at the College. The entire archive can be found in the *O'Connor Papers*, Box 42, Folder: *Increased Costs NAC*.

were to be prepared both in Rome and New York City, because he believed the reports of the architect, lawyer, and Spellman should themselves provide the clearest picture of costs and deficits. Deep down, neither he, nor Spellman, nor O'Connor understood how this could have occurred.[450]

Both autographed reports by Galeazzi and Silvestri were submitted by the end of June. Galeazzi showed that there were three reasons why this 246,985,000 lire [$2,895,684.36] overrun of the original 1949 budget existed: price revisions for labor and materials by Ravello & Mengarini, which totaled approximately 150,000,000 lire [$1,758,642.20]; contract revisions for labor by the subcontractors; and design and construction changes from the original plans, as construction proceeded.[451]

Silvestri's financial report was quite simple, stating that an extra 240,000,000 lire or $400,000 [$3,446,966.29], would be required to complete the College. Ever the clear-headed pragmatist, the College lawyer concluded his report by commenting:

> This additional percentage is rather minimal in relation to a construction project begun in 1947 and that will come to an end, with most of it paid for, in 1954; in other words, more than seven years; a long period in which the rise in costs reflected above, in light of the unique market conditions created following upon various international events, whose repercussions have affected both the construction work and the administration of the College.[452]

O'Connor sent both reports with a cover letter to Mooney, reminding the President of the Episcopal Board about the additional

---

[450] Brighton, MA June 18, 1953, Sennott to O'Connor, KC, *Enrico Galeazzi Papers, No. Amer. Coll. Financial Management, 1953-1954*, Box 13, File 9.

[451] Vatican June 25, 1953, Galeazzi Memorandum: *Aggiornamento del preventive di spesa al 30 aprile 1953*, CUA, *O'Connor Papers*, Box 42: *NAC subfile*, Folder: *Increased Costs NAC*.

[452] Rome June 30, 1953, Silvestri to O'Connor, CUA, *O'Connor Papers*, above ref.

expenses connected with the *avviamento*, or opening of the new College. This was not simply the cost for the dedication day ceremonies and reception, as Spellman misinterpreted it. Rather, it included the transfer of the students and entire College to the new site; the purchase of all necessities for daily life in the new building, as well as the opening ceremonies; along with the inevitable operational deficits for the first years of the College in the new building on the Janiculum. The Rector was concerned, since the Board had made no decisions about any of this, despite his repeated requests through the years.[453] He cabled Monsignor Sennott on July 1st, alerting him that the "signed reports airmailed today."[454]

On July 3rd, O'Connor wrote Mooney a letter marked "<u>Personal</u>". O'Connor relayed Mooney's bullet points of instruction from his earlier letters to the Rector, and reported that he spoke with Sennott, Galeazzi and Silvestri about the costs for the decoration of the new chapel, and the costs for the new work in the Casa San Giovanni and the Umiltà property. He agreed with Mooney that the decoration of the College chapel had to proceed, especially since contracts had been signed the previous December, as the Board had approved. Likewise, the Casa San Giovanni had to be adapted to house the nuns who were arriving to staff the College. Only the complete rehabilitation of the Umiltà property for graduate priests might be held in abeyance, limited to essentials, and that might cost $50,000 [$430,870.79]. He continued:

> In spite of the disappointment it seems that we should feel very grateful for the opportunity to purchase blocked lire as the profit here has spared a great drain

---

453 Rome June 30, 1953, O'Connor to Mooney, CUA, *O'Connor Papers*, above ref. Attached to this is O'Connor's penciled note to Galeazzi on a personal note card, dated June 27, 1953, asking "Please let me know if this is satisfactory." He attached it to his penciled draft of his letter to Mooney, as well as a copy of Silvestri's report, asking the architect to look it over and to translate the lawyer's report into English. Galeazzi responded on the same note card, "I think it is perfect."

454 Cable Rome July 1, 1953, O'Connor to Sennott, CUA, *O'Connor Papers*, above ref.

from home. The general opinion seems to be among Americans who have seen the whole project that for the cost in America we could multiply our cost here by three if we were anxious to know what the expenses would be over there. With the completion of these projects the church in America has large and valuable holdings in Rome and I am sure that you will be favourably impressed in the Fall even though this set back is not a pleasant prelude.[455]

The Rector concluded asking Mooney's advice on the three-day inauguration ceremonies he was planning.

Sennott wrote the Rector on July 12th, that he had spoken by phone with Maguire before O'Connor's reports arrived. He wrote to Mooney, relaying that:

Monsignor Maguire professed no advance knowledge of the impending situation when I contacted him by phone on the day I received your reports. He professed great horror and indignation that this situation exists, he felt it could not have come on suddenly and that it should have been indicated in previous reports. I tried to work out a plan of action with him but we made no progress. I tried to find out how much money was still receivable on pledges but he said he did not have the information. He did give me the amount spent for the last lire transaction which occurred since I left Rome but I do not know if he was using round figures or not. He concentrated on the fact that the Building Fund is now in debt since money had to be borrowed to raise the purchase price of this latest lire transaction. I was trying to determine just how much we would be in debt or clear if all the pledges were paid. He does not wish to talk in these terms—he thinks we should discuss things on the basis of the

---

[455] Rome July 3, 1953, O'Connor to Mooney, CUA, *O'Connor Papers*, above ref.

cash on hand. We agreed that I was to call him when I received a reply to my cable to you—or he was to contact me in the meantime if he wishes here at the Chancery [in Boston].[456]

The College *Economo* continued that, since the Roman team and Mooney now knew the amount required to complete the project, all they needed was a report on the actual amount of money available in New York, and that could be had only from Monsignor Maguire, who was not cooperating. Sennott had observed some discrepancies in Silvestri's report: 68,000,000 lire [$797,136.81] taken from both the new and old College accounts for operating expenses, which was 13,000,000 lire [$152,502.41] more than originally reported. Silvestri claimed this to have been transacted in 1950: "I never found any record of it." The second item was 61,000,00 lire [$ 623,961.22] taken from the Credito Italiano accumulated interest: "I have no figures to support this amount. Our last report to the Bishops from the lawyer showed only 12,500,000 lire [$146,547.77] transferred to the College." Sennott told O'Connor there were other points to discuss, but he would speak about them when he returned to Rome, preferring now to "proceed to the solution of the problem of obtaining this extra $400,000"[$3,446,966.29].

Monsignor Maguire analyzed Sennott's reports and sent a memorandum to Cardinal Spellman on July 31st. Two copies of this informative document can be found, one in the Archives of the Archdiocese of New York, and one at The American Catholic History Research Center and University Archives at The Catholic University of America. The latter copy was sent to Cardinal Mooney by Spellman. Mooney penned his comments and instructions on it, and enclosed it with his letter to O'Connor of August 5th. This letter and the copy of Maguire's report bear Mooney's notations, comments, and instructions to O'Connor.[457]

---

[456] Brighton, MA July 12, 1953, Sennott to O'Connor, CUA, *O'Connor Papers*, above ref.

[457] New York July 31, 1953, *Memorandum for His Eminence*, Maguire to Spellman, NYC, Box SC-74, Folder 3: *To Card. Spellman, N. Amer. Coll.*

Maguire observed that the unexpected cost overruns could be explained. For instance, no allowance had ever been made for new furnishings for the new College, for any new supplies, provisions or equipment. Galeazzi's report stated that cost was 205,000,000 lire [$2,403,500.66]. An allowance for 200,000,000 lire [$2,344,798.82] had been made, in fact, in Sennott's March 1953 report. Silvestri reported that 135,000,000 lire [$1,583,631.11] had been paid for operational deficits of the College. Maguire observed that this had no bearing on cost overrun for construction, "because it is offset by interest earned on Lire deposits which was not considered in the March report." This was a large deficit, however. [Mooney noted here that O'Connor should "check +EM" the numbers]. Silvestri also allowed for 17,720,000 lire [$200,578.97] for the transfer tax for the title to the Umiltà property, which sum had never been entered into any budget. [Mooney noted here: "Naturally—it was not foreseeable +EM"]. Silvestri mentioned an allowance for 60,000,000 lire [$703,465.50] for *avviamento*, which continued to be a touch stone of annoyance on New York's side, who saw this as symbolic of all they considered wrong with O'Connor's administration. This, Maguire explained, was composed of all expenses needed to open the College. "It seems a very high estimate", Maguire observed, telling Spellman that "no previous allowance was made for this." [Mooney noted, "and for expected deficits during the years before full enrollment is attained! +EM"]. The total estimate required, including the various unbudgeted costs, totaled 240,000,000 lire [$2,813,861.99].

While Spellman had repeatedly complained about operational deficits, the fact is that he himself had added his own big-ticket items to the College operational and construction expenditures. Likewise, this report of failures in budgeting for the basic huge costs for furnishings, equipment, and provisions; for the transfer of students the ceremonial opening; and the first years of the new College, raised more questions about Spellman's role as Treasurer and his New York team's work of overseeing the College finances,

---

This is also found in CUA, *O'Connor Papers*, Box 42: *NAC subfiles*, Folder: *Increased Costs NAC*.

than about the work of O'Connor as Rector, or of Galeazzi's, or Silvestri's work during the previous six years.

On July 13th, Cardinal Mooney responded to four earlier letters by O'Connor.[458] After reading through the reports by Galeazzi and Silvestri, Mooney reported that he:

> took the matter up by phone through regular channels [Spellman] and, after some discussion of points relevant and irrelevant, achieved agreement on the desirability of a conference between Msgr. McGuire [sic] and Msgr. Sennott for the purpose of reconciling definitively the accounts in New York and Rome and thus setting up a basis for a possible meeting of the Board in the very near future.[459]

Mooney told O'Connor he had second thoughts about leaving the arrangements in New York's hands, and phoned Sennott, asking that he take the initiative and phone Maguire, suggesting a meeting to discuss the two reports just received. "This was done in view of remarks made in the previous telephone conversation" [Mooney's to Spellman]. The first and clearest point made by the Cardinal President was his reference to Silvestri's report and to the same questions that Sennott had already expressed to the Rector. He understood the financial discrepancies in the College lawyer's report were not the result of any criminal activity, or even of mismanagement on the part of Silvestri or his staff. Rather, he understood that Silvestri's summary, translated from Italian into English by another Italian [Galeazzi] contained "some items . . . which I thought were rather unfortunately expressed."

While he listed those same numbers that had raised Sennott's curiosity, Mooney understood what they were, much more clearly than did the College Business Manager. He did foresee the necessity

---

458   The letters from O'Connor were of June 16th, 19th, 30th and July 3rd in above ref.

459   Detroit July 13, 1953, Mooney to O'Connor, CUA, *O'Connor Papers*, Box 42: *NAC subfile*, Folder: *Increased Cost NAC*.

of clarification, for he was more concerned how these numbers could be misinterpreted, and manipulated by some, because Spellman was aching for a fight:

> Of course, I took these items to refer to expenditures for furniture or some other expense that involved capital expenditure but was not part of the building itself. But I immediately saw here the possibility of the kind of enquiry we are familiar with and that would possibly connect these expenditures with operational costs. I know that it will not be difficult to answer the inquiries in a satisfactory manner, but it struck me that Silvestri's accountant was, in circumstances that we know better than him, a bit too general in his terminology.

Mooney turned to the inauguration ceremonies of College, about which O'Connor had asked him. The Rector and Board suggested three days of ceremonies and banquets to be held in mid-October, 1953 for the dedication. The centerpiece of the third day would be a pontifical Mass for the deceased alumni of the College. O'Connor had invited Spellman to be the celebrant of the Mass, but Spellman suggested Mooney be the celebrant instead, as the President of the Board. Mooney's health was not the best, and he informed the Rector that "I am trying to avoid Pontifical Masses, as I cannot always count on being 'at the top of my game' in the morning."

Mooney then suggested that O'Connor repeat his invitation to Spellman:

> This will give you an opportunity to insist with Cardinal Spellman—which he may like. You can say that I prefer that he should take it. If he really does not want to do so, it may give us an opportunity to do something that may really help our public relations. That would be to have some Bishop who is not an alumnus of the College take part in the Dedication program. This would be highly appropriate

particularly in view of the wonderful support the Hierarchy as a whole has given the project and the desire, I am sure we share, to promote ever more the idea that the College belongs to all the Bishops.

Mooney wrote that he had spoken to Stritch about this, and Stritch "cordially approves the idea of getting some non-Roman on the program and is utterly indifferent as to what part he [Stritch] plays." Stritch and Mooney thought Archbishop Keough of Baltimore would fit the bill perfectly. Mooney then addressed O'Connor whom he knew well, and it is worth quoting at length:

My own present experience furnishes me with a good argument. I have just let the contract for the chapel at St. John's [Seminary] which is 35% more than the firm bid I received in 1948! Even the Stepinac High School cost 25% more than the original estimate.

So, while you 'keep your chin up', we will look forward to an interesting meeting of the Board—probably here at St. John's Seminary.

Our greatest difficulty in going to the Bishops is that unfortunately a certain competition has been set up between the solicitation for the College and for the Shrine at the University—for which we have a big collection on December 8th. But we will get through in the end. So don't worry.

And, as if Mooney were writing the script for the extraordinary Episcopal Board meeting that would take place in Rome on October 14th, the Cardinal President predicted:

Again let me repeat—perhaps *ad nauseam*—my counsel not to let all this get you down—or unduly lower your blood pressure. It will all come out alright and probably in the end the party that objects most

strenuously [Spellman] will make the motion of
approval—and possibly add a vote of thanks!!

O'Connor could do little else but worry, while Sennott and
Maguire conferred by phone and letter, preparing their own analyses
of the Galeazzi and Silvestri reports for Spellman and Mooney.
Sennot's three analyses of the reports, along with his own *dubbia*,
were sent out to all the principals by late July, showing a surprising
positive balance of nearly $34,000 [$292,992.13], resulting from
increased New York resources and the benefit from the third blocked
lire transaction.[460]

Sennott had been busy speaking with Maguire by phone and
reporting to Mooney. He relayed Mooney's message to Maguire
asking for fundraising suggestions. That obviously had an immediate
effect on Spellman. While visiting his ailing brother in a Boston
hospital, Sennott ran into Dr. John Spellman, who told him that
his brother had sent out a letter urging bishops and lay people to
complete their pledge payments.[461]

Sennot also reported to O'Connor that Mooney wanted the
Rector "to cable a reply to me asserting that these estimates will
hold; that all needs are cared for and so no further requests will
occur." Once he had O'Connor's cable, Sennott was to contact
Maguire to formulate concrete plans for a Board meeting. "The
Cardinal [Mooney] is quite anxious to bring this problem to as quick
a solution as possible but he stressed that he does not want to act
unless his act will be conclusive."

In the midst of this, O'Connor wrote the Pope, repeating the
invitation to preside over the College inauguration that he made
verbally during his audience with Pius the previous October:

---

[460] Brighton, MA July 27, 1953, Sennott to O'Connor, KC, *Enrico Galeazzi
Papers, No. Amer. Coll, Financial Management, 1953-1955*, Box 13, File 9.

[461] Brighton, MA July 30, 1953, Sennott to O'Connor, CUA, *O'Connor Papers*,
Box 42: *NAC subfiles*, Folder: *Increased Costs NAC*. Sennot wrote O'Connor
a second letter on July 30th, reporting a phone conversation with Maguire who
told him a Board meeting in Rome might be preferable. In above ref.

The presence of Your Holiness would be a tremendous encouragement to thousands of priests and religious men and women who have prepared students for the priesthood and who have a profound attachment to their national seminary in Rome, whence many young and zealous apostles have gone forth to spread through the United States an ever increasing love and steadfast loyalty to the Vicar of Christ.[462]

Mooney wrote again on August 5th. In this five page, handwritten letter, he apologized for the tardiness of his reply to O'Connor's letter, saying this was "delayed all too long because it is so hard to get down to my desk" because of his schedule. "Your letter of July 29th conveying the answer given to your invitation to the Holy Father is interesting in that it does not close the door completely. That is something."[463]

He then answered O'Connor's question about commissioning a commemorative medal for the College inauguration. Mooney first said that something simpler and less expensive would be preferable, in light of the present controversy. A simple holy card of the Madonna dell'Umiltà, the College patroness with a small picture of the new building, might fit the bill:

If the card were pliable and not stiff, it would have a permanent place in our breviaries. The expense would be negligible and the effect, I think, better than that of a medallion—on the American in contrast to the

---

[462] Rome July 24, 1953, O'Connor to Pope Pius XII, KC, *Enrico Galeazzi Papers, No. Amer. Coll, Corresp Most Rev Martin J. O'Connor, 1953-1954*, Box 30, File 13.

[463] Detroit August 5, 1953, Mooney to O'Connor, CUA, *O'Connor Papers*, Box 42: *NAC subfiles*, Folder: *Increased Costs NAC*. Detroit August 27, 1953, Mooney to O'Connor, CUA, above ref: Mooney's August 5th letter appeared to have been lost in the mails. It's delay caused misunderstandings about subsequent communications, until it was delivered in mid-September. It's delayed delivery was due to a seminarian's having failed to put airmail postage on the envelope.

Italian mentality. In any case, the only way to keep the medallion expense from becoming a subject of possibly acrimonious discussion would be to be able to list it as a donation. [In the end, a small bronze commemorative medal was struck]

The "acrimonious discussion" might come from the Spellman camp. Mooney observed that the results of the Sennott-Maguire consultations, albeit only by phone and letter, revealed that if the bishops all paid their full pledges there actually would be no deficit, "—provided Galeazzi does not come up with further unforeseen obligations." If there was no deficit, there was no problem. The arrangement worked out by Mooney with Spellman was that, following the completion of the discussions by Sennott and Maguire, Spellman would inform Mooney of the results in order to decide when or if a Board meeting should take place:

> To date I have no further word from him—but there may be a letter from him in the mail from the house [Mooney was writing from the Seminary] which will be brought out to me tomorrow.

> Evidently Msgr. Maguire's view that a meeting now would not be advisable reflects the views of the Treasurer—after hearing from Maguire that he does not now feel in a position to give a complete and definitive report to the Board. Tactically there are many advantages in having the meeting in Rome with Galeazzi and Silvestri present. In regard to the curtailment of the new projects [transforming the Casa San Giovanni into a convent, and the Umiltà property for graduate priest use]—reference to which by Maguire is, I feel certain, an echo of remarks by the Treasurer—I am prepared to defend the proposition that the chapel decoration and work on the Casa S. Giovanni just had to go on. But I do think it would be a good gesture to defer—possibly for a year—the

remodeling of the Umiltà Residence. It will be no serious inconvenience to the priests to have adjoining rather than connecting rooms.

He continued writing:

Later—I just received as I expected a letter from Card. Spellman suggesting that our meeting of the Board be deferred until we get to Rome. I have talked with him by phone and we agreed that he inform the Board members that the meeting be held at the College on Oct. 13 [sic] at 4:30 P.M.

Mooney told O'Connor that Spellman had enclosed Maguire's memorandum about the two reports, which Mooney sent along with this letter to O'Connor.

Mooney wrote that he had explained the term *avviamento* to Spellman, and that it had been raised and approved during an earlier Board meeting. He closed by instructing O'Connor to tell Sennott to determine what questions he should ask Galeazzi and Silvestri about their reports, because those answers would be needed to prepare for the questions Spellman would invariably ask during the October meeting. Likewise, Mooney insisted that a final cost be determined for the furnishings of the College, "in the face of a vanishing surplus, we have to try to be as definite as possible." He confessed that the one item Silvestri listed under *Gestione Collegio* for 135,000,000 lire [$1,582,786.60] "stumps me . . . . Possibly some burse funds or other operational receipts were put through Silvestri's books. In any case that is an item that Silvestri ought to be prepared to explain in more detail."

The Roman team kept working throughout the summer, sending clarifications to Mooney, Maguire, and Sennott, who was still in Boston attending to his ailing brother. Writing to O'Connor in August, Sennott relayed Mooney's observations expressed during a recent telephone conversation:

In my conversation with Cardinal Mooney I could find reflection of some of the remarks made to me when talking with New York. Monsignor Maguire had complained of several points in the reports of the Architect and Lawyer about which I had written previously to you, e.g., the difference between the figures used by the Lawyer in 'Uscita' and in 'Spese Techniche'; the error in balance; the high account for 'Gestione'; and the dubious 9% figure. He [Mooney] had considered the report 'careless' and felt the Board could not have confidence when dealing with the request for $400,000.00.[464] [$3,446,966.29]

On August 10th, Spellman sent Maguire's analysis of Sennott's report to the College Episcopal Board members. He did not include Sennott's original reports, sending only Maguire's analysis. The Cardinal Treasurer was not going to back down, writing, "If you will compare this memorandum with the analysis of the previous reports you will realize why the situation has suddenly become disturbing."[465]

Mooney, in contact with O'Connor and his Roman team, including Sennott in Boston, answered Spellman's letter on August 17th. He defined *avviamento* for Spellman once again. Then he proceeded to the question of the operational deficit, borrowing from O'Connor's June 30th letter to him:

> Personally I am in agreement with the idea that we cannot definitely fix a reasonable fee for board and tuition in the new College until the enrollment at least approaches the capacity of the building;—or the number we are going to get. In the meantime there will be a deficit and we—unlike a diocese—have no other

---

[464] Brighton, MA August 9, 1953, Sennott to O'Connor, KC, *Enrico Galeazzi Papers, No. Amer. Coll, Financial Management, 1953-54*, Box 13, File 9.

[465] New York August 10, 1953, Spellman to Episcopal Board Members, NYC, Box SC/74, Folder 3: *To Card. Spellman, N. Amer. Coll.*

resort but to try at least to provide for it beforehand if that is possible. Surely, this consideration ought to enter into our figuring and *avviamento* brings it in. In the meantime, *pax et bonum*.[466]

Spellman's response was brief; "I thank you for your explanation but what we all need is an explanation of how we got this far in this way so suddenly and an explanation of what we can do about it."[467] He was impatient with bishops who seemed not overly troubled by the cost overrun, having had similar experiences in cost increases in their own diocesan capital projects. Spellman would not let up, as seen in his response to Bishop William Mulloy, Bishop of Covington, Kentucky:

> I regret that I must differ with you as I think it is most distressing in an expenditure of three million dollars, for which through negotiations and the acquisition of blocked lire we obtained the equivalent of four million dollars, to find within a few months before the completion of the work and only a few months after we were assured that we would have a cushion of approximately half a million dollars, that we are facing a several hundred thousand dollar deficit.

> This is a big difference from your statement 'that it is impossible for any human being to estimate to the last cent just what it is going to cost for remodeling and repairing a building', and I for one am distressed and depressed at the shocking situation.[468]

---

[466]   Detroit August 17, 1953, Mooney to Spellman, NYC, Box SC/74, Folder 3: *To Card. Spellman, N. Amer. Coll.*

[467]   New York August 24, 1953, Spellman to Mooney, NYC, above ref.

[468]   New York August 26, 1953, Spellman to Mulloy, NYC, Box S/C-74, Folder 3: *To Card. Spellman, N. Amer. Coll.*

Today, in an age when we can instantly communicate electronically with people around the world, and can overnight letters and packages, it is difficult to imagine a world when communication was not so convenient or instantaneous. But, during the 1950's there was no overnight mail, nor was the placing of a long distance telephone call an easy or inexpensive task. The delays in the international mail, letters and answers to letters crossing each other in the mail, and a flurry of cables, all caused numerous misunderstandings and misinterpretations.

These, and his own questions about the various reports, urged Sennott to request further clarifications of Galeazzi and Silvestri throughout the summer. But, as the summer wore on, Sennott observed that the situation had changed. He told O'Connor that all the information was required only if a final decision were to be made in the United States by the College Board. But, since plans for the emergency Board meeting had changed to mid-October in Rome, the analytical gymnastics by Maguire, Sennott, O'Connor and Mooney and the other members of the Roman team were unnecessary, because Galeazzi and Silvestri, Sennott and Maguire, O'Connor and Lacy, Spellman and Mooney, would all be at the Roman meeting, and could talk with each other face-to-face, and answer all questions, personally.[469]

By September 1st, all letters, reports and cables had arrived at their intended destinations. Mooney requested a final and clear report be made, and that the report "be the latest possible", meaning no further changes be made, and include the most up-to-date figures. So, Sennott suggested that O'Connor use the forum of his annual report, usually dated August 31st. If necessary, "we can bring it up to an even later date", so that the Board members could have no grounds to complain that the final numbers were not actually the most recent. Galeazzi, Silvestri, and Maguire were to be asked to submit their final figures to Sennott as well, in order to prepare for the Roman Board meeting.[470]

---

[469]   Brighton, MA August 29, 1953, Sennott to O'Connor, CUA, *O'Connor Papers*, Box 42: *NAC subfile*, Folder: *Increased Costs NAC*.
[470]   Brighton, MA September 1, 1953, Sennott to O'Connor, CUA, above ref.

The Rector prepared his report in anticipation of the meeting, which was actually held at the Umiltà property on the afternoon of October 14th, following the dedication ceremonies. The report would later be sent to all members of the American Hierarchy with an explanatory letter, and served as the basis for the Rector's usual detailed annual report for the College for the annual November bishops' meeting in Washington, D.C.

In his opening letter, dated October 13th, O'Connor gave a brief list of the attached documents by the members of his Roman team. Since the report took the form of the usual annual report submitted to the American bishops, O'Connor included the individual reports about each aspect of seminary life for the year, construction projects, and progress of the seminarians and graduate studies priests, as well as the financial report of operating costs for the academic year.[471]

The report then moved to the heart of the matter and the reason for this extraordinary meeting. This was taken up by the ten page *Confidential Report* written by Monsignor Sennott giving in detail the total cost of the entire building program for all the College construction and restoration projects, as well as all other "expenditures made or to be made from the Building Funds." He continued, "By combining the expenditures to date with the estimated future expenditures, the total cost of the program is attained."[472] The Board members received this report after they arrived in Rome, a few days prior to October 14th, so they might consider its contents before the opening of the meeting.

---

[471] Ibid, p 31: For the benefit of the Cardinal Treasurer, a page entitled "Estimated Deficit" was included, showing the total estimated deficit for the year was $15,110. Likewise, page 42 was entitled "Gifts", in answer to Spellman's earlier and repeated insistence that the Rector should be raising funds through the audience office. The total gifts received for the year was $3,266.00.

[472] Ibid, p 32: "These include money allotted to the College and to the Casa San Giovanni for capital expenditures and for normal operating deficits, legal expenses not only for the Building Program but also for the transfer of the title of College Property, which has been in negotiation with the Propaganda, New Projects not provided for at the beginning of the Building Program, expenses connected with the Dedication of the New college and a provision for the expected deficit of the first years of operation among others."

The Rector also reported that 15 religious women of the Teaching Sisters of the Holy Cross of the Third Order of St. Francis of Menzingen, Switzerland, were hired to oversee the domestic services of the College. The Superior and two Sisters had been living in the new College infirmary for the previous three months, completing last-minute purchases and preparations for the opening of the "domestic department", kitchen, laundry and infirmary. They would be transferred into the Casa San Giovanni shortly. He also reported that 18,000 Americans had been received by the College Audience Office since January 1st. The number could be expected to rise dramatically during the 1954 Marian Year.

Finally, the Rector reported, he had been informed on September 30th by Monsignor Carlo Toraldo and Monsignor Nasalli Rocca that the Holy Father would visit the College on the dedication day.[473]

---

[473] *Rector's Report North American College, October 13, 1953*, CUA, *O'Connor Papers*, Box 44 NAC, Folder: *Rector's Report (October 1953)*.

Chapter 7

Dedication Day, October 14, 1953

*"For several years now We have followed with keen
interest the preparations and the construction of your
new seminary. Our Venerable Brother, the Rector,
devoted, courageous, vigilant of every detail, kept Us
informed of its progress, until with Our own eyes We
saw it, reflecting the morning sun, like a city seated
on a mountain."*

—Pope Pius XII

October 14, 1953 was no common Wednesday for the American
cardinals, archbishops, bishops, College alumni priests, religious
sisters and brothers, seminarians, and College guests in Rome. No
matter what other business might be pressing, that morning nothing
else mattered, other than the dedication of the new College on the
Janiculum Hill, to be blessed by the Holy Father himself.

Two invitations had been sent: the first by the College, in the
name of the American hierarchy and the Rector, inviting guests to
a 4:00 p.m. ceremony;[474] the second by the Vatican, in the name
of Pope Pius XII, who invited those same guests to be present as
he visited the new College. This was sent on October 10th, with
the rescheduled time of *ore 10 precise*. Each bishop, including the
Rector, and all those invited by the College to attend, received a
papal invitation, marked *strettamente personale*.[475]

---

[474] KC, *Enrico Galeazzi Papers, No. Amer. Coll, Dedication invitation, 1953*,
Box 13, File 6.

[475] NAC, #5, *Pope Pius XII.*

The College invitation bore the newly devised College coat of arms on the front,[476] below which were the year of College founding, 1859, and the year of the new College opening, 1953. On the interior were two Latin inscriptions from the exterior of the new College: the first on the highest point of the College facing Rome:

> *O Roma Felix Quae Duorum Principum*
> *Es consecrata Glorioso Sanguine*[477]

The second, over the exterior door of the Rector's reception room [*The Red Room*], facing Saint Peter's Basilica:

> *Qui huc appulerunt iuvenes*
> *E longinquis Americae oris*
> *Vaticanum respicientes Collem*
> *Suam roborant Fidem*
> *Suumque in Romanum Pontificem*
> *Amorem*[478]

The Holy Father was driven to the City from Castel Gandolfo, arriving at the College a few minutes prior to *ore 10 precise*. Among those accompanying the Holy Father from Castel Gandolfo were Prince Carlo Pacelli and Count Enrico Galeazzi. Arriving at the

---

[476] The College coat-of-arms was designed by Mr. William F.S. Ryan, an expert in ecclesiastical heraldry, and by Bishop James Henry Griffiths, one time chancellor for the Military Ordinariate, and later auxiliary bishop to the Archbishop of New York, whose hobby was ecclesiastical heraldry. The lengthy correspondence can be found in KC, *Enrico Galeazzi Papers, No. Amer. Coll, Bids-Contracts Gianicolo, Works & Reports on Works, 1950: Coat of Arms: 1950. 1953*, Box 13, File 1; Oversize Box 001, File 3; also, KC, above ref, *No. Amer. Coll, Corresp Martin J. O'Connor, 1950-1953*, Box 30, File 19; also, KC, above ref, *No. Amer. Coll, Corresp Martin J. O'Connor, Jan-June 1951*, Box 50, File 13.

[477] "O Happy Rome, you have been consecrated by the glorious blood of two princes" [Saints Peter and Paul].

[478] "The young men who have come here from the distant shores of America, looking upon the Vatican Hill, strengthen their faith and their love for the Roman Pontiff."

formal entrance of the College, facing Saint Peter's, the Pope was met by the Rector, who escorted him into the formal reception room.[479]

Gathered behind the processional cross, the Holy Father, and Bishop O'Connor, was a rather crowded and loosely formed procession of various and sundry Vatican officials, cardinals, bishops and *monsignori,* moving toward the new chapel. As the procession made its way along the corridors of the *Piano Nobile,* the new College bells, *Holy Savior, Immaculata,* and *SS. Peter and Paul* rang out,[480]and the assembled guests and seminarians lining the halls applauded, genuflecting for the Holy Father's blessing.

The student choir sang Ravanello's *Tu Es Petrus* as the Pope entered the chapel, greeting the assembled cardinals, prelates, 200 American alumni priests; the American Ambassador to the Italy, Mrs. Clare Booth Luce; members of the diplomatic corps accredited to the Holy See; and many other guests.[481]

After kneeling in prayer, the Pope moved to the throne erected on the Gospel side of the sanctuary to address the American seminarians, who had entered the chapel and stood lining the aisles. Just as his predecessor Pope Pius IX had done during his inaugural address at the newly-opened College in 1860, so now Pope Pius XII expressed the same hope for the Church in the United States as he spoke to a new generation of *Nordamericani* in their new chapel and home. The address was delivered in Italian, with a few personal remarks in English, and special notice made of Bishop O'Connor and their mutual friend, Count Galeazzi:

> For several years now We have followed with keen interest the preparations and the construction of your new seminary. Our Venerable Brother, the Rector, devoted, courageous, vigilant of every detail, kept Us

---

[479] McNamara, Robert, *The American College in Rome,* Rochester, NY, 1956, pp. 662-666.
[480] See Appendix IV for the inscriptions on the College bells.
[481] Ashton, John P., *Memories of Memorable Days: The Dedication Ceremonies,* in *Roman Echoes,* 1954, pp. 1-12, contains the full details of the ceremony.

informed of its progress, until with Our own eyes We saw it, reflecting the morning sun, like a city seated on a mountain. Let us tell you some of the thoughts it stirred within Our soul.

This is a building that has its foundation set deep on the generous and often trying sacrifices of the Bishops, the Alumni and the loyal faithful whom they serve. God reward them. Its large and majestic though severe lines, drawn by an architect of rare distinction in his profession, have been measured by the far-seeing wisdom of a zealous hierarchy. Its completion lights a stronger flame of hope for the Church in the United States of America and in the world. All this, it seemed to Us, adds up to a grave and sacred responsibility that rests on you, Our dear young seminarians, and on those who are to follow you. Will the sacrifice cheerfully offered for your sake be repaid in kind and with interest? Will the hopes and plans cherished by your Bishops, cherished by Us, be fulfilled? Your eager hearts are quick to answer: yes. But reflect a moment. That will be true only under one condition, that you become priests worthy of the name.[482]

The Holy Father then returned to the faldstool, was vested with a stole, and intoned the *Veni Creator Spiritu*, which was taken up by the choir and congregation. He offered a prayer and walked down the chapel aisle and into the corridors, sprinkling the new building with holy water. Returning to the chapel, the Pope intoned the prayers for the blessing of a seminary, newly composed for the occasion, written on a beautifully illuminated parchment. He then bestowed his apostolic blessing upon all.

---

[482] *Program for Dedication of the North American College*, October 14, 1953, NAC, *NAC Construction, 1925-1954*, #224, H-34. The Holy Father's entire address can be found in Appendix III.

The choir sang Antonelli's *Oremus pro Pontifice* as the Pope left the chapel, made his way around the east side of the courtyard along the *Piano Nobile* and into a reception room, today part of the library, in which he received the cardinals.

Finally, the Rector escorted the Holy Father down the southern corridor of the *Piano Nobile*, as the guests applauded him, and the seminarians sang the College song, *Ad Multos Annos*. Passing again through the Red Room, the Pope entered his car and returned to Castel Gandolfo. The entire visit lasted nearly one hour.[483]

The extraordinary meeting of the Episcopal Board opened in the afternoon of October 14th at the Via dell'Umiltà. Those Board members present were Cardinals Mooney, Spellman, and Stritch; Archbishops Keough and Binz; Bishops White [NAC 1910], Mulloy, and Brady. Also attending were Bishop O'Connor, Monsignors Maguire and Sennott, Count Galeazzi, and Mr. Silvestri.

Cardinals Stritch and Mooney had already prepared for this meeting, phoning each other and other Board members during the summer months. Most of the Board was already on-board, having grown to respect and trust the Rector's ability and judgment, as displayed repeatedly during his past seven years of hard work. Mooney also prepared them for the meeting. Likewise, all were exhilarated, having played a part in this their singular achievement on the Janiculum, and all wanted to be sure of one thing only: that the College opened and the construction project, plans for which had begun in the 1920's, was finally completed and paid for, no matter what the cost, no matter what the method. No blame was to be meted out to anyone for oversights or cost overrun. It was a great day to be an American Catholic in Rome, and nothing was going to spoil that.

---

[483] All then returned to the chapel for Benediction of the Most Blessed Sacrament at noon, with Archbishop Francis Keough of Baltimore as the celebrant, followed by a brief, yet chaotic, light reception in the new refectory. The next day, Cardinal Stritch was the celebrant for the first Pontifical Mass in the chapel for the living alumni and benefactors of the College, followed by a formal dinner attended by over 500 prelates, alumni, seminarians and guests. The third day, Pontifical Mass was offered for the souls of the deceased alumni and benefactors, and the celebrant was Cardinal Spellman.

Besides, all had attended the Holy Father at the dedication ceremony that morning, and all were moved by it, regardless of their rank, as Catholic Americans. And, following the praise the Holy Father bestowed upon Bishop O'Connor and Count Galeazzi for their superb work and devotion to the College, and the thanks they themselves had received from the Pope for their sacrifices to complete the project, there could be only one outcome of the meeting, no matter what the personal feelings of any individual present at that meeting might be.

Spellman began, asking for a clarification of the financial picture of the College building projects, "particularly the large difference between estimates submitted in March of this year and the revision of these estimates received after the completion of the last Lire transaction."[484]

The response was reduced to simply defining two Italian words used repeatedly in the summer's correspondence and reports generated during the past months: *Gestione* was not merely the deficit for ordinary College expenses, but also included the cost of the furnishings purchased for the Umiltà, Casa San Giovanni, Villa Santa Caterina, and for the new College. "In the future these expenses will be set up in an account for capital expenses". *Avviamento* represented all costs related to the dedication of the new College; the moving of the students and faculty into their new home; and also included the deficit anticipated for the first years until the new College and the Umiltà would operate at full capacity—a one-time extraordinary expense.

Then it was the turn of the architect and the lawyer, whose reports had raised so many questions. Galeazzi explained that the original estimated cost was, by nature, tentative, because of unforeseen circumstances during the years of planning and construction, "such as the deaths of the two partners in the contracting firm", and he

---

[484]   *Minutes of the Special Meeting of the Episcopal Board of the American College of the Roman Catholic Church of the United States held in the Casa S. Maria dell'Umiltà, Rome, on October 14th, 1953*, NYC, Box S/C-74, Folder 2: *To Card. Spellman, N. Amer. Coll.*

hoped the higher costs would be within 10% of the actual cost of the completed project.

Silvestri explained his accounting of cash receipts and expenditures as part of the "intricate system employed in making all disbursements" in post-war Italy.

Sennott concluded, stating that for the completion of all the projects and the requested amount for the *avviamento*, the Board would be asked to provide $380,000 [$3,274,617.98], in addition to the amount already sent to Rome. However, if all the pledges were paid there would be a surplus, not a deficit, of about $65,000 [$560,132.02].

As planned, Cardinal Stritch then moved that "we proceed to the completion of the projects including the allowance of $100,000 [$861,741.57] for *avviamento*." Spellman seconded the motion, and it was passed unanimously, with the caveat that any further expenses would require Board approval.

Bishop Mulloy then moved that the Board delegate Bishop O'Connor and Count Galeazzi the authority to determine what items of work should be deleted to keep within the limits established by the above resolution. Archbishop Keough seconded the motion, and this was unanimously approved.

Spellman then announced that he had secured a contribution of $27,000 [$232,670.22] from the Knights of Malta and the Knights of the Holy Sepulcher to defray the cost of the bronze Stations of the Cross in the new chapel, "to commemorate the visit of the Holy Father on the day of the Dedication of the New College."

The last motion made during this meeting had been predicted by Mooney when this final scuffle began in June. The Minutes of the meeting record,

> Cardinal Spellman moved a vote of thanks to the Rector and his staff, to the architect and the lawyer for the magnificent success of the building projects undertaken since the war and culminating in the dedication ceremonies of the morning. The Rector was asked to seek an audience with the Holy Father to voice the thanks of the Administrative Board of

the College, of the hierarchy of the United States and of American Catholics for His historic visit to the College for the Dedication.

The motion passed unanimously.
The Rector had completed his task.

Dedication Day, October 14, 1953: Pope Pius XII is welcomed to the new College by Bishop Martin J. O'Connor.

(courtesy Pontifical North American College Archives)

October 14, 1953, Dedication Day.
Pope Pius XII enters the new College

October 14, 1953: Bishop O'Connor escorts Pope Pius XII
through the new College to the chapel

October 14, 1953: Monsignor Giovanni Montini (center),
the future Pope Paul VI, with other visiting prelates and seminarians.

October 14, 1953: A light reception following the dedication ceremony
In the new College refectory.

Bishop O'Connor blesses the new College bells.

*College bronze bust of Pope Pius XII before the marble plaque with his
February 18, 1948 letter to the American Hierarchy,
re-establishing the College.*

Main courtyard, facing south.

Main courtyard, facing north.

College Refectory.

Pontifical North American College postcard:
Rector's entrance and St. Peter's.

The College Chapel.
(photograph by Christopher Brashears)

Count Galeazzi's tomb in the chapel crypt.
(photograph by Christopher Brashears)

Pontifical North American College, Rome 1956. Aerial View towards St Peter's.

Postscript

> *"Today the Holy Father blessed the new American College. He spoke briefly in English. Sixteen Cardinals were present and forty American bishops, besides several Europeans. They are still at work on the new building and it will take months to complete. Indiana has its name above a window and Evansville is also found on the walls."*
>
> —Bishop Henry Grimmelsman
> of Evansville, 1953.[485]

It was true. Along the walls on the *Piano Nobile* are the coats of arms and the names of all American dioceses extant when the new College was dedicated, grouped in their ecclesiastical provinces; across the corridor, above the cortile windows, are the names of the States. Those American seminarians, alumni, bishops, and cardinals were proud that great day when the dream of a new seminary was realized, and when the Pope came to bless their work.

On November 2, 1953, Monsignor Burns spoke with Count Galeazzi, informing him that O'Connor had entered the Blue Nuns' clinic near San Stefano Rotondo a few days earlier, and had undergone surgery the week before for the removal of a growth on his tongue, which had developed a serious infection. The Count explained that O'Connor's doctors had insisted he undergo surgery earlier. He refused, until after the dedication ceremonies, during which he endured great pain, without mentioning this to anyone, not even to his Vice Rector, Monsignor Burns.

Galeazzi informed the Pope of the Rector's surgery, and immediately visited O'Connor in the hospital. He was told that

---

[485] Postcard, Citta del Vaticano October 14, 1953, Bishop Henry Grimmelsman to the Sisters of Saint Benedict, NAC, *NAC Construction, 1925-1954*, #224, H-34.

O'Connor was to remain in the hospital at least another ten days. The hospital sisters were quite concerned with his condition, since the growth on his tongue was pronounced, and they feared it might be cancerous.

The next day, O'Connor sent his friend a handwritten note thanking him for his visit.[486] "Your message brought me much joy and I appreciate your kindness in securing the blessing of the Holy Father. If the opportunity presents itself, please tell His Holiness that I am truly grateful for his sympathetic interest and Apostolic Benediction." Galeazzi also told the Rector that the Holy Father would soon present the College with a gift, a memento of his visit on the dedication day, October 14th. O'Connor asked Galeazzi to inform the Cardinal Treasurer of his surgery, and to say that the Rector asked to be excused for health reasons from attending the November Board meeting, and that there might be a delay in the sending of the reports because of his health condition. He added, "N.B. (*Pro hae vice*—he is not responsible!!!)".

Galeazzi wrote Cardinal Spellman notifying him of O'Connor's surgery and present condition, adding that he and the other members of the American hierarchy should recall the "Spartan serenity when faced with various difficulties" that the Rector had shown, and that they might ponder what the present surgery means when considering the man's mettle, especially since he had refused to inform anyone that he needed surgery, lest that information mar the entire dedication ceremony, or influence the results of subsequent the Board meeting. Galeazzi ended by suggesting that Spellman write the Rector a kind note.[487]

Spellman wrote that note to O'Connor on November 25th, one week after the annual Board meeting in Washington, D.C. He told the Rector that Galeazzi had informed him of the surgery and thanked the Rector for his "kind letter" acknowledging Spellman's

---

[486] Rome November 3, 1953, O'Connor to Galeazzi, KC, *Enrico Galeazzi Papers, No. Amer. Coll, Corresp Most Rev Martin J. O'Connor, 1953-1954*, Box 30, File 13.

[487] Vatican November 3, 1953, Galeazzi to Spellman, KC, *Enrico Galeazzi Papers, No. Amer. Coll, Card. Spellman Corresp, 1953-1954*, Box 12, File 10.

participation in the dedication ceremonies. He ended by mentioning that the American bishops had unanimously passed a resolution during their recent annual meeting, "praising you for the work that you have done during the re-birth of the College."[488]

The promised gift to the College from the Holy Father was given to the Rector on March 23rd. O'Connor expressed his deep gratitude to the Holy Father and to Galeazzi the next day:

> My dear Friend, It is difficult for me to tell you how grateful I am for the priceless gift of the beautiful Rochet which Our Holy Father wore on the occasion of the inauguration of the College.
>
> Perhaps I didn't express myself as well as I should have done yesterday but I am overjoyed with this testimonial of His benevolence and I am deeply appreciative of your intercession and ever personal and unselfish interest in everything that concerns the welfare of the College as well as its prestige.
>
> As you know I have been very discouraged at times and you have been of great help to me. The Holy Father's coming on October 14th last was of course a great tribute to the United States but for me personally it meant so much in the way of approval and vindication that I will owe Him a debt of gratitude all my life. Ever since His illness began I have said Mass for Him in honor of the Holy Spirit. When I could not, on a few occasions, I supplied with another priest.
>
> This letter is just for yourself but you know my sentiments. I will write a letter soon in thanks for

---

[488] New York November 25, 1953, Spellman to O'Connor, KC, *Enrico Galeazzi Papers, No. Amer. Coll, Corresp Francis Card. Spellman, 1950-1951, 1953-1954*, Box 30, File 17.

the Rochet. I hope you will be able to find the correspondence of Mrs. Brady about its material worth. If you see no objection later on the garment could be photographed, described and published in the American Catholic press as His tribute to Catholic America and the College. We can preserve it in a glass case in the large reception room.[489]

As the months passed, even Spellman appeared to be more conciliatory toward the Rector, asking O'Connor to represent him and the American bishops at the upcoming consecration celebrations of the Basilica of St. Therese in Lisieux, France on July 14th,[490] and even offering to pay for O'Connor's travels! "Perhaps we have surmounted a barrier [in his relationship with Spellman], and St. Therese is doing something for me. I have her roses in my coat of arms but the first few years she has been too busy with missionaries."[491]

Whatever of that, any apparent *rapprochement* lasted only a short while, and may simply have served to put the Rector off his guard. For Spellman succeeded in appointing his own man, Monsignor Frank Reh, as Vice Rector of the College, just as O'Connor was embarking on his Lisieux pilgrimage.[492] Reh would succeed O'Connor as the Rector.

During these past and busy years in Rome, along with the support of Pope Pius XII, O'Connor gained a good friend in Count Galeazzi,

---

[489] Rome March 24, 1954, O'Connor to Galeazzi, KC, *Enrico Galeazzi Papers, No. Amer. Coll, Corresp Most Rev. Martin J. O'Connor, 1953-1954*, Box 30, File 13. To insure no one other than the Count opened and read his note, the Rector marked the front of the envelope "Personal Urgent", and on the back flap, sealed it, signed it over the flap, and stapled the top right hand corner.

[490] Rome June 21, 1954, O'Connor to Galeazzi, KC, *Enrico Galeazzi Papers*, in above ref.

[491] Rome July 5, 1954, O'Connor to Galeazzi, KC, *Enrico Galeazzi Papers*, in above ref.

[492] Washington, D.C., July 16, 1954, Msgr. Joseph P. Christopher [NAC 1916] to Msgr. Florence D. Cohalan, NYC, Box S/B-15, Folder 7: *About Card. Spellman*: "The appointment of Frank Reh is a victory of course for Spellie, and will serve as a pipeline—it may mean the end of Bishop O'Connor, whom Spellie does not like, to put it mildly."

as is evident in their correspondence, quoted above, but also in these last two examples, the first from 1954, and the second from 1965:

> My dear Friend, I know that you have received 'official' greetings for Christmas. These are 'personal'.
>
> We have been so fortunate in the last eight years as to have planned and worked together for the program of the American College. I shall always acknowledge your professional discretion and most prudent personal counsel as elements without which I would have abandoned my efforts long ago.
>
> The more I think of it, the graces of the Marian Year [1954] are evident in my own life. I think they must also be in yours.[493]

*   *   *

> My dear Friend: During the past months I have been going through files of the last 18 years, selecting material for the College and for history.
>
> I am amazed at the amount of correspondence we had with each other. There were so many difficulties and without your sympathy and practical assistance, I would have not been able to achieve the purpose for which I was asked to come to Rome.
>
> The interest and support of His Holiness, Pope Pius XII is more than ever evident in retrospect. And now, as you must know (as it was with your approval

---

[493] Rome December 3, 1954, O'Connor to Galeazzi, KC, *Enrico Galeazzi Papers, No. Amer. Coll, Corresp Most Rev Martin J. O'Connor 1953-1954*, Box 30, File 13.

undoubtedly) I have the furniture from the [Pope's] private apartment that was a gift of the Prussian Bishop to Cardinal Pacelli.[494]

But, O'Connor did not accept the position as the Rector of the Pontifical College with an eye to making friends. He accepted because he loved the priesthood and the Church and the College that trained him; and his students understood that well, as expressed in a letter by one of them:

On September 17, 1949 I first had the privilege of meeting you—my impression—your kindness—persists throughout fifteen years. I have been the recipient of your thoughtfulness and patience, your experience and tact—for these my life has been richer. You need not be concerned about what you have done for your students. We, your students, have spoken so often of all you have given us. Whatever has been accomplished by priests formed under your direction, has been done by the policy established by you, by your ideals and thanks be to God, your perseverance. The American College has stature because you have stature. Thank you so very much.

These past three years I have grown to know you and admire you ever more as a bishop, superior and above all as a friend. I know your sufferings—I wonder how many men could have endured these? You are a man of faith. One familiar phrase I often meditate upon—'God will take care of us'. God raised you up for the good of the College and through you He has

---

[494] Rome January 24, 1965, O'Connor to Galeazzi, KC, *Galeazzi Papers, Corresp Most Rev Martin J. O'Connor 1950, 1965-1970*, Box 264, File 31.

been good to the College for 18 years, and He has taken care of us—He <u>will</u> take care of us.[495]

Even O'Connor understood and admitted that his accomplishments at the College were part of team work, and the fruit of the dedication of Galeazzi and Silvestri, and it was apparent to others as well, as clearly described by Father Joseph Lacy in a letter to Galeazzi:

Bishop O'Connor, Msgr. Burns and myself know as no one else possibly could the debt the American College owes you. The New College is not just a monument of concrete and steel but it is a lasting memorial of the loving care and spiritual devotion which you, as architect and builder, put into it. I know that after the encomium of the Holy Father on the day of dedication, there is nothing that can be added in praise of your work. However, I feel that as one who watched the work develop from its conception to its magnificent completion I should add my personal word of gratitude and thanks. The work was not easy and the technical details were just one part of it. I could say that you were the right hand of Bishop O'Connor in this work, but you were more than that. You and the bishop and the lawyer made an unbeatable team in facing every problem, whether it was technical, legal or diplomatic. It does not lessen the part that any one of you played to say that without the three working in unison the splendid results would not have been obtained.

You should realize that every priest who is trained at the North American College will have something of

[495] Rome October 11, 1964, Fr. James Chambers [NAC 1952] to O'Connor, CUA, *O'Connor Papers*, Box 23: *MJ O'Connor Misc & Unfiled Corresp*, Folder: *Correspondence (Sent to Washington 1973)*, 2: *Important letter of Msgr. Chambers to Abp O'Connor*.

you in his priesthood, and I pray that this part of you may make their priesthood more bountiful and more blessed.[496]

On November 15, 1964, a dinner was held to honor the "Eleventh Rector of the Pontifical North American College". It was the last time Bishop O'Connor set foot inside his beloved handiwork. On that occasion, he gave thanks to three Popes whom he had served, Pius XII, John XXIII, and Paul VI. During his brief remarks, he expressed that which was at the heart of his priesthood and work for the College he loved so very much:

In my time as Rector it has been my privilege to witness from a unique vantage point a new and exciting era in the world. The aftermath of war, the resurrection of Europe and the increasing prosperity here and in the United States accompanied the second foundation of the American College. In 1947 the Bishops unanimously approved the project of restoration and building and supplied me with necessary funds. Since then four hundred and eighty eight young men have been ordained to the priesthood here while the numbers of priests who studied at the Casa San Giovanni and Casa Santa Maria has reached a total of four hundred.

While it has been in Rome for more than a hundred years [the College] will become more and more a part of the American seminary, preparing young Americans for the problems and mentality of the American people of today while preserving and adapting to that end the lessons of Roman life.

[496] Rome June 23, 1964, Lacy to Galeazzi, KC, *Enrico Galeazzi Papers, No. Amer. Coll, Notice Reports of Work, 1951-1955*, Box 13, File 11.

And to the present generation of students, the hope of the Church, I dare to recall again the inscription over the west door of this building, that 'the young men who come here from the distant shores of America looking on the Vatican Hill strengthen their Faith and their love for the Roman Pontiff.'[497]

---

[497] O'Connor was made an Assistant at the Pontifical Throne in 1953; named to the Congregation of Seminaries and Universities in 1954; named President of the Pontifical Commission for Motion Pictures, Radio and Television in 1959, and promoted to the titular archiepiscopal see of Laodicea in Syria on September 5, 1959; in 1960 he was named head of the Vatican press secretariat, and attended all sessions of the Second Vatican Council, drafting the original constitution on social communications; he was named Nuncio to Malta in 1965. The press speculated that O'Connor was in line to fill various important American sees and Vatican posts: *N.Y. Times*, June 18, 1958: O'Connor was rumored to become the Cardinal Prefect of the Congregation de Propaganda Fide, following the death of Cardinal Stritch; *N.Y. Times*, September 3, 1964: repeated rumors that O'Connor would be named a cardinal; *N.Y. Times*, December 4, 1967: listed O'Connor as a possible successor to Spellman in New York. The Rector died on December 1, 1986. The text on the front of the gravestone, below an engraved cross and his archiepiscopal coat-of-arms reads: "Most Reverend Martin J. O'Connor D.D. Titular Archbishop of Laodicea, Former Auxiliary Bishop of Scranton." On the back of the stone: "Archbishop Martin J. O'Connor, D.D. Born May 18, 1900 Ordained March 15, 1924, Episcopal Ordination January 27, 1943, Died December 1, 1986."
Scranton November 6, 1995, Msgr. Joseph G. Quinn [NAC 1985] to Brother Randal Riede, CFX, NAC Archives, #168: Martin J. O'Connor, 1900-1986: "Dear Brother, I've enclosed pictures you requested of Archbishop O'Connor's grave. As always, you're right! There is no reference to his tenure as rector at the College. One cannot imagine that that was by his request."

APPENDIX I

Letter from Pope Pius XII to the American Hierarchy, February 18, 1948

The approaching reestablishment here in Our dear Rome of the North American College, the knowledge of whose reopening has been communicated to Us by the rector, affords Us the welcome opportunity of addressing Our paternal words to you, the Members of the Hierarchy of the United States. We rejoice not only in the fact that after a lapse of eight years you are once more sending your chosen young men to study in Our beloved city, to imbibe the sacred wisdom of Holy Mother the Church at its very source and to be nourished at the very heart of the Catholic world, but that you are also planning to erect in the very shadow of Our own dwelling a new and greater seminary to care for ever more young Levites from America.

It was Our predecessor of blessed memory, Pius IX, who, nearly one hundred years ago first proposed to the American Bishops that they establish a national seminary in Rome, and it was the same Pontiff who purchased and graciously granted the use of the edifice that has housed the American students ever since that time.

Surely there is evident the hand of Divine Providence in the fact that the very first steps were taken on the occasion of the definition of the dogma of the Immaculate Conception and that the College itself was opened for the first time on the very eve of the feast, on December 7th, 1859. And since that day Our Heavenly Mother, Queen of the Clergy, has never ceased to bless with every manifestation of Divine favour a work that is of necessity so close to her maternal heart. The students nurtured in tender love of their Mother and Queen developed in the image of Her Divine Son, enlightened in the sacred sciences learned at the feet of Christ's Vicar, made strong and courageous by their close association with the places sanctified by the Prince of the Apostles and the martyrs, have returned to their own country to win ever greater triumphs for Christ and His Holy Spouse. As pastors and teachers, as administrators and also as bishops of the

Church in America, the men trained here have always been marked with an especial loyalty to Us and to Our illustrious Predecessors, an inevitable consequence of their sojourn in this City, the See of Peter and of Peter's Successors.

Today as We look about the City of Rome we see on all sides the flower of the youth of the world, even from the most distant nations, drawn here by a common faith, sustained by common ideals, being trained in the same doctrine, sharing the same Divine Sacrifice, and all united by the same bonds of attachment to Us. Surely they are giving to the leaders and to the peoples in every land a magnificent example of unity and of the ability of mankind to live together in Christian peace and concord. The concurrence of so many thousands of men, later destined to play such an important part in the salvation of souls over the whole face of the earth, is a great consolation to Us; and it should be to you, Beloved Sons and Venerable Brethren, a reason especially appealing at this time, to be prompt in making every sacrifice to maintain and even to enlarge the national seminary of your country.

So it is with particular joy that We have learned of your proposals to erect an even finer seminary and to plant your roots even closer to Us. Your wisdom and courage to look to the future and to plan for almost three hundred of your seminarians to study in Rome represent a most worthy initiative that can elicit only Our warmest commendation. At the same time you are keeping a tie with your old and honoured traditions in putting the former college building to use as a house of studies for priests wishing to train themselves in the higher branches of the sacred sciences. Both of these projects call forth Our heartiest approval and support and the return of grace and wisdom that will accrue to the Church in America will amply reward the expenditures and the sacrifices that are necessarily involved in their realization.

The united action taken in this matter by the American Hierarchy, always so ready and generous in their support of all measures for the extension of the Kingdom of Christ, once more demonstrates the flourishing condition of the Faith in your great nation. We are sure that the bishops and priests and people will rally to the support of a cause that promises so much for the Church and which is so close to Our own heart. Already an abundant and fruitful harvest for God and souls has been garnered from the past eighty-nine years of the existence of the North American College: and now your decisions for the future give abundant hope that succeeding generations will continue, in greater measure and with more ample facilities, to enjoy the richest blessings stemming from a priesthood nourished in the Eternal City.

With great joy then we give Our blessing to the plans that have been made known to Us by the rector for the future of your seminary. We shall follow their unfolding and their realization with intimate pleasure and personal interest and, as a token of Our encouragement in the great task that lies ahead, We impart to you, Beloved Sons and Venerable Brethren, as also to the priests and the faithful of the United States, Our paternal Apostolic Benediction.

Given at the Vatican, on the eighteenth day of February, one thousand nine hundred and forty-eight, the ninth year of Our Pontificate.

Pius PP. XII

APPENDIX II

Bishop Martin J. O'Connor's Vatican Radio address, Sunday, October 11, 1953[498]

Roma Sacra, as you are doubtless all aware by this, is to witness on Wednesday next the dedication of a new and discreetly imposing home for the Pontifical North American College. It has been built deep into the rock of that storied Janiculum Hill nearby, which overtops protectively Bernini's Colonnades with the familiar approaches to Saint Peter's and the Vatican on its Western flank, while to the East it looks down with Goethe and many a greater than he on 'the history of the world spread out at its feet'.

Could you be present, with the distinguished group of clergy and laymen that is to see the new edifice presented, in the name of the American Catholic Hierarchy, to the Vicar of Christ in person—for His Holiness has done us the inestimable honor of promising to bless the seminary—you might be tempted, like so many others whose comments we have heard already, to view this modest contribution of ours to the spiritual grandeur of Eternal Rome in terms of triumph, a dream come true, an answer well-nigh perfect to a nation's urgent need and anxious prayer. We shall not here anticipate the judgment of the experts on what we have come to call so coldly the "physical plant." I should like rather to speak with you heart-to-heart to-night, by way of vigil to our solemn opening, of what I cannot but feel to be the real core of our achievement—in the only sense that matters, of your achievement.

From start to finish, the building of the new North American College, like the maintenance of its century-old first home on Humility Street in the heart of Ancient Rome, has been a labor of love. Be that said in pride and affection for all those generous souls, from the Sovereign Pontiff and His Brethren in the American episcopate down to the nameless least of our workmen with his trowel, chisel or bucket of cement, who have treated the roadblocks

---

[498] NAC #224, H-34. This was reprinted in the College Dedication booklet.

of these decades of planning, of these four last difficult years of construction, as so many challenges to their zeal, rather than as mere tests of their patience and ingenuity. Be that said, too, in gratitude to each of you, my listeners, who have followed and sustained us along the arduous way—perhaps better than you knew—with the precious aid of your prayers, your work and your suffering.

Labor of love for whom? Zeal for what so absorbing cause? The question will have its simple yet eloquent answer, if any be needed, on Wednesday, when the builders and benefactors of the new North American College kneel beside 190 seminarians from the United States—the largest number in our history, and the largest single group, I believe, in the Eternal City—in the living Presence of their Eucharistic Lord, to beg with them His blessing on a new scholastic year of preparation for their priestly ministry to souls. There you have it: our planning and our labor, like your prayers, have all been for love of Him, the High Priest Whose life and mission we prolong in His Mystical Body, Whose doctrines we preach, Whose grace He would have us dispense to a world that never needed it more sorely than at this hour.

No other design was behind the designing of our new Roman seminary on the Janiculum. No other ambition than His could have carried it through to completion: that this eager legion of His Levites from America might have His life and live it more abundantly, as they approach in studious prayer and prayerful study the altar of His perfect Sacrifice.

The Supreme Pontiff himself will be the first to agree. He will not have forgotten for a moment the words he wrote to us during the very first weeks of his Pontificate, in the Encyclical Letter *Sertum Laetitiae* (*Crown of Your Joy*) commemorating the Sesquicentennial of the establishment of our Hierarchy in the United States; words in which we found the force of a command, even more than an encouragement from the paternal heart of our Universal Shepherd:

"We heartily share your desire to see erected in Rome a more worthy and convenient building for the Pontifical College charged with the formation of ecclesiastical students from the United States. If it is indeed true that travel abroad can do much to round off the training of our youthful elite, long and happy experience makes it plain that candidates for the priesthood derive quite exceptional advantage from an education here close to the See of Peter, where the spring of faith is purest to drink from, where so many monuments of the Christian ages and so many footprints of the Saints awaken in generous hearts the burning desire for a life of heroic achievement."

Pope Pius XII in 1939, as on a hundred occasions public and private since that time, was but repeating the cordial invitation to share his own labor of love first extended to us by his immortal predecessor Pius IX a little less than a hundred years ago, when in his reply to an enquiry of the archbishops and bishops attending the First Provincial Council of New York, he formally proposed the establishment of a North American College in Rome. In a matter of months the project was enthusiastically accepted as a national responsibility, and the Pope himself greatly eased the burden of our first beginnings by purchasing for us in 1857 the old Visitation Convent of the Umiltà, then used as a barracks for the French garrison in Rome. The College was formally opened in 1859 with a student body of thirteen American pioneers.

The rest, up to to-day, is history. What fruits were to ripen from these early days of our labor of love, what "heroic achievement" it inspired in the thousand American priests (including forty bishops, nine archbishop and seven Cardinals) it has formed during these first hundred years, we had best leave to others. This week, meanwhile, we are sure to hear the highlights and the heartburns of the story retold by the homecomers,—parish priests, prelates and Princes of the church who lived and loved their Roman student days "close to the See of Peter": within the sheltering walls and before the altar of the chapel on the Via dell'Umiltà, with classes in the hallowed halls of Propaganda and the Gregorian, unforgettable vacations at lovely Villa Santa Caterina in the Alban hills, and ordinations—heart's desire!—at the end of the journey, in the college chapel or in an ancient Basilica.

There will be little time, alas! For more than generalities, enlivened by incident and anecdote. But of two things we may speak. Looking backward, past two world wars and six Pontificates to the Vatican Council and well beyond, one and all will be happy, and perhaps a little proud, to realize that "youthful and ardent America"—as the Popes with so many others persist in describing us—has long since linked her spiritual destiny solidly and intimately with the destiny sublime of Roma Sacra; has long since found herself completely "at home at Rome" beside her sister nations, old and young, of one world united in Christ. Looking forward, as we must with our new College extending its welcome to ever greater numbers of the Lord's American elect, no one will be disposed to sit back or kneel down complacently with the air-pilot's sense of relief for a 'mission completed' in his heart or on his lips. Least of all the Americans, with the Holy Father's anxious call to arms, and the world's more desperate challenge to "moral leadership" for priest and layman, ringing loudly in their ears. Like every labor of love in the Christian economy of grace, this one is always just beginning.

Which brings us, in closing, back to the heart of our story. To complete the explanation and point out the significance of what our earnest effort at the North American College has thus far achieved, as to quicken our hopes for the immense task ahead, there is a second love, like unto the first, which one can never forget nor undervalue; I mean, of course, the love of Our Lady.

The economy of grace, which after all is only a synonym for the careful planning of our lives by a just and merciful God, would have it that our every labor of love for Christ is supervised, protected and sweetened by the intercession of Mary, His Virgin Mother. And how soon and how well the New world, after the example of the Old, learned to "fly to her protection, implore her help and seek her intercession!" It was surely no causal, passing impulse that led our first North American martyrs, who were to baptize our country in their blood as it emerged from savagery, and whom we have commemorated in this new building, to consecrate it first to Our Lady of the Immaculate Conception two full centuries before the dogma was defined. No accident, either, was the profusion of later American tributes to Mary's beauty and goodness, of official appeals to her power and compassion, listed by our Daniel Sargent in his precious little volume, *Our Lady and Our Land*.

Among these official developments, the founding and growth of the North American College at Rome may well seem to have been, and to be still to-day, an object of special affection and vigilance for our country's Immaculate Patroness—in return, we like to hope, for the filial trust we have always placed in her. Are we to call it just a coincidence that the bishops who first expressed to Pope Pius IX our yearning for an American seminary at Roma Sacra to take rank with the other national colleges in the Eternal City, had crossed the ocean to be present at the Proclamation of the Dogma of the Immaculate Conception? Or the fact that we took formal possession of the College, in 1859, on her Feast-day, December the eighth? Or the circumstance that the beloved building and Alumni chapel where so much of our spiritual testing has been done ever since it had been founded by the Daughters of Our Lady's Visitation?

The Marian feasts and favors that grace the pages of our College Chronicle are simply, like Our Lady's titles to our love, without number. And here, this coming Wednesday, within the Octave of today's feast of her Divine Maternity, we are to offer for the blessings of His Holiness the "more worthy and convenient" quarters he begged for his cherished North Americans in such fond terms as his glorious Pontificate began! The labor of love continues on the Janiculum just where we left off at Our Lady's Shrine in Rome.

We haven't of course, left off at all. The new school term begins on the eve of Mary's own Jubilee Year, which also marks the centenary of the birth of the North American College project in the apostolic hearts of Pius IX, Archbishop Hughes of New York and Archbishop Kenrick of Baltimore. Shall all this, too, be written off as mere coincidence? Let it rather be accepted humbly and gratefully by our students, staff and alumni alike as one more reassuring sign from the Sacred Hearts of Our Lord and His Mother that the path to 'heroic achievement' in America's portion of the vineyard still beckons us on from Roma Sacra and beyond; that our labor will be lightened and our apostolate more fruitful in the measure of our abiding love for Them. And tomorrow as to-day may *Their* satisfaction, and no other, be our reward exceeding great.

APPENDIX III

Pope Pius XII's sermon at the College Dedication, October 14, 1953

For several years now We have followed with keen interest the preparations and the construction of your new seminary. Our Venerable Brother, the Rector, devoted, courageous, vigilant of every detail, kept Us informed of its progress, until with Our own eyes We saw it, reflecting the morning sun, like a city seated on a mountain. Let us tell you some of the thoughts it stirred within Our soul.

This is a building that has its foundation set deep on the generous and often trying sacrifices of the Bishops, the Alumni and the loyal faithful whom they serve. God reward them. Its large and majestic though severe lines, drawn by an architect of rare distinction in his profession, have been measured by the far-seeing wisdom of a zealous hierarchy. Its completion lights a stronger flame of hope for the Church in the United States of America and in the world. All this, it seemed to Us, adds up to a grave and sacred responsibility that rests on you, Our dear young seminarians, and on those who are to follow you. Will the sacrifice cheerfully offered for your sake be repaid in kind and with interest? Will the hopes and plans cherished by your Bishops, cherished by Us, be fulfilled? Your eager hearts are quick to answer: yes. But reflect a moment. That will be true only under one condition, that you become priests worthy of the name.

In the priesthood man is elevated to an almost staggering height, a mediator between a world in travail and the celestial kingdom of peace. Christ's ambassador, steward of God's mysteries, he exercises a divine power. Heir to the priestly and kingly offices of the divine Redeemer, he is commissioned to carry on the task of salvation, bringing souls to God and giving God to souls. Never, then, unmindful of the supreme importance of such a vocation, the priest will not busy himself with useless things. Modeling his life on that of Him he represents he will gladly spend and be spent on behalf of souls. Souls he seeks everywhere and always, not what the world can offer him. "To be a priest and to be a man dedicated to work is one and the same thing", wrote Pope Blessed Pius X; and he liked to quote the words of the synod presided over by Saint Charles Borromeo: "Let every cleric repeat again and again: he has been called not to a life of ease and leisure, but of hard work in the spiritual army of the Church."

Those words, beloved sons, recall another fact one dare not forget. We belong to the Church militant; and she is militant because on earth the powers of darkness are ever restless to encompass her destruction. Not only in the far-off centuries of the early Church, but down through the ages and in this our day, the enemies of God and Christian civilization make bold to attack the Creator's supreme dominion and sacrosanct human rights. No rank of the clergy is spared; and the faithful—their number is legion—inspired by the valiant endurance of their shepherds and fathers in Christ, stand firm ready to suffer and die, as the martyrs of old, for the one true Faith taught by Jesus Christ. Into that militia you seek to be admitted as leaders.

Imprisonment and martyrdom, We know, do not loom on the horizon that spreads before your eyes. In an atmosphere of untrammeled freedom, where "the word of God is not bound", the Church in your country has grown in numbers, in influence, in strength of leadership in all that makes for the good of the commonwealth. The college on the Via dell'Umiltà has seen your priests increase from twenty-five hundred to forty-five thousand and more-proud and glorious tribute to the unselfish, clear-visioned Catholic family life that prevails among you; a mission country become a seminary of apostles for foreign fields. But the Church militant is "one body, with one Spirit . . . with the same Lord, the same faith, the same baptism". And that Spirit calls for more than a dash of heroism in every priest who would be worthy of the name, whatever the external circumstances of time and place.

The spirit of the martyrs breathes in every priestly soul, who in the daily round of pastoral duties and in his cheerful, unrelenting efforts to increase in wisdom and in grace, gives witness to the Prince of shepherds, who endured the cross, despised the shame "when He gave Himself up on our behalf, a sacrifice breathing out fragrance as He offered it to God."

We raise a fervent prayer to Mary Immaculate, under whose patronage you have placed your country, to Mary gloriously assumed into heaven, whom you have wished to honor in your chapel here, that she would always show a mother's loving care to the clergy of America, and guide you, beloved seminarians, bearers of such high hopes, along the way that leads to holiness which will bring her to recognize in you a greater and greater resemblance to her own divine Son.

Pius PP. XII

APPENDIX IV

The College Bells

Each of the three North American College bells bears a Latin inscription.[499]

The bell dedicated to Our Lord:

Divini Redemptoris Vocem
Quasi Saeculorum Fluctus Supervolantem
Refero
Sacris Alumnis
Monitum Hortamentum Gaudium
A. MCMLIII

I sound an echo of the Redeemer's Voice,
winging, as it were,
over the Waves of Time for Seminarians:
Warning, Encouragement, Joy.
1953

The bell dedicated to Our Lady:

Quae a Suo Conceptu
Semper Immaculata Exstitit
Hostis Maligni Repellat Insidias
Innocentiam Foveat
Sempiternam Tandem Impetret
Beatitatem
A. MCMLIII

---

[499] Tournier, Francis, *The North American College*, private printing, 1955, pp. 34-35

May She, who from the Moment of Her Conception,
was Ever Immaculate,
Ward off the Snares of the Wicked Foe,
Foster Innocence,
and
Procure Eternal Happiness.
1953

The bell dedicated to Saints Peter and Paul:

Apostolorum Principes
Qui Suo Urbem Consecrarunt Sanguine
Civibus Populis Gentibus
Romam Praedicant
Catholicae Veritatis Magistram
A. MCMLIII

The Princes of the Apostles,
Who have Consecrated [the] City by Their Blood,
Proclaim Rome to The Citizens, Peoples and Nations,
As the Teacher of Catholic Truth.
1953

INDEX